SHEM FLEENOR

Mad Men

and the Specter of American Fascism

1848 Publishing Company

New York and Melbourne

ISBN: 978-1-951231-05-7

Table of Contents

Introduction 3

Chapter One

"Mad Men and Cold War American Racism" 30

Chapter Two

"Jackie, Marilyn and Masculine Anxiety in Mad Men" 57

Chapter Three

"Neoliberalism, Mad Men, and American Opposition to Marxism"
.... 97

Chapter Four

"Mad Men, Violence, and the Banality of Evil in 1960s America"
.... 130

Chapter Five

"The New Man, Nationalism, Militarism, and the Menacing Fetish for Youth" 163

Chapter Six

"Mad Men and the American Empire" 191

Chapter Seven

"Death, Religion, Consumerism and Utopianism" 212

Chapter Eight

"Mad Men, the Culture Industry, and the Vanishing Border Between High and Low Art" 238

Epilogue 270

Introduction

Mad Men is a cultural phenomenon. The groundbreaking drama about the inner workings of a 1960s Madison Avenue advertising agency and the inner lives of the company's employees featured ninety-two episodes in seven seasons between 2007 – 2015 and was awarded a record four consecutive Emmy Awards for Outstanding Drama Series. As recently as 2017, *Business Insider* referred to the series as the best show to come out of television's Golden Era.[1]

Mad Men is perhaps most explicitly about individual identity. In season two, Freddy Rumsen (Fred Murray), for instance, soon after being put on leave for drunkenly soiling himself just prior to presenting an ad campaign to a client says, "If I don't go in that office every day, who am I?"[2] Dr. Faye Miller (Cara Buono), a psychologist hired by Sterling & Cooper in the interest of better serving the needs of the agency's clients, tells protagonist, Don Draper (Jon Hamm), that "in the end," identity "all comes down to what I want versus what is expected of me."[3]

The theme of personal identity is particularly elaborated via names on *Mad Men*. "What's in a name?" Don asks in the final season of the series.[4] The question is seemingly off the cuff, but

---

[1] Carrie Witmer, "Why 10-year-old 'Mad Men' is still the best show to come out of television's Golden Age," *Business Insider*, July 19, 2017.

[2] Season 2 episode 9 "Six Month Leave" September 28, 2008.

[3] Season 4 episode 2 "Christmas Comes But Once a Year" August 1, 2010.

[4] Season 7 episode 11 "Time & Life" April 26, 2015.

actually gets to the satirical heart of the show, which is about how conflicted and ever changing one's identity is. Names are, in fact, essential in *Mad Men*. They are depicted to be as fluid as individuals' identities, which is evidenced by protagonist Don Draper, who is actually named Dick Whitman, yet once refers to himself in season two, as "Tilden Katz" – the name of his former mistress's husband.[5] Adam Whitman, Dick's half-brother, mails a package to Donild [sic] Draper in season one.[6] In season two, Don calls his secretary, Allison (Alexa Alemanni), "Donna." A season later the Draper's housekeeper, Carla (Deborah Lacey), calls Sally Draper (Kiernan Shipka) "Jessica."[7] There's also a character named Johnny Mathis (Trevor Einhorn), but not the popular singer, though one of the pop star's tunes, "What'll I Do?" concludes episode eleven of season two. Martinson Coffee changes its name to appear hipper in season two,[8] but a dog food company rocked by a horsemeat scandal refuses to change its name to rebrand in season three.[9] The ad agency's difficulty naming itself and subsequent identity crisis in the wake of the merger between Sterling, Cooper, Draper, Campbell & Pryce with Cutler, Gleason, and Shaw is also a central feature of an episode in season six.[10]

[5] Season 2 episode 4 "Three Sundays" August 17, 2008.

[6] Season 1 episode 5 "5G" August 16, 2007.

[7] Season 3 episode 8 "Souvenir" October 4, 2009.

[8] Season 2 episode 7 "The Gold Violin" September 7, 2008.

[9] Season 3 episode 8 "The Gypsy and the Hobo," October 25, 2009.

[10] Season 6 episode 10 "A Tale of Two Cities" June 2, 2013.

Numerous *Mad Men* characters created by executive producer, Matthew Weiner (who one could easily imagine was likely teased relentlessly as a kid due to his last name), share names with other characters, which is especially uncommon in theatrical storytelling. For instance, there is Don and his secretary Dawn, and Don's son, Bobby, and also Don's mistress, Bobbie. Three different actors, in fact, play Bobby Draper in seven seasons of *Mad Men*. There are also two Gene Hofstadts in the show.[11] There are also two doctors surnamed Arnold. Betty Draper (January Jones) and Peggy Olson both have friends named Joyce, which is the same name as Duck Phillips' (Mark Moses) secretary. There are two men named Henry on the show and several people named Rosenberg – a name most commonly associated in postwar American history with Jewish-American parents executed by the United States in 1953 for treason after passing along atomic secrets to the Soviet Union. In season six, a Manischewitz executive confesses to Roger Sterling (John Slattery) that he is "afraid" that people will think he is related to the infamous parents executed during the Red Scare.[12] The fact that there are so many references to the Rosenberg execution as well as peripheral characters on the series named Rosenberg seems a clue to *Mad Men's* critique of fascism deeply embedded in postwar American society.

Identity in *Mad Men* is also often very much shaped by tragedy, trauma, and the necessity of actively forgetting and transcending the past, all of which are also prominent features of the show. The persistent theme of actively forgetting and

[11] Season 3 episode 4 "The Arrangements" September 6, 2009.

[12] Season 5 episode 9 "Dark Shadows" May 13, 2012.

transcending trauma and its impact on individual identity surfaces again and again throughout the series, most prominently when Abraham Menken (Allan Miller), Rachel's (Maggie Siff) father, who escaped the Russian Pogroms for turn-of-the-century America, seems pained to remember that "it was hard in the old days" and "people are jumping to forget it."[13] Three seasons later Allison, Don's jaded secretary, laments that her boss is "a drunk" who gets "away with murder" because he forgets "everything."[14] In an expository flashback, Don visits Peggy at St. Mary's Hospital after she gives birth to Pete Campbell's (Vincent Kartheiser) son. Don insists that Peggy put the ordeal behind her and move forward. "This never happened," he says. "It will shock you how much it never happened." Later in the episode Peggy reluctantly asks him to repay her $110 she paid to bail him out of jail after he drunkenly crashed his car while cheating on his wife with Bobbie Barrett (Melinda McGraw). "I guess when you forget," Don apologizes to Peggy as he reimburses her, "you have to forget everything."[15]

Mad Men also, as alluded to above, often compels viewers to consider the Jewish Holocaust. Matthew Weiner, *Mad Men's* creator, in fact, compares Dick Whitman's American experience to Jewish-Americans in the postwar period. "Their identity is the same story as Don's identity," Weiner said in a 2014 interview. "How do we become white? How do I get my kid to go to Wesleyan so he can be in that law firm? What's it going to

[13] Season 1 episode 10 "Long Weekend" September 27, 2007.

[14] Season 4 episode 4 "The Rejected" August 15, 2010.

[15] Season 2 episode 5 "The New Girl" August 24, 2008.

take?"[16] Don, as a metaphor for the Jewish-American experience in the postwar era, surfaces very early in the series. In season one, for example, he is especially taciturn about his childhood, but reluctantly and cryptically admits to Roger and his wife, Mona (Talia Balsam), to think of him as "Moses in a basket," which likewise alludes to the fluidity of individual identity (Moses was adopted by an Egyptian princess) and collective identity (Moses was as Jewish as Don was American).[17] Don, as a metaphor for the Jewish-American experience, is also a clue that *Mad Men* is as much about the specter of fascism deeply embedded in postwar America's collective identity as it is about the individual identities of the characters. In other words, *Mad Men* is as much about postwar American identity as it is about the fluid and hidden identities of characters such as Don and Peggy.

There are a number of clues that help to illuminate Weiner's depiction of American identity being deeply conflicted by an inveterate tension between liberty and justice versus technocratic corporatist authoritarianism. One such clue is that numerous characters on *Mad Men* are of Italian or German ancestry or express interest in Italy and Germany, which were two fascist allies in World War II. For instance, Salvatore's last name is Romano. In season one, Sterling & Cooper is tasked with marketing Israel to American tourists. "If Lebanon is the Paris of the Middle East," a member of the Israeli Tourist Bureau says to Don, "we'd like to

[16] Gilbert Cruz, Dave Itzkoff, and Kathryn Shattuck, "*Mad Men* and Its Love Affair With '60s Pop Culture," *The New York Times,* April 3, 2015.

[17] Season 1 episode 2 "Ladies Room" July 19, 2007.

think Haifa is Rome."[18] Close to the end of season one Joan Holloway (Christine Hendricks) says, "If I let you in the supply closet, it will not be the sack of Rome," to Kenny Cosgrove (Aaron Staton), who aches to get into the storeroom for more booze to fuel a raucous office party set during election night in 1960.[19] An episode later Rachel Menken, Don Draper's reluctant Jewish-American mistress, takes a three-month sabbatical and goes on a trip to Rome and Paris to presumably get over her heartache towards the dashing but married ad man she had been seduced by in earlier episodes.[20] *A Funny Thing Happened on the Way to the Forum"* also plays on Broadway in season two of *Mad Men*.[21] The storyline of the Tony-winning Stephen Sondheim musical depicts a Roman slave who tries to win his freedom by helping his master get the girl he desires, which likewise seems to be an homage to Billy Wilder's *The Apartment* (1960), which is prominently alluded to in the season one storyline of *Mad Men*. Also in season two, Paul Kinsey (Michael Gladis) throws a well-attended soiree in New Jersey where he explains to Joan that he had purchased one of the shipwrecked but recovered "casques of Rome."[22] Father John Gil (Colin Hanks) tells parishioners that he recently returned from Rome, where he learned to play the mandolin and soccer.[23] In

---

[18] Season 1 episode 6 "Babylon" August 23, 2007.

[19] Season 1 episode 12 "Nixon vs. Kennedy" October 11, 2007.

[20] Season 1 episode 13 "The Wheel" October 18, 2007.

[21] Season 2 episode 5 "The New Girl" August 24, 2008.

[22] Season 2 episode 2 "Flight 1" August 3, 2008.

[23] Season 2 episode 4, "Three Sundays" August 17, 2008.

season three, viewers learn that Sally Draper's teacher, Suzanne Farrell (Abigail Spencer), has an epileptic brother, Danny (Marshall Allman), who informs Don that "Julius Caesar had epilepsy and he ran Rome."[24] Suzanne, who is also Don's mistress in season three, reminisces to her philandering lover about the spaghetti she enjoyed in Little Italy, where she was treated "very nicely" due to the attractiveness of her features – her dark hair and eyes (like an Italian's).[25] "Rome wasn't built in a day," creative director Lou Avery (Allan Havey) says to Shirley (Sola Bamis), his new secretary, as they leave the office on Valentine's Day in season seven.[26] In season four, Roger Sterling tells Lane Pryce (Jared Harris) that the Christmas party to be thrown for Lee Garner, Jr. (Darren Pettie) of Lucky Strike Cigarettes needs to be a "Roman orgy."[27] A painting of an ancient Roman ruin, the sketch of a Roman bust, and Knight's armor all adorn the wall of Lane's office.[28] When Saint John Powell (Charles Shaughnessy) compliments Lane for streamlining the agency so soon after it having been acquired by Putnam, Powell and Lowe, the latter of the two responds by uttering "Pax Romana."[29] In season five,

[24] Season 3 episode 10 "The Color Blue" October 18, 2009.

[25] Season 3 episode 11 "The Gypsy and the Hobo" October 25, 2009.

[26] Season 7 episode 2 "A Day's Work" April 20, 2014.

[27] Season 4 episode 3 "The Good News" August 8, 2010.

[28] Season 5 episode 5 "Signal 30" April 15, 2012.

[29] Season 3 episode 6 "Guy Walks Into an Advertising Agency" September 20, 2009.

Harry Crane's office wall is adorned by a painting depicting a Roman victory arch.[30] An episode later a Roman marble steele hangs over the clawfoot bathtub in Roger Sterling's luxury midtown-Manhattan apartment as he and his young wife, Jane (Peyton List), come down from an LSD trip.[31] A season later, Roger's psychiatrist has a bust of a Roman emperor on the bureau in his office.[32] In the premier episode of season seven, Joan visits an economics professor at his office at what is, due to its neoclassical architecture, presumably Columbia University; a Roman bust rests atop his desk.[33] In season two, Duck Phillips's daughter, Patricia (Gina DeVino), excuses herself because, as she tells her father, she has German vocabulary homework.[34]

    While these are not explicit clues that depict postwar America as a fascist state, the fact that there are Little Italys in American cities, fetishization of Italian and German culture, etc. speaks to cultural synchronicity between Americans, Italians (particularly Romans), and Germans. As banal as that may seem, it actually seems to speak volumes that Betty seems proud to speak Italian and Duck's daughter is learning to speak German, of all languages. The fact that so many of the characters on the show have German or Italian surnames and/or are enamored with

[30] Season 5 episode 5 "Signal 30" April 15, 2012.

[31] Season 5 episode 6 "Far Away Places" April 22, 2012.

[32] Season 6 episode 1 "The Doorway" April 7, 2013.

[33] Season 7 episode 1 "Time Zones" April 13, 2014.

[34] Season 2 episode 6 "Maidenform" August 31, 2008.

German and Italian culture likewise seems to allude to cultural syncretism, and also to the fact that Germanic and Italian culture has deep roots in American society, particularly in regard to the centrality of Protestantism and Catholicism.

An especially good clue that *Mad Men* conscientiously compares European fascism to postwar America's consumerist and militarist society can perhaps best be detected in season two as Betty throws a dinner party for her husband's coworkers and their wives. "We stop in Spain for gazpacho," she says to the guests assembled at the dining room table, "then Japan for rumaki, and then Dutchess County for leg of lamb, and then a mint jelly accompanied with egg noodles the way my grandmother from Germany used to make them."[35] The pairing of Dutchess County, one of the richest suburbs in the United States, with Spain, Japan, and Germany does not seem to be by happenstance. The pairing, in fact, seems to be a clue that *Mad Men* is a thinly veiled critique of fascism embedded in Cold War American society.

Uber-nationalist Betty seems especially enamored with Italy. She, for example, flips through a book about Italy while babysitting Glen Bishop (Marten Holden Weiner) in season one.[36] Early in the series she tells her neighbor, Francine Hanson (Anne Dudeck), that she modeled in Italy after she graduated from Bryn Mawr College.[37] Three episodes later she hails Michelangelo for painting

[35] Season 2 episode 8 "A Night to Remember" September 14, 2008.

[36] Season 1 episode 8 "The Hobo Code" September 6, 2007.

[37] Season 1 episode 3 "Marriage of Figaro" August 2, 2007.

the Sistine Chapel while "pigmies were still living in caves." [38] In season seven, Betty says to her husband, Henry Francis (Christopher Stanley), "I'm not stupid. I speak Italian."[39] Arthur Case (Gabriel Mann), the young and engaged man who has a flirtatious relationship with Betty at the Country Club's horse stables in season two, calls her "sad." Betty coolly responds by explaining that she is "not sad," her "people are Nordic."[40]

Betty, whose maiden surname is Hofstadt (a German name), has pristine blond hair and icy blue eyes. She, thus, appears to be the ideal Aryan housewife, as well as the Cold War paragon of American housewifery. There are, in fact, several characters with German surnames in the show, including the Hofstadt family, and also Pete's father-in-law, Tom Vogel (Joe O' Connor) of Vicks Chemical. Harry Crane's (Rich Sommer) secretary is named Hildy (Julie McNiven). The point seems particularly underscored in season two by the fact that business partners Kurt (a German) and Smitty (an American) share the same last name – Smith.

As anecdotal as all of these allusions to Italy, Rome and Germany might seem, they actually offer subliminal clues to illuminate that *Man Men* is actually a critique of the fascism deeply embedded in, yet often overlooked, in Cold War American society and identity. It is important to note that *Mad Men* has been regarded for the show's painstaking attention to detail, including ice cubes hand-cut to smaller 1960s dimensions; nicotine stains

[38] Season 1 episode 6 "Babylon" August 23, 2007.

[39] Season 7 episode 5 "The Runaways" May 11, 2014.

[40] Season 1 episode 13 "The Wheel" October 18, 2007.

painted on the fingers of actors; furniture, clothing, kitchenware, and whiskey tumblers that are all genuine vintage items, not replicas; even real fruit, when used, was selected to match the size of produce from a bygone era that predates genetic modification.[41] It thus, in short, seems evident that the numerous references to Germany and Rome were by no means anecdotal or incidental.

The conflation of German, Italian, and American names, as well as the relationship between the Smiths, likewise point viewers to the fact that postwar American and German economies were increasingly entwined in the decades following World War II, thanks largely to the Marshall Plan. Late in season three, Don takes Betty to Rome, while Pete saves his neighbor's German nanny by buying her a new dress to replace the one she ruined, which was owned by her boss' wife. Late in season seven, Don's daughter plans a trip to Francisco Franco's fascist Spain.[42] Both instances evoke the Marshall Plan, which both salvaged the European economy and made business partners and bedfellows of American companies and fascist regimes such as Franco's. The many instances of Americans taking vacations to fascist countries, such as Spain, likewise speaks to Madison Avenue's curious relationship with fascists such as Volkswagen and Franco. *Mad Men's* critique of American fascism thus illuminates that Americans in the Cold War were increasingly seduced into taking vacations by multinational corporations such as Hilton Hotels and ad men such as Don Draper

---

[41] Yi-Ping Ong, "Smoke Gets in Your Eyes: *Mad Men* and Moral Ambiguity," *Philosophy And New American TV Series*, Vol. 127, No. 5, (December 2012), pp. 1013-1039, p. 1017.

[42] Season 7 episode 13 "The Milk and Honey Route" May 10, 2015.

and were thus complicit in both conformity and fascism around the world. The intervention of American tax dollars made countries like Spain (a fascist regime until 1975) and Italy (where fascists' purge of leftists in the Interwar Era was comparable to the purge of leftists in postwar American society)[43] into trendy tourist destinations amongst America's burgeoning middle class in the decades after World War II.[44] As organized religion increasingly lost its mystique, aura, and value in the context of an increasingly secularized and militarist postwar American consumer culture, in which nuclear holocaust seemed a genuine possibility, vacation destinations such as Hawaii, California, Italy, and Spain were, as *Mad Men* elaborates, increasingly depicted as utopian anecdotes to New York City, especially in the season four finale when Don takes his kids to Disneyland, which was owned by a man named Walt Disney who, along with Ronald Reagan, named names to the House Un-American Activities Committee during the McCarthyist purges of American leftists in the 1950s.[45]

The fact that American tax and tourist dollars kept companies such as Volkswagen and Franco's regime alive and

[43] Andrea Mammone, "Is fascism back on the rise in Italy?: How Italy's far right became mainstream — and what it means for the United States" *The Washington Post*, January 27, 2018. For more historical context see Richard Beyler, Alexei Kojevnikov and Jessica Wang, "Purges in Comparative Perspective: Rules for Exclusion and Inclusion in the Scientific Community under Political Pressure," *Osiris* 2nd Series, Vol. 20, Politics and Science in Wartime: Comparative International Perspectives on the Kaiser Wilhelm Institute (2005), pp. 23-48.

[44] Season 3 episode 8 "Souvenir" October 4, 2009.

[45] Season 4 episode 13 "Tomorrowland" October 17, 2010.

thriving, in the interest of fueling consumer capitalism as a Cold War anecdote to communism, grows more poignant in season four when Don jokingly asks Roger if he "enjoyed the fuehrer's party?" Don's quip was in reference to the sadist southerner, Lee Garner, Jr., who was an executive of Lucky Strike Cigarettes. "May he live for a thousand years," Roger drunkenly retorts in a German accent reminiscent of Peter Sellers performing Dr. Strangelove.[46] The fact that Sterling & Cooper's corporate overlord is the grandson of a former Confederate soldier, who knows his product gives people cancer and yet cares only for profits and nothing of the lives imperiled, speaks to the deep strain of corporatist fascism deeply embedded, but often ignored, in Cold War American society and identity that stretches back to slavery.

The historical memory of the antebellum era and especially World War II in American history, as alluded to above, which is remembered far less fondly in Great Brittan than in the United States, also looms heavily over *Mad Men*. In season three, for example, Lane Pryce rehearses his speech for the agency's Fortieth Anniversary Party. "It was very rousing," his assistant, John Hooker (Ryan Cartwright), says of the speech. Lane then queries his underling: "Churchill rousing or Hitler rousing?"[47]

The specter of fascism in postwar American consumer culture likewise looms especially large when Don Draper likens Jaguar, which proves to be a particularly difficult client, to Munich.

---

[46] Season 4 episode 2 "Christmas Comes But Once a Year" August 1, 2010.

[47] Season 3 episode 10 "The Color Blue" October 18, 2009.

"You're always saying that," frustrated Pete, who was too young to have fought in the war, snarls; "what does it mean anyway?" Roger explains, "it means we gave the Germans whatever they wanted to make them happy and they just wanted more." Pete rhetorically asks, "Well, who won the war?"[48] Pete's comment seems to indicate that the Americans had subsumed the Germans in terms of imperial avarice in the decades after World War II. The notion of always wanting more yet never being fulfilled likewise seems to be a not-so-veiled critique of the nature of consumerism in which more is never enough.

In season five, Lane and his wife dine with newfound friends, English expatriates all. They celebrate their national team beating "the Gerry's" in the 1966 World Cup, which alludes to the complex, yet largely overlooked ways in which extreme nationalism and fascism had been repackaged into consumer culture in the decades after World War II.[49] Fascists, it is also interesting to note, founded the World Cup.[50] Later in season five, Michael Ginsberg (Ben Feldman) pitches an idea to sell ice cream by depicting a cartoon version of Adolf Hitler being smashed in the face with a snowball, which, he explains, kids would find very funny. Ginsberg's ad, like the unabashed celebration of nationalism associated with the World Cup, satirically illuminates ways in which fascism had been absorbed into and, in many ways

---

[48] Season 6 episode 3 "Collaborators" April 14, 2013.

[49] Season 5 episode 5 "Signal 30" April 15, 2012.

[50] Simon Martin, *Football and Fascism: The National Game Under Mussolini*, (London, Berg, 2005).

repackaged in, consumer culture in the decades after World War II.[51]

All these allusions are not by happenstance. For example, *Mad Men's* creator, Matthew Weiner, told Michael Renov in an interview for the book *From Shtetl to Stardom* (2016) that there was a group of boys he went to middle school with in Southern California who called themselves the "Sons of Hitler."[52] Weiner's memory seems to speak to the fact that he sees many similarities between the Southern California cultural milieu of his affluent youth (Governor Reagan's California) and what he learned about European fascism as a student. It is also interesting to note that Weiner's father was Reagan's physician.

Mad Men, in short, is as much about Weiner's experience growing up in Cold War America and his historical memory of the nation's collective identity, which was profoundly shaped by consumerist conformity, the advertising industry, a revamped Christian Evangelism, and militarism.

Fascism, in short, is not, according to its depiction in *Mad Men*, bound by ideology, which is particularly alluded to in season one when Abraham Menken (the owner of a mid-level Jewish department store that neighbors Macy's), upon leaving Sterling & Cooper's offices, says to his daughter in the wake of a cordial yet

[51] Season 5 episode 9 "Dark Shadows" May 13, 2012.

[52] Steven J. Ross and Michael Renov, "An Outsider's View of Sixties America: Matthew Weiner Talks with Michael Renov about the Jews of *Mad Men*" in *From Shtetl to Stardom*, (West Lafayette, IN, Purdue University Press, 2017), p. 168.

tense meeting with Don Draper and Pete Campbell, "This place reminds me of a czarist ministry. No matter what decision you make, you don't feel as though it was yours."[53]

Further evidence that *Mad Men* is as much about fascism embedded in postwar America's collective identity as it is about the individual identities of the characters on the show can be especially detected in season one as Don tells Pete that Sterling & Cooper has "more failed artists and intellectuals than the Third Reich."[54] Earlier in the season, Paul Kinsey asks Peggy, soon after she returns from eating lunch with Harry Crane, Ken Cosgrove, and Joan Holloway, if she "had fun with the Hitler youth?"[55] The viewer also learns that Volkswagen, a company long associated with Adolf Hitler, who ceremoniously opened the company's first factory in 1937, was growing more popular in postwar America due to its clever and minimalist advertising campaign. Roger notes that Birkbock, a Jewish ad agency, was skittish at the prospect of reindustrializing Germany, but worked with Volkswagen anyway. "Everybody has their price," Salvatore Romano (Bryan Batt) then sneeringly quips.[56] Helen Bishop (Darby Stanchfield), the Draper's neighbor from down the street, also drives a Volkswagen. One of the men attending a party hosted by Betty early in the inaugural season of the show jokes that, "the last time" he saw a Volkswagen he "was

[53] Season 1 episode 10 "Long Weekend" September 27, 2007.

[54] Season 1 episode 6 "Babylon" August 23, 2007.

[55] Season 1 episode 2 "ladies Room" July 19, 2007.

[56] Season 1 episode 4 "New Amsterdam" August 9, 2009.

throwing a grenade in it."[57] Sterling & Cooper also do business with Kodak and United Fruit in season one, both of which likewise did business with the Nazis. The Central Intelligence Agency also waged a coup in Guatemala in 1954 on behalf of United Fruit, which was that country's largest landowner. This alludes to numerous fascist dictators the U.S. backed economically and militarily all around the world during the Cold War. In later seasons of the show, Don's ad agency is consumed with trying to land the General Motors account, which spent more on advertising than any other company in the world during the 1960s. GM also did business with the Nazis all through the 1930s, and even sued the federal government and won reparations for property destroyed by allied bombing raids during World War II. The company was also, Weiner reminded readers of *TIME*, bailed out by American taxpayers after the 2008 global economic collapse, which underscored the corporate welfare endemic to America's militarized and consumerist society, which, not inconsequentially, also led the world in incarceration rates by the turn of the twenty-first century.[58] There is a prison guard named Hobart and also an advertising agency executive named Hobart, which seems to indicate a correlation between Cold War America's increasingly militarized/consumerist society and its prison industrial complex.

The specter of postwar American consumerism (soft power) exhibiting hallmarks of fascism is even more explicit in season four when Pete lands a meeting with Honda Motorcycles, a Japanese

[57] Season 1 episode 3 "Marriage of Figaro," August 2, 2007.

[58] James Poniewozik, "Making History: A Q & A with *Mad Men's* Matthew Weiner." *TIME*, March 27, 2014.

company. Roger, who is still deeply traumatized as a result of his time in the South Pacific as a member of the United States Navy during World War II, refuses to do business with the Japanese company. "If Birkbock can do business with Volkswagen," Pete says, "we can do business with anyone."[59] Later in season four, Peggy has a new leftist love interest named Abe Drexler (Charlie Hoffheimer) who makes his living as a journalist for underground publications such as *The Village Voice*. Abe writes a story entitled, "Nuremberg on Madison Avenue," which is one of the most explicit references *Mad Men* makes to postwar American consumerism being fascistic.[60]

Mad Men, in short, makes it seem as though the advertising industry is deeply complicit in the sadistic specter of Cold War nuclear holocaust, which could supposedly be alleviated by the utopian pleasure promised by conformity to a militarized/consumerist society. Mrs. Blankenship (Randee Heller), Don's geriatric secretary says to Peggy "this (the advertising industry) is the business of sadists and masochists," shortly before she, who is long past the age of retirement, keels over and dies at her desk. Just after the sixteenth minute in the same episode, Sally Draper (Don and Betty's oldest child) sits in the lobby of the midtown Manhattan high-rise where her father's agency is located. Outside the window is a subliminal "666" in big bold black print just above Abe's head as he waits to give Peggy "Nuremberg on Madison Avenue," which he hopes will enlighten her to the evils of

---

[59] Season 4 episode 2 "Christmas Comes But Once a Year" August 1, 2010.

[60] Season 4 episode 9 "The Beautiful Girls" September 19, 2010.

her industry and its complicity in America's war in Indochina. Abe is, not inconsequentially, an unabashed Jewish-American leftist who ultimately dumps Peggy because he comes to see her as "the enemy." Two seasons later Ted Shaw tells a tableful of attendees at the Clio's, an advertising industry award show, that "they're going to fire off a canon when the atrocities begin."[61] In season five, Roger laments that Jane, his twenty-year-old secretary turned wife, daftly asked, "Which one is Mussolini?" Later in the episode, Michael Ginsberg, who told Peggy he was born in a Nazi concentration camp, is first introduced to viewers. Peggy examines his portfolio and says, "You really have a voice." Ginsberg snidely replies, "That's what they said about *Mein Kampf*, 'Hitler really has a voice.'"[62] In season seven, McCann-Erickson's Jim Hobart (H. Richard Greene) tells Joan Holloway that he could get *The New York Times* to "print *Mein Kampf* on the front page" due to the amount of ad space his corporate and publicly traded agency buys during the course of a year.[63]

Also, twelve Caesar's eagles made of granite, which traditionally signified new territory gained by the Roman emperor, peered down on the entrance of Pennsylvania Station in midtown Manhattan for five decades. The Roman Eagle was also a symbol of the Italian, German, and American empires. In season three, controversy regarding the tearing down of Penn Station to build Madison Square Garden seems to become Sterling & Cooper's

[61] Season 6 episode 5 "The Flood" April 28, 2013.

[62] Season 5 episode 2 "A Little Kiss" March 25, 2012.

[63] Season 7 episode 12 "New Horizons" May 3, 2015.

public relations cross to bear on behalf of its corporatist real estate developer client, which alludes to Robert Moses. Kinsey shows one of the besieged developers of the proposed stadium an article critical of the endeavor with a headline that reads "Stop Fascism" in bold print.64 The controversy surrounding the tearing down of Penn Station on *Mad Men* seems to allude to Jane Jacobs's classic, *The Death and Life of Great American Cities* (1961), which championed ad-hocism in city building rather than the corporatism and Hausmannization hailed by Robert Moses and Madison Avenue, which, historian Fitzhugh Brundage argues, "left a trail of desolation, like a latter-day Sherman" dividing the recent past into "before and after" the New Deal.65

Mad Men also rightly depicts a longtime duplicity inherent in American identity between liberty and equality-for-all in epic tension with the United States as a bastion of capitalism. The mangled duality between freedom and authoritarianism embedded in America's collective identity in the postwar era is thus evident throughout the show. For instance, in the premier episode of season six Sandy (Kerris Dorsey), a virtuoso violinist whose mother recently died, says to Betty in reference to the beatnik squatters in Manhattan's East Village, "people are naturally democratic if you give them a chance."66 The adolescent's romantic notion is starkly contrasted with pessimistic Don's view of humanity. In season

---

64 Season 3 episode 2 "Love Among the Ruins" August 23, 2009.

65 Fitzhugh Brundage, *The Southern Past* (Cambridge, Mass.: Belknap Press of Harvard University Press, 2005, p. 269.

66 Season 6 episode 1 "The Doorway," April 7, 2013.

three, for instance, he engages in pillow talk with his daughter's former teacher, Suzanne Farrell, whose character seems inspired by Leonard Cohen's song, "Suzanne." She fawns over a question posed to her earlier in the day by a bright-eyed eight-year-old in her art class: "'How do I know if what I see as blue is the same as it is to you?'" the curious child asked the awed teacher. Suzanne, a free-spirited idealist, is thrilled by the simplicity yet complexity of such a seemingly innocent question. Don, conversely, answers the question as if he were one of the failed Third Reich artists that he described to Pete in season one. "The truth is," Don says matter-of-factly, "people may see things differently but they don't really want to."[67] Don likewise seems to ape an authoritarian discourse when he tells a beatnik at the Gaslight Café in season one that, "people want to be told what to do so badly that they will listen to anyone."[68]

Another hint that *Mad Men*, particularly Don, is a critique of the duality between freedom and authoritarianism embedded in postwar American society is the show's thematic similarity to Simone de Beauvoir's *Les Belles Images* (1966), a novel about a professionally accomplished yet spiritually unfulfilled ad woman in postwar Paris. Beauvoir's protagonist seems like she may have been part of the inspiration for Don Draper's character. Beauvoir, like so many critical theorists of the postwar era, including her husband, Jean-Paul Sartre, as well as Hannah Arendt, Michel Foucault, Frantz Fanon, and the members of the Frankfurt School, dedicated their careers to exploring ways in which fascism was

[67] Season 3 episode 9 "Wee Small Hours," October 11, 2009.

[68] Season 1 episode 6 "Babylon" August 23, 2007.

deeply embedded in, but often overlooked or ignored, in places such as The U.S., Great Brittan, and France.

Another obvious but heretofore overlooked clue that *Mad Men* is as much about the character and identity of the nation as much as it is about the inner lives of the characters on the show is the numerous references to the tension between being urban and agrarian that exists in America's collective identity. There is certainly an obvious and unmistakable glorification of Manhattan on the surface of *Mad Men*. The series is, for example, a product of a "golden age" in American television, as well as set in a "golden age" of the advertising industry, and a "golden age" of New York City history. The glitzy mid-century modern style of the show creates a kind of nostalgia and desire for New York City, and Madison Avenue in particular. But there are also several couched allusions to the anti-urban populist discourse championed by both American and German conservatives. In the decades before and after World War II urban space was often depicted by Europeans and Americans as a place where traditional cultural norms were perverted and, ultimately, collapsed.

Victor C. Ferkiss's "Populist Influences on American Fascism," like *Mad Men's* depiction of populism, helps to elaborate the deep strain of anti-urbanism espoused by reactionary conservatives in twentieth century American history. The widespread mistrust of urbanism and celebration of populism amongst rural folks common to both American and German popular culture and politics is especially critiqued in *Mad Men*. Both Richard Nixon and Ronald Reagan were, the creators of the show often remind viewers, populists from California, a state which was depicted to be new, improved, utopian, and was especially central to America's postwar military industrial complex, in stark contrast to decaying New York City.

Populism is also detected in the suburbanization depicted in *Mad Men*. "Our husbands are infinitely better out here (in the suburbs) Betty says to Francine in season one.[69] "I don't like Manhattan on my own," Betty says to Don four episodes later, "it's harsh."[70] Early in season two, Paul Kinsey says, "this (New Jersey and not New York City) is (the real) America."[71] An episode later, Bobbie Barrett forces herself on Don. Bobbie is depicted as an unapologetically urbane and sophisticated Jewish femme fatale in glaring contrast to Betty, who is depicted as the quintessential Aryan suburban housewife dutifully aching for her husband to come home from the big bad city after a long day of work.[72] In season three, Don's father-in-law, Gene, snidely asks Don, "how was Babylon" (in reference to Manhattan)?[73] In season five, Lane Pryce and his wife dine with a Jaguar executive and his spouse. The Jaguar executive's wife explains to the other expatriates that she prefers "New York to London because fifty miles away they are infinitely more wholesome." The Jaguar executive assuages his wife's urban-induced anxiety by assuring her that, "you'll have your farmland someday."[74] The anti-urban/populist theme is

[69] Season 1 episode 3 "Marriage of Figaro" August 2, 2007.

[70] Season 1 episode 9 "Shoot" September 13, 2007.

[71] Season 2 episode 2 "Flight 1" August 3, 2008.

[72] Season 2 episode 3 "The Benefactor" August 10, 2008.

[73] Season 3 episode 3 "My Old Kentucky Home" August 30, 2008.

[74] Season 5 episode 5 "Signal 30" April 15, 2012.

evident in season seven, too, when Roger's daughter, Margaret, leaves her husband and young son behind in Manhattan (Babylon) to live on a commune in upstate New York. "I used to think the country was lonely," she tells her Knickerbocker father, who she accuses of being a terrible parent, "now I think the city is."[75] Late in season seven, Bob Benson bails a General Motors executive visiting New York from Pontiac, Michigan, out of jail. The GM executive, whose face is battered and bloody as a result of trying to fellate an undercover police officer in a department store bathroom, wonders aloud, "how could you live in this city, there's so much temptation?" Bob admits, "It was hard."[76] The exchange seems to particularly speak to populists' fears that Judeo-Christian civilization inevitably dissolves in multicultural melting pots such as New York City (Babylon).

      Walter Veith (Randy Oglesby), an executive for Bethlehem Steel, and Conrad Hilton both personify the rural populism commonly, and sometimes comically, aped by American industrialists in the twentieth century. Walter, for example, does not like the ads pitched to him by Don and Salvatore in season one because they seem like they are selling cities such as New York and Chicago, rather than Bethlehem Steel. Walter especially chafes at the notion of being a "middleman" for the marketing of cities. The steel magnate explains to Don that he is "not from the city," so the WPA-style minimalist ads that champion his corporation as the

[75] Season 7 episode 4 "The Monolith" May 4, 2014.

[76] Season 7 episode 6 "The Strategy" May 18, 2014.

"backbone" of America's cities "bother" him.[77] Two seasons later Don meets Conrad Hilton at a Jay Gatsby-esque party hosted by Roger. Don informs Hilton that he is from rural Pennsylvania by way of rural Illinois because his family lost their farm and ended up in coal country.[78] The fact that Don appears like a quintessential blue collar salt-of-the earth populist, who could be a character in a Steinbeck novel, quickly endears him to Hilton, who proudly hails from a homestead in New Mexico (before it was a state). Ten episodes later Hilton, however, sours on Don and explains that he can no longer do business with the ad man's agency because, as the hotel baron explains, he "earned everything" he has "on his own" and thus cannot "deal with people who complain."[79] Hilton's line reeks of the "pull yourself up by your bootstraps" ethos and discourse weaponized by conservatives in the postwar era to denigrate poverty-stricken Americans as lazy and stupid, rather than victims of socioeconomic factors beyond their control.

But the most concealed, yet, perhaps, most glaring clue that *Mad Men* – a show about the American advertising industry – is a Trojan Horse of a critique of consumerist and militarized society as fascistic – can be found buried late and very fleetingly in the final season of the show. Don, who is "riding the rails" west in his Cadillac an attempt to escape from the stultifying conformity at Jim Hobart's corporatist agency, McCann-Erickson, which had recently acquired Draper's agency, sees a woman sunbathing by a motel

[77] Season 1 episode 4 "New Amsterdam" August 9, 2007.

[78] Season 3 episode 3 "My Old Kentucky Home" August 30, 2009.

[79] Season 3 episode 13 "Shut The Door. Have a Seat" November 8, 2009.

pool. She reads, of all things, *The Woman from Rome* (1947), a novel by Alberto Moravia about the intersecting lives of many characters, most notably a prostitute and an idealistic scholar who, after an interrogation by fascist officers, during which he betrays his colleagues for reasons he himself is not able to understand, becomes completely disillusioned and nihilistic.

Although Moravia's novel examines the identities of a prostitute, an intellectual, and a fascist henchman, the story is, like *Mad Men*, ultimately a study of individual identity in the context of the wider society. *The Woman from Rome* is also thematically similar to *Mad Men* in terms of exploring individualism in the context of the wider cultural milieu that shapes individuals' personal identities. Both *The Woman from Rome* and *Mad Men*, in short, are as much about the individuals' environment (the militarized corporatist nation-state) as they are about the individual characters' inner lives. Both stories also depict cultures in which fascism, in one form or another, is deeply entrenched in the day-to-day lives of the characters, but those characters are often ambivalent to the fascism that dictates their thoughts and actions and conscribes their agency.

Although anti-urban populism is depicted in early seasons of *Mad Men*, mass mobilization to the capitalist system, which is especially fueled by consumerism, is the most central theme of postwar America's collective identity, as depicted throughout the show. In other words, whether examining racism, sexism, imperialism, or art, mass mobilization to the capitalist system, which was fueled primarily by consumerism in tandem with militarism in postwar America's Affluent Society, is the most prominent theme that runs across seven seasons of *Mad Men*.

The chapters that comprise *Mad Men and the Specter of American Fascism* focus especially on the depiction of American identity during the Vietnam Era/Space Age, most particularly on elements of fascism deeply rooted in American postwar consumer culture, as depicted in *Mad Men*. There is, however, no universally accepted definition of fascism. Since the end of World War II, political scientists and historians have struggled to get at the "fascist minimum" that characterizes all fascisms.[80] Fascism is, however, most commonly associated with values that are contrary to those often associated with the Enlightenment (liberty, fraternity, equality, and social justice) in contrast to "political realists" who view all life as a Darwinistic struggle for survival, power and domination in a global jungle in which human beings are basically beasts masquerading as spiritual beings. Fascism is, however, for the purposes of this study, most commonly characterized by mass mobilization, racism, sexism and misogyny, homophobia, opposition to Marxism, a glorification of violence as regenerative, militarism, extreme nationalism, imperialism, and a fetishization for a youthful "New Man" and warrior culture. These themes and concepts provide the parameters for the chapters that comprise this study.

Chapter one uses *Mad Men* as a lens with which to examine racism in postwar American society. Chapter two examines sexism, misogyny, and second-wave feminism in postwar American

---

[80] Matthew Wills, "Do You Know Fascism When You See It? *JSTOR Daily*, July 6, 2006. Roger Griffin, "The Primacy of Culture: The Current Growth (Or Manufacture) of Consensus within Fascist Studies" *Journal of Contemporary History*, Vol. 37, No. 1 (Jan., 2002), pp. 21-43.

society. Chapter three features Cold War American opposition to Marxism and the subsequent perpetuation of the American social system (including class, racial and gender). Chapter four examines the heightened violence associated with the Vietnam Era in American history. Chapter five explores American militarism and the lecherous fetish for youth in postwar American consumer culture. Chapter six examines the United States at the height of its imperial powers, paying particularly close attention to the soft power of consumerism. Chapter seven explores the anxiety associated with death, and the conflation of religion and consumerism as tandem utopias vying for Americans' hearts and minds at a time in human history when nuclear annihilation seemed a very real possibility. Chapter eight examines the character, Michael Ginsberg, as the personification of Allen Ginsberg's poem, *Howl*, which, like *Mad Men*, alludes to postwar American consumerism and militarism exhibiting myriad elements of technocratic fascism. The final chapter also explores the paradox of trying to create revolutionary high art made for the masses by elaborating Theodor Adorno and Max Horkheimer's concept of "the culture industry." The study concludes with an epilogue that elaborates that *Mad Men* is as much about the Digital Age and anxiety associated with notions of the decline of the American Empire in the twenty-first century as it is about the Space Age, Vietnam Era, and the zenith of the American empire in the 1960s.

Chapter One

"Mad Men and Cold War American Racism"

Steven Horwitz's essay, "Fascism: Italian, German, and American" helps to illuminate that racism was a central feature of each of those nation's politics, society and collective identity during the Interwar Era.[81] The Nazis, as is well known, blamed Jews for almost everything that had gone wrong in Germany in the years between World War I and World War II, everything from the Great Depression and the rise of Marxism to the evils of international capitalism. Mussolini was also anti-Semitic and used scientific racism to justify Italy's invasion of Ethiopia in 1935. Harold Brackman argues in "'A Calamity Almost Beyond Comprehension:' Nazi Anti-Semitism and the Holocaust in the Thought of W.E.B. Du Bois," that the vilification and oppression of the Jews of Eastern Europe, who lived in the lands occupied by the Nazis in the late-1930s and early 1940s, could be compared to the vilification of black Americans all through the history of the United States.[82] *Mad Men*, likewise, quite rightly depicts the United States as having deep strains of fascist racial customs and practices deeply embedded in postwar American society and identity, including the nation's laws. This chapter examines *Mad Men's* depiction of the prevalence of racism in 1960s America, paying close attention to Jewish-Americans, Native Americans, Asians, and most predominately, African Americans. All told, *Mad Men* depicts postwar American racism to be eerily similar to Nazi and Italian racism in the Interwar Era.

[81] See Steven Horwitz, "Fascism: Italian, German, and American," *The Independent Review*, Vol. 13, No. 3 (Winter 2009), pp. 441-446.

[82] See Harold Brackman, "'A Calamity Almost Beyond Comprehension:' Nazi Anti-Semitism and the Holocaust in the Thought of W. E. B. Du Bois," *American Jewish History* Vol. 88, No. 1, America and the Holocaust: New Perspectives-I (March 2000), pp. 53-93.

Mad Men depicts 1960s America, both the North and South, as being racially segregated. The hegemonic white culture in Mad Men is also depicted as woefully ignorant of and chauvinistic towards racial "others," most conspicuously Jews, which seems explicitly intended to draw comparisons between the Nazi's and postwar American WASPs. Very early in season one of Mad Men, for instance, there is a crisis at Sterling & Cooper because the agency does not employ anyone Jewish. The company executives, most notably Roger Sterling, scramble to find an employee of Jewish ancestry so as not to risk offending the potential client, Menken's Department Store. "Have we hired any Jews?" Roger nervously asks Don Draper. Don snidely replies, "Not on my watch." Later in the episode, shrimp cocktail is served during the meeting with Rachel Menkin (although shellfish is not kosher). Rachel, a Jewish-American woman, seems somewhat offended as she uses the shrimp cocktail as an ashtray.[83] Two episodes later Francine Hanson (Anne Dudeck), Betty Draper's friend from the neighborhood, chafes at the high percentage of Jews in Boca Raton, Florida. She laments that she was not able to relax on her vacation in Boca because she felt "outnumbered" (by Jews).[84] In season four, Pete Campbell tells Peggy that Sugarberry Ham is testing their product in markets that are predominately Jewish. But the company executives cannot understand why sales are flat, as if they simply did not know that ham also was not kosher.[85]

[83] Season 1 episode 1 "Smoke Gets in Your Eyes" July 19, 2007.

[84] Season 1 episode 3 "Marriage of Figaro" August 2, 2007.

[85] Season 4 episode 1 "Public Relations" July 25, 2010.

In the latter part of season one, Sterling & Cooper is tasked with creating an ad campaign to attract American tourists to Israel. Salvatore Romano laments that the "Jews here (New York City) don't look like the Jews there (Israel)," essentially calling Israeli women glamorous and beautiful in contrast to Jewish-American women, who he seems to consider homely. Later in the episode Don plops a magazine depicting a sultry Israeli woman atop stark black and white photos of the starved skeletal remains in Buchenwald, a liberated Nazi concentration camp. Moments later, Rachel takes umbrage with Don referring to Israelis as "those people." She insinuates that Don inherently, perhaps subconsciously, dislikes Jewish people, a charge he flatly denies. She also mentions the recent capture of Adolf Eichmann and indicates that Don (the glib advertising agent) and the infamous Nazi taskmaster are not as dissimilar as he might like to think.[86]

Three seasons later, Roger marries a 20-year-old Jewish girl and is bound by unapologetic nepotism to hire her cousin as a copywriter. "You're such a Jew," Harry Crane says to Jane's cousin, Danny Siegal (Danny Strong), as he complains of the exorbitant price of a ticket to watch the Cassius Clay versus Sonny Liston title bout scheduled to be played live at the Lowe's movie theater in Manhattan. "Your friends in Hollywood know you talk that way?" Danny, who later becomes a motion picture producer, asks Harry -- the head of television operations at Sterling & Cooper. "And let me tell you something," Danny adds, "You're the Jew for trying to make thirty dollars off something you didn't pay for."[87] The

[86] Season 1 episode 6 "Babylon" August 23, 2007.

[87] Season 4 episode 7 "The Suitcase" September 5, 2010.

stereotype of Jews being too miserly to be trusted surfaces again a season later when Roger enlists the creative genius of Michael Ginsberg, a Jewish-American man, who claims to have been born in a Nazi concentration camp, to craft an ad campaign that might attract Manischewitz's business. "It (the ad) has to be cheap," Roger snidely tells Ginsberg, "surprise…"[88]

The specter of the Holocaust, as the gruesome images atop Don's desk and Rachel's allusion to Eichmann in the show's inaugural episode illuminate, looms over the series like an atomic mushroom cloud, particularly the early seasons of the show. The creators of *Mad Men* poignantly point viewers to the fascist racial attitudes and practices deeply embedded in postwar American society, especially in the realm of consumerism. Genocide, however, is depicted as an atrocity that has happened throughout human history, not merely in 1940s Europe.

The wanton destruction of Native American cultures is, for example, sardonically alluded to on a number of occasions. In season one, McCann-Erickson's Jim Hobart alludes to the postwar American fetish for cowboys versus Indians when he tries to woo Don to his agency by saying, "you want to sell corn? We do an Indian show?" In the following scene, Betty refers to the "Indian Trading" Don had to do to buy her a fur coat when they first met.[89] In season two, Don says, "when one is in Indian country one needs a man who knows Indians," as he refers to young people recently hired by the agency during a meeting with Martinson executives

[88] Season 5 episode 9 "Dark Shadows" May 13, 2012.

[89] Season 1 episode 9 "Shoot" September 13, 2007.

eager to seduce kids into drinking coffee.[90] Also, in season two, the audience learns that Mohawk Airlines is a client of Sterling & Cooper. Not only is it racially insensitive to name a company after a culture that was the victim of genocide comparable to the Jewish Holocaust, but Paul Kinsey, a young and paradoxical pseudo-liberal Princeton graduate copywriter at Sterling & Cooper who also wrote a utopian short story about white folks and black folks getting along just fine in his depiction of a utopian New Jersey,[91] incongruously cheers for Richard Nixon when the Vice President wins Ohio in the 1960 General Election.[92] He, in fact, crafts a number of insensitive and stereotypical taglines in the hopes of marketing Mohawk. One such tagline he authors includes, "Mohawk Airlines, there's a new chief in the sky…" and "Most routes to Boston, circle the wagons, we've got it surrounded." Peggy then suggests using Pocahontas (not a Mohawk) to market the airline.[93] Two episodes later, shock comic Jimmy Barrett (Patrick Fischler) jokes that Mrs. Edith Schilling (Jan Hoag), the obese wife of the owner of Utz Potato Chips, might be of interest to "Sitting Bull" because she is the "last buffalo."[94] The line alludes to the destruction of the buffalo and subsequent displacement and annihilation of myriad cultures native to North America in the name of the "progress" associated with manifest destiny and the

[90] Season 2 episode 7 "The Gold Violin" September 7, 2008.

[91] Season 1 episode 5 "5G" August 16, 2007.

[92] Season 1 episode 12 "Nixon vs. Kennedy" October 11, 2007.

[93] Season 2 episode 1 "For Those Who Think Young" July 27, 2008.

[94] Season 2 episode 3 "The Benefactor" August 10, 2008.

"settling" of the West. Three seasons later, Sitting Bull is depicted as being hit in the face with a snowball as a means of marketing ice cream to kids. Michael Ginsberg explains that kids hate Indians, which makes the joke "funny."[95]

Mad Men is set in the 1960s, a time when Westerns were the most popular genre on *NBC, ABC,* and *CBS* -- the only three channels on American television during the decade. Native Americans were routinely depicted on primetime and daytime television as communal bad guys that were mostly one-dimensional and barely-human obstacles often conflated with nature and standing in the way of America's hyper-masculine white cowboy settling the frontier and paving the way for capitalism's conquering of the Transcontinental West. Betty's father, Gene Hofstadt (Ryan Cutrona), who "let one of the black caddies at the Golf Course have it" in season two,[96] cuts a John Wayne-like grizzled figure as he complains in season three that Sally and Bobby's rowdiness and roughhousing is like a bunch of "wild Indians."[97]

There are also several concealed instances of racism directed towards Asians in *Mad Men*. Early in season one, for example, some of the younger men employed by Sterling & Cooper, which has a frat house dynamic, play a gag on Pete Campbell, who has just returned for his first day back at work after his honeymoon with Trudy in Niagara Falls. Pete's officemates hire a family of

[95] Season 5 episode 9 "Dark Shadows" May 13, 2012.

[96] Season 2 episode 10 "The Inheritance" October 5, 2008.

[97] Season 3 episode 2 "Love Among the Ruins" August 23, 2009.

"Chinamen" ("Orientals" to Peggy) who are dressed as if they just stepped off a wooden boat or time machine to occupy his office. The episode is set just seven years after the end of the Korean War and around the time of the Sino-Soviet split.[98] Roger, a season later, cryptically jokes that he has to "give a Chinaman a music lesson" as he drunkenly parts ways with Freddy and Don at the conclusion of an evening filled with heavy drinking and illegal gambling.[99] In season three, Betty and Don's son, Bobby, runs inside the house laughing gleefully because the cab driver "is Chinese."[100] In season four, Roger refuses to do business with Honda Motorcycles, a Japanese company and calls them Pete's "little yellow buddies."[101] Later, Roger rudely interrupts a meeting attended by Honda executives and his partners at Sterling & Cooper and callously makes light of the fact that the United States dropped two atomic bombs (weapons of genocide) that killed hundreds of thousands of Japanese civilians during World War II. Close to the conclusion of the series Don attends a fundraiser frequented by dozens of drunken American Veterans of Foreign Wars, one of whom does a crude impression of a perverted "Jap" doctor.[102]

The depiction of Roger speaks to the complex ways in which the Japanese were viciously racialized in American propaganda

[98] Season 1 episode 3 "Marriage of Figaro" August 2, 2007.

[99] Season 2 episode 9 "Six Month Leave" September 28, 2008.

[100] Season 3 episode 10 "The Color Blue" October 18, 2009.

[101] Season 4 episode 5 "The Chrysanthemum and the Sword" August 22, 2010.

[102] Season 7 episode 13 "The Milk and Honey Route" May 10, 2015.

during World War II, especially compared to the far more humane depictions of the Nazis by the likes of Walt Disney studios. Whereas Japanese people tended to be depicted as anthropomorphic bucked-tooth rats and apes, Germans were often depicted, most notably by Disney cartoonists, to be doughy-eyed victims who had been duped by a madman, rather than racially inferior mongrels. Japanese Americans were also rounded up and forced into internment camps somewhat comparable to Nazi concentration camps. German Americans, conversely, were not interned.

The residual racial animus towards the Japanese viscerally experienced by American veterans of World War II was sometimes transferred from fathers to sons in postwar American history, which helped facilitate the dehumanization of the Vietnamese in the 1960s and 1970s. This dehumanization of Asians is alluded to in the premiere episode of season six when Don and Megan Draper (Jessica Paré) visit Hawaii. Don meets Private First-Class Dinkins (Patrick Mapel), an American G.I. on leave in Hawaii. The G.I. drunkenly laments that Hawaiians make him uneasy because they "look just like the enemy."[103] American G.I.s also, it is important to note, often likened the Vietcong to Native Americans. Vietnam was, in fact, often referred to as "Indian Country" by American troops, thereby illuminating continuity in terms of racialization of peoples that stood in the way of the United States' ascendance as a

---

[103] Season 6 episode 1 "The Doorway" April 7, 2013.

continental empire in the nineteenth century and a global empire a century later.[104]

Like Jews, Native Americans, Asians, and Latin Americans are likewise depicted as victims of Anglo-American racism in *Mad Men*. In season three, for example, Horace Cook, Jr. (Aaron Stanford), a young heir to a shipping magnate's fortune, tells Pete, a fraternity brother from Dartmouth College, that his father made a fortune as a war profiteer who rented out troop transports to the federal government in the 1940s, but "didn't care about the Germans (as an enemy)." Horace, Jr. further elaborates that his father (David Selby), like the Nazis, is devoutly anti-immigration and called star Jai Alai player, Padgie, a "wetback."[105]

There's also veiled racism expressed towards Africans in season three. Rebecca (Embeth Davidtz), Lane Pryce's wife, who recently moved to New York City from London, laments that the expatriated couple's new apartment is in Sutton Place, which is quite near the United Nations complex in midtown Manhattan. "There are plenty of Africans," she laments, which might allude to the Cold War era in American history also being an era of anti-colonialism in many parts of the world, including Vietnam and the U.S.[106] The following season the audience learns that Lane's patrician father would not approve of his son dating a black girl,

---

[104] See Paul C. Rosier, *Serving Their Country: American Indian Politics and Patriotism in the Twentieth Century*. (Cambridge, Mass., Harvard University Press, 2009); p. 248.

[105] Season 3 episode 4 "The Arrangements" September 6, 2009.

[106] Season 3 episode 2 "Love Among The Ruins" August 23, 2009.

thereby alluding to the centrality of racism to imperialism in both the United States and England, as well as fascist Germany and Italy during the Interwar Era.[107]

American race relations, which is evidence of the moral ambiguity in the United States throughout World War II and the Cold War, is as central to *Mad Men* as is the Vietnam War. Late in the final season of the show, for example, a *TIME Magazine* featuring a cover story about "Black America," which was published in 1970, sits atop Don's coffee table. The subliminal messages in *Mad Men*, which critique the advertising industry, seems to correlate consumerism, the Jewish Holocaust and white backlash to black civil rights.

Many African Americans, especially the National Association for the Advancement of Colored People and the African-American World War II veterans who were vital to toppling Nazi, Italian, and Japanese fascism also championed the "Double Victory" campaign begun in 1942, which was designed to expose and defeat the ever-present specter of fascistic racial mores that existed in Cold War American society and collective identity. Many political leaders in the United States in the decades after World War II saw the Cold War and the modern civil rights movement and decolonization around the postcolonial world as a many-headed hydra. African American leaders such as Martin Luther King, Jr., who had been deeply inspired by Mahatmas Gandhi and India's non-violent struggle to win independence from the British Empire during the 1920s through 1940s, was acutely

---

[107] Season 4 episode 10 "Hands and Knees" September 26, 2010.

aware of the global dimensions of African Americans' quest for economic and political equality during the 1950s and 1960s.

Although overt and institutional racism is expressed by white Americans depicted in *Mad Men* towards Jews, Native Americans, Asians, Latinos, and Africans, by far most racism is aimed squarely at African Americans as they struggle to win civil rights during what many scholars refer to as America's Second Reconstruction. There are three main areas of racism directed towards black Americans in *Mad Men*: in business, in politics, and culturally at a grassroots level; all of which overlap from time-to-time. *Mad Men* thus makes plain that the struggle for civil rights in the decades after World War II is evidence of a deep strain of racism comparable to that associated with European fascism during the Interwar Era.

Entrenched racism in American business is first introduced to viewers early in season one when Pete Campbell's patrician father, Andrew (Christopher Allport), denigrates his youngest son's industry as synonymous with boozing and whoring and, therefore, "no job for a white man."[108] A season later Roger tells Don that a rival agency "hired a colored kid." Don's response: "I'm glad I'm not that kid," as if to illuminate that the young man's struggle will be comparable to the backlash Jackie Robinson suffered as he integrated Major League Baseball in 1947.[109] The exchange between Roger and Don thus underscores how racially segregated American industries, including in the North, continued

[108] Season 1 episode 4 "New Amsterdam" August 9, 2007.

[109] Season 2 episode 9 "Six-Month Leave" September 28, 2008.

to be in the 1960s. As Joan notes in season six, The Federal Commission on Human Rights investigated the American advertising industry in the late-1960s due to pervasive racial and gender discrimination.[110]

The racial segregation of postwar American business is further elaborated in season three; Pete probes Hollis, an African-American elevator operator at Sterling & Cooper, for information about why Admiral Television might be so much more popular amongst African-American consumers than with white consumers. Hollis is reticent to engage Pete. Pete, however, persists by saying, "it's just Hollis…" Hollis abruptly replies, "and *Mister* Campbell… I don't even watch the damn thing (television). We (African Americans) have bigger things to worry about than TV." Pete replies, "you're looking at this very narrowly; the idea is that everyone will have a house and car — the American Dream."[111] Hollis dares to look long, hard, and accusatorially at Pete as if the latter is childishly naïve. The fact that Pete abruptly stops the elevator manned by Hollis seems to indicate that the former thinks that the successful performance of his job is more vital than Hollis successfully performing his, despite the fact that Hollis literally pushes the button that gets Pete where he needs to go. And the fact that Hollis is compelled by what he perceives to be Pete's ignorance and indifference to African American suffering alludes to the growing frustration and rage of African Americans during the 1960s. The icy interaction between Pete, whose employment is far more secure than a black service worker like Hollis' would be,

[110] Season 6 episode 3 "To Have and To Hold" April 21, 2013.

[111] Season 3 episode 5 "The Fog" September 13, 2008.

particularly underscores the farce of a "post-racial" America, which some American conservatives and centrists mistakenly believed Barack Obama's presidency represented. The tense interaction between Pete and Hollis, in which the latter makes a point of referring to the former as "Mister," indicates a white blindness towards entrenched class and racial hierarchies that Pete seems completely oblivious to, but of which Hollis is all too painfully aware. Later in the episode, Pete explains to executives at Admiral Television that *Jet Magazine* and *Ebony Magazine* are "by Negroes for Negroes." He elaborates that "ads are much cheaper in Negro publications." Admiral, however, refuses to be "an integrated company." An Admiral executive seems particularly peeved as he rhetorically asks Pete, "Who is to say Negroes aren't buying Admiral because they think white people want them?" Bert Cooper, Pete's boss, chastises his young underling by saying, "Admiral has no interest in being a colored television company." Pete is frustrated as he replies, "But, they are! I can't understand why a company wouldn't want to make more money."[112]

The theme of postwar America's racially divided "free" market economy is explored further in season four. Peggy suggests employing African American Harry Belafonte to sing Fillmore Auto Parts' new jingle. Peggy offers the suggestion as a veiled criticism because she knows that the auto parts company refuses to hire black workers at the Fillmore stores in the American South. "Have you ever been to the South?" Stan Rizzo (Jay R. Ferguson) asks Peggy. "They have a certain way of doing things and it does not include Harry Belafonte." Don says to Peggy, "Our job is to make

---

[112] Season 3 episode 5 "The Fog" September 13, 2008.

men like Fillmore, not make Fillmore like Negroes."[113] Fillmore is based in Boston, which speaks to the fact that postwar American racism is not merely a southern problem, and simultaneously alludes to the federal government's attempt to force integration by bussing kids from predominately black and Latino urban schools to mostly white suburban schools and vice versa, which stoked vicious and often violent backlash towards African Americans all throughout the country in the early 1970s, most notably in Boston, which experienced some of the most vitriolic white backlash towards integration and civil rights.

Season five begins in the summer of 1967, which witnessed dozens of race riots. Employees of Young and Rubicam, a rival agency to Sterling, Cooper, Draper & Pryce, say things such as "get a job" as they gleefully toss paper bags full of water from the window of the high-rise that is home to the company on African-American protestors below, who are marching against pervasive racial segregation in the advertising industry. One of the protesters, an aging black woman, says, "Is this what Madison Avenue represents?" Another woman says, "and they call us savages." The recently renamed Sterling, Cooper, Draper, and Pryce, which does not employ a single African American, places an ad in *The New York Times* declaring SCDP an "equal opportunity employer" as a barb against Y&R. An unintended consequence of the joke, however, is that several African Americans seeking employment show up at the agency, which underscores the ignorance of and ambivalence towards racial inequality amongst the white men who work on

[113] Season 4 episode 9 "The Beautiful Girls" September 19, 2010.

Madison Avenue. Y&R meanwhile sends an artifact depicting an African warrior donning only a loincloth to SCDP which arrives at the very moment the company's lobby is packed with African American job seekers.[114]

In season seven, Bert Cooper's ire is stoked after Joan assigns a recently hired black secretary to man the front desk of the agency. "I'm all for the national advancement of colored people," Cooper tells Joan, "but I do not believe they should advance all the way to the front of this office. People can see her from the elevator."[115] Cooper is made uneasy by the notion that the company he founded might be perceived as having a black face, which is especially ironic considering his partner's Al Jolson-like blackface performance of "My Old Kentucky Home" in season three. Cooper seemed especially amused by Roger's racist performance.[116] Close to the conclusion of the series, Shirley, a young African-American woman hired by the agency tells her boss, Roger, she is leaving the agency for a position with Traveler's Insurance. "Advertising is not a comfortable place for everyone," she concedes to Roger, underscoring how inhospitable the industry is for black women workers in particular.[117]

The wider context of pervasive postwar American racial segregation is the centrality of racism in American politics during

[114] Season 5 episode 1 "A Little Kiss" March 25, 2012.

[115] Season 7 episode 2 "A Day's Work" April 20, 2014.

[116] Season 3 episode 3 "My Old Kentucky Home" August 30, 2009.

[117] Season 7 episode 12 "New Horizons" May 3, 2015.

the Second Reconstruction. Close to the end of season three Don drives from the suburbs to Manhattan early in the morning. An excerpt from Martin Luther King, Jr.'s "I Have a Dream" speech plays on the radio as Don stops the car to offer Suzanne Farrell, who is jogging, a ride home. Suzanne, who was Sally's teacher the prior school year, tells Don she plans to read King's speech to her class the first day of the new school year. Don expresses that he thinks the kids are most likely too young to understand it. The teacher, conversely, says that she thinks children inherently understand the message, thereby evoking Nina Simone's "Turning Point," a song in which a little white girl is taught to see the world through a racist lens by her mother.[118] Later in the episode Betty's friend and neighbor, Francine, expresses that she is interested in finding out how presidential candidate Nelson Rockefeller, whose assistant is scheduled to visit the Draper home for a fundraiser, would "handle the South." Another of Betty's friends says, "You know what my father says about the South? It's not 1963. It's 1863."[119] This could be considered one of many allusions to Barry Goldwater winning the 1964 presidential nomination at the Republican National Convention over Rockefeller and George Romney by successfully stylizing himself as a champion of "state's rights" in contrast to the federal government's backing of Civil Rights legislation. Goldwater was defeated by Lyndon Johnson in a landslide in the 1964 general election. But Goldwater's campaign had a profound impact in terms of reshaping American political discourse along racially coded lines. The South and American

[118] Nina Simone, "The Turning Point," *Silk & Soul*, 1967.

[119] Season 3 episode 9 "Wee Small Hours" October 11, 2009.

"heartland" has been solidly Republican ever since the 1968 general election due in large part to Richard Nixon's "southern strategy" in which the Republican Party successfully turned the more rural regions of the country deep red by couching racism in a language of taxes, state rights, and law and order in opposition to urban riots, civil rights and welfare chiselers.

In season four, the viewer is first introduced to Stan Rizzo, a progressive artist who worked on a controversial commercial on behalf of Lyndon Johnson's 1964 presidential campaign that never aired. The commercial, which was actually made and can be viewed on youtube.com, depicts Ku Klux Klan members parading around a fiery cross as a voiceover of Robert Creel, a grand wizard of the Alabama Klan, professes his admiration for Barry Goldwater as well as his racist hatred for all "isms."[120] The KKK is a white supremacist organization founded at the end of the American Civil War. The organization was revived in 1915 after the premiere of D.W. Griffith's incredibly popular film, *A Birth of a Nation* (1914). The Klan displayed some of the fascist characteristics associated with the Nazis, who likewise preached the supremacy of the white race. The Klan had a kind of revival during the postwar civil rights movement as white supremacy and racially coded language such as "state's rights" became the cornerstone of racially coded "post-racial" American politics, in which racism remains a defining, yet often ignored, feature of the American polity.

In season six, a producer and actress on Megan Draper's soap opera says, "status quo antebellum," as if to allude to the fact that postwar America is not too terribly dissimilar to the America

[120] Season 4 episode 6 "Waldorf Stories" August 29, 2010.

that existed prior to the Civil War.[121] In season four, viewers learn that Lee Garner, Jr's grandfather fought in the Civil War and "never surrendered," which further underscores the fetishization for the antebellum South in American popular culture (including politics) and the centrality of racism to American society in the decades before and long after World War II.

In addition to the pervasive racial discrimination central to postwar American business and politics, *Mad Men* does very well to elaborate the centrality of racism at a grassroots cultural level. Early in season seven, for instance, the two black secretaries employed by the agency, Dawn (Teyonah Parris) and Shirley, jokingly call each other by the others' name, thereby underscoring that the white workers at the agency tend to confuse them.[122] Early in the show's existence Betty Draper and Mona Sterling do not tip black bathroom attendants at an upscale Manhattan restaurant, eliciting the following response from one of the African-American workers: "if those purses get any smaller we're going to starve," underscoring the fact that millions of black Americans in the postwar American North as well as South were second-class citizens largely dependent on the largesse of well-to-do white Americans for survival. It likewise underscores the increased retreat from liberalism by the likes of Mona and Betty.[123]

It should come as no great shock that almost all of the service workers depicted in *Mad Men*, including maids, delivery

[121] Season 6 episode 10 "A Tale of Two Cities" June 2, 2013.

[122] Season 7 episode 2 "A Day's Work" April 20, 2014.

[123] Season 1 episode 2 "Ladies Room" July 26, 2007.

people, elevator operators, caddies, movers, et cetera, tend to be African American. In season five, Gail Holloway (Christine Estabrook), Joan's mother, tells her daughter to hire a "colored girl" as a housekeeper because "they are used to being bossed around."[124] In season two, Kinsey is visited in the office by Sheila White (Donielle Artese), his African-American girlfriend (who works at a grocery store in New Jersey). The quick kiss between Sheila and Kinsey elicits hardly concealed contempt and disgust from Allison, a white secretary.[125] Earlier in the season, Sally Draper visits the agency and notices the picture of Sheila on Kinsey's desk and asks, "Is that your maid?" It is an innocent question, especially considering that nearly every maid on the show through seven seasons, including the maid at her own suburban home in Ossining, New York, is African American. Black nursemaids were highly desired by well-to-do white families in both the North and South during the Jim Crow era. In fact, one of the most profound ironies of the Jim Crow era is that wealthy white children were predominately looked after by African-American women, especially in the Deep South.[126] Sally is likewise predominately raised by Carla, a black maid. Six episodes after being introduced to Carla the audience learns that Betty, the quintessential blond haired and blue-eyed Aryan depiction of

[124] Season 5 episode 11 "The Other Woman" May 27, 2012.

[125] Season 2 episode 10 "The Inheritance" October 5, 2008.

[126] Season 2 episode 4 "Three Sundays" August 17, 2008.

domestic womanhood, was also raised by a black maid named Viola.[127]

In season two, Peggy, Salvatore, and Harry watch television in the office; James Meredith's admittance to The University of Mississippi (Ole Miss) flashes on the screen. "It's strange, isn't it?" Pete rhetorically asks. Meredith's controversial admittance elicited violent white backlash including riots and Meredith being shot, although he survived the assault and ultimately graduated from the university. The fact that Meredith's integration of Old Miss is mentioned on *Mad Men* underscores how deeply entrenched fascist racial mores were in postwar American society, and that the creators of the show consciously seek to make viewers connect the proverbial dots.[128]

In season three, Don waits at the hospital while Betty gives birth to their third child. News of Medgar Evers, an African American World War II veteran who was murdered by a white man for trying to register black voters in Mississippi, being laid to rest at Arlington National Cemetery plays on the waiting-room television. Don is joined by Dennis Hobart (Stan Bushell), a gruff corrections officer who says, "Being a guard is like being a king… All these animals, they all blame their mother and father."[129] The fact that Hobart is, of all things, a corrections officer as Evers' funeral flickers on the television screen seems to allude to incarceration rates in the United States, which spiked drastically in

[127] Season 2 episode 10 "The Inheritance" October 5, 2008.

[128] Season 2 episode 11 "The Jet Set" October 12, 2008.

[129] Season 3 episode 5 "The Fog" September 13, 2009.

the 1960s concomitant to the civil rights movement and in the wake of urban race riots, which were racially coded as a lack of law and order, which helped justify white backlash all through the 1970s and 1980s to the civil rights gains of the 1960s.

The viewer of *Mad Men* gets a profound sense of how ambivalent so many white northerners were to civil rights in the 1960s and decades after. "I don't know why they (civil rights activists) keep stirring up trouble," Harry Crane says in season two, "it's bad for business."[130] In season four, the agency partners attend a meeting; the 1965 March on Selma, Alabama, and subsequent police brutality is on the front-page of *The New York Times*. "Why aren't they (African Americans) happy," Bert Cooper grunts, "they got what they wanted."[131] Northern white ambivalence to black suffering is echoed in season two by Kinsey, who would rather take a trip to the "Rocket Fair" in California with Pete than go on a Freedom Ride to the Deep South to register voters with Sheila. "Why can't it wait?" Kinsey asks his black girlfriend on the elevator, which seems to chafe both Hollis and Sheila.[132] The following season Carla, the Draper's maid, nervously turns off the radio as Betty enters the kitchen. A news broadcast describing the four little black girls killed in a church bombing in Birmingham, Alabama seems to have upset Carla. Betty says, "Maybe civil rights is not supposed to happen right now." Carla is clearly perturbed by

[130] Season 2 episode 11 "The Jet Set" October 12, 2008.

[131] Season 4 episode 5 "The Chrysanthemum and The Sword" August 22, 2010.

[132] Season 2 episode 10 "The Inheritance" October 5, 2008.

the statement and wants to respond, but her agency is diminished by the fact that she needs to keep her job looking after her racist boss's privileged white children.[133]

A season later Betty fires Carla after the maid had the temerity to let Glen Bishop say goodbye to Sally as the family prepares to move to Rye, New York, where Henry Francis' mansion is located. "Someone has to raise those children," Carla, who is finally liberated by unemployment to honestly express herself to Betty, says. "Oh really," Betty, who does not have to work and lives a life of idle luxury, sardonically replies, "and I suppose your children are all doctors and lawyers?" The glaring irony is that Betty could presumably raise her kids without the assistance of Carla -- her black status symbol. Carla, conversely, is presumably forced by socioeconomic forces beyond her control -- most notably systemic and institutionalized racism and poverty (never mind sexism) -- to earn a living raising Betty's kids, which pulls the maid away from her own family, which adversely affects her own children's chances of social mobility. The irony, however, is completely lost on Betty, who is as blind to her white privilege as Pete Campbell is to his.

Two episodes after Carla is fired Don's geriatric secretary, Miss Blankenship, jokes, "If I wanted to watch two Negroes fight I'd drop a dollar bill out my window," in reaction to the excitement at the agency regarding the impending Cassius Clay versus Sonny Liston title bout.[134] In season five, Gail, Joan's mother, is critical of

---

[133] Season 3 episode 9 "Wee Small Hours" October 11, 2009.

[134] Season 4 episode 7 "The Suitcase" September 5, 2010.

52

black rioters (in the summer of 1967). Greg Harris (Gerald Downey), an Army surgeon embedded in Vietnam but home on leave, says, "there are plenty of Negroes in Saigon that are plenty brave," which underscores the fact that poor Americans, most notably black men from blighted American ghettos that had been ravaged, in part, as a result of white-flight suburbanization, being second-class citizens at home, yet forced by the Draft to fight in order to, ostensibly, bolster the pervasive racist status quo, which has existed in the United States since the nation was founded as a bastion of the peculiar institution of chattel slavery, followed by Jim Crow, and then the rise of the prison industrial complex.[135]

The topic of the sad irony of black men being sent to risk their lives, limbs, and mental health to fight a people whom Muhammad Ali (formerly Cassius Clay) famously said he had "no quarrel with" is explored further, late in the final season of the show, when Glen Bishop informs Sally that he is going to Vietnam. "Are you fucking stupid?" Sally seethes. "You're against the war! What about Kent State? You were crying and going to join the movement." Glen, who in season five writes a paper about Nat Turner, a man who led a slave revolt in Virginia in 1831,[136] responds to Sally by asking, "What about a bunch of Negro kids dying while we stay at home and get stoned? It's immoral." Sally pleads for her friend to regain his sanity. "You're going to die," she says, "and for what?" Nationalist and patriotic Betty defends Glen by saying, "Don't listen to Jane Fonda here. It's a very brave thing to do." Sally fires one more volley, "Just remember, those kids (at

[135] Season 5 episode 4 "Mystery Date" April 8, 2012.

[136] Season 5 episode 12 "Commissions and Fees" June 3, 2012.

Playland) are the same age as the kids you'll be killing in Vietnam."[137]

    Midway through season seven Sally likewise criticizes the twenty-five billion dollars spent sending white American men to the moon when "people are going hungry" back on earth, which might allude to Gil Scot-Heron's sardonic poem, "Whitey on the Moon." The lyrics are as follows:[138]

"A rat done bit my sister Nell
(with Whitey on the moon)
Her face and arms began to swell
(and Whitey's on the moon)

I can't pay no doctor bill
(but Whitey's on the moon)
Ten years from now I'll be payin' still
(while Whitey's on the moon)

The man jus' upped my rent las' night
('cause Whitey's on the moon)
No hot water, no toilets, no lights
(but Whitey's on the moon)

I wonder why he's uppin' me?
('cause Whitey's on the moon?)
I was already payin' 'im fifty a week
(with Whitey on the moon)
Taxes takin' my whole damn check,

---

[137] Season 7 episode 10 "The Forecast" April 19, 2015.

[138] Season 7 episode 7 "Waterloo" May 25, 2014.

Junkies makin' me a nervous wreck,
The price of food is goin' up,
An' as if all that shit wasn't enough

A rat done bit my sister Nell
(with Whitey on the moon)
Her face an' arm began to swell.
(but Whitey's on the moon)

Was all that money I made las' year
(for Whitey on the moon?)
How come there ain't no money here?
(Hm! Whitey's on the moon)
Y'know I jus' 'bout had my fill
(of Whitey on the moon)
I think I'll sen' these doctor bills,
Airmail special
(to Whitey on the moon)"[139]

Scott-Heron, who is perhaps best known for his critique of American postwar consumerist conformity and co-opting of the revolution by Madison Avenue to sell products in his classic, "The Revolution Will Not Be Televised" (1971), underscores Bert Cooper's assertion in season one that the central issues in American politics are healthcare and communism, both of which were often racialized, as evidenced by numerous billboards erected across the country in the 1960s that assailed Martin Luther King, Jr. as a communist and the civil rights movement, including socialized medicine, as a Soviet plot to subvert the American economic and

---

[139] Gil Scott-Heron, "Whitey on the Moon," *Evolution*, 1970.

political system, which was rooted in a long history of white supremacy. The pervasive postwar American racial tension is alluded to further in *Mad Men* when Don takes his son, Bobby, to see *Planet of the Apes*, which, like "Whitey on the Moon" and the teleplay for *Star Trek* written by Kinsey that features "Negrons,"[140] is a metaphor for the centrality and power of racism in American society.[141]

The prevalence of racism to postwar America's real estate industry also seeps into the series in later seasons of *Mad Men*, which broaches the subject of gentrification. In season six, Peggy and her leftist lover Abe buy a rundown apartment building in the West 80s in the hopes of fixing it up and renting space.[142] Three episodes later, Abe is mugged and stabbed as he gets off the MTA train. He, however, refuses to cooperate with the police. "Can you believe those questions ('were the perpetrators colored or Puerto Rican')?" Abe, who seems exasperated, says to Peggy, in response to a stereotypical-white ethnic New York City beat cop questioning him about the assault. "Fascist pig!" Abe says. "This is a fucking police state! We're going to have to fight… They did it in Prague, they did it in Paris, and, like it or not, we're going to have to do it here, too." Abe, ultimately, does not want to "give the cop an excuse to shake down every kid that walks by," which alludes to the incredibly unconstitutional and arguably fascist violation of basic civil rights associated with the stop-and-frisk racial profiling

---

[140] Season 5 episode 10 "Christmas Waltz" May 20, 2012.

[141] Season 6 episode 4 "To Have and Hold" April 21, 2013.

[142] Season 6 episode 6 "For Immediate Release" May 5, 2013.

established in the 1960s by Governor Nelson Rockefeller (who Henry Francis works for) that had become pervasive in twenty-first century New York City. Peggy expresses anger that Abe is "protecting criminals." Abe, however, defends the muggers as victims of a legacy of entrenched American white supremacy and socioeconomic circumstances beyond their control when he says, "those kids have no other recourse in this city," and "they were brought here in slave ships!"[143] The irony is that Abe, despite his best intentions, is a kind of pioneer in terms of the gentrification of the West 80s and thus financially invested in the white supremacy deeply embedded in postwar America's, especially New York City's, real estate industry.

In *Mad Men, Mad World: Sex, Politics, Style and the 1960s*, Jeremy Varon and Clarence Lang note the absence of representations of characters engaged in 1960s social movements in the show. Lang argues that *Mad Men* "naturalizes a black quietude that did not actually exist" in the North. Varon likewise notes that marginal characters who are engaged in social protest or counter-culture are portrayed as cynical or shallow, so that the narrative remains "captive to the condition it diagnoses." Kent Ono similarly argues that despite being self-reflective about race, *Mad Men* "unnecessarily and objectionably produces the irrelevance" of non-white characters in a way that mirrors the racism it seeks to critique.[144] With all due respect to the scholars mentioned above,

---

[143] Season 6 episode 9 "The Better Half" May 26, 2013.

[144] See Ono, Varon and Lang in Lauren M. E. Goodlad, Lilya Kaganovsky, and Robert A. Rushing, eds. *Mad Men, Mad World: Sex, Politics, Style and the 1960s*, (Durham, NC: Duke University Press. 2013) p. 258 and p. 306.

the pervasive racial segregation depicted on *Mad Men,* in fact, mirrored the reality of the situation in postwar American society, as illuminated by the fact that the ad industry was investigated by the federal government for a glaring lack of diversity. While it is easy to criticize the show as being akin to whiteness studies in terms of "being captive to the condition it diagnoses," it would have been disingenuous of the creators of *Mad Men* to force black power activists into the show other than globally famous civil rights activists such as Medgar Evers and Martin Luther King, Jr., both of whom were widely publicized and therefore impossible to ignore, even by the wealthy white New Yorkers *Mad Men* largely focuses on. Shoehorning counter-culturalists onto the show would have been incredibly disingenuous in a series about the conformity of postwar consumer culture. In fact, the banality of evil in postwar American racism depicted on the show is what makes it so timely and effective in the context of twenty-first century American politics. Plus, neither Sheila, who goes on Freedom Rides, or Abe, seem at all quiet, cynical, or shallow, especially compared to the many Protestant and Catholic characters depicted.

The fact is, despite a scarcity of black characters on *Mad Men,* in seven seasons the series indeed provided a searing critique of the pervasive racism entrenched and yet largely overlooked and ignored, in both the 1960s and twenty-first century American economics, politics, and culture writ large. *Mad Men,* which originally aired mostly during Obama's presidency, also skewers the notion of a post-racial America. It thus seems clear that the critique of postwar American racism and blatant cultural insensitivity towards and denigration of Jews, Native Americans, Asians, Latinos, and especially African-Americans as depicted on the show is meant to underscore the point that American racism is a similar brand of racism to that proudly exhibited by German and Italian fascists in the decades prior to World War II.

Chapter Two

"Jackie, Marilyn and Masculine Anxiety in *Mad Men*"

Charu Gupta's "Politics of Gender: Women in Nazi Germany," Jo Fox's "'Everyday Heroines:' Nazi Visions of Motherhood in *Mutterliebe* (1939) and *Annelie* (1941)," and Ara H. Merjian's "Fascism, Gender, and Culture," each examine the depiction and role of women under fascist regimes, which tended to be as unabashedly sexist and misogynistic as the postwar masculine American power structure depicted in *Mad Men*.[145] Gisela Bock's "Racism and Sexism in Nazi Germany: Motherhood, Compulsory Sterilization, and the State," and Greg Castillo's "Domesticating the Cold War: Household Consumption as Propaganda in Marshall Plan Germany" likewise elaborate a great deal of cultural continuity in terms of gender and class norms in interwar Germany and postwar America.[146] The idea that women's

---

[145] See Charu Gupta "Politics of Gender: Women in Nazi Germany" *Economic and Political Weekly* Vol. 26, No. 17 (Apr. 27, 1991), pp. WS40-WS48; and Jo Fox, "'Everyday Heroines:' Nazi Visions of Motherhood in *Mutterliebe* (1939) and *Annelie* (1941)," *Historical Reflections/Réflexions Historiques*, Vol. 35, No. 2, The politics of French and German Cinema, 1930-1945 (SUMMER 2009), pp. 21-39; and Ara H. Merjian "Fascism, Gender, and Culture" *Qui Parle* Vol. 13, No. 1, Fascism, Gender, and Culture (Fall/Winter 2001), pp. 1-12.

[146] See Gisela Bock, "Racism and Sexism in Nazi Germany: Motherhood, Compulsory Sterilization, and the State," *Signs* Vol. 8, No. 3, Women and Violence (Spring, 1983), pp. 400-421; and Greg Castillo, "Domesticating the Cold War: Household Consumption as Propaganda in Marshall Plan Germany,"

proper place was confined to the domestic sphere was, for example, pervasive in both Germany and the United States before and after World War II.

Mad Men does well to depict the anxiety and backlash of American men towards women's liberation during the second-wave feminism of the 1960s. The notion that men (traditional breadwinners) were widely considered to be more valuable in the context of postwar American consumer society is also explicitly critiqued throughout *Mad Men*, perhaps never more obviously than in season four when Trudy's exultant father, who has been apprised by his son-in-law, Peter Campbell, that he will soon be a grandfather, promises, "$1000 if it's a boy and $500 if it's a girl." Close to the end of the final season of *Mad Men,* Joan Harris, who became a partner at Sterling & Cooper as a result of sleeping with Herb Rennet (the head of the Auto Dealers' Association), threatens Jim Hobart (the head of McCann-Erickson, an advertising agency that acquired Sterling & Cooper) with loaded language including, "equal opportunity employer, ACLU, and Betty Friedan." She also references "*Ladies Home Journal* and *Newsweek*," both of which in the 1960s actually had suits filed against them by the Federal Commission on Human Rights due to pervasive gender and racial discrimination. Hobart requites Joan's not-so-veiled threat with, "Do you have any idea how much space we buy in *The New York Times* a year?" His rhetorical question highlights the fact that he, despite Joan's threat, has the balance of power in the relationship.

Journal of Contemporary History Vol. 40, No. 2, Domestic Dreamworlds: Notions of Home in Post-1945 Europe (Apr., 2005), pp. 261-288.

"I could get them to print *Mein Kampf* on the front page," he adds.[147] Hobart tries to convince Joan to quit and relinquish half her shares in the company for fifty cents on the dollar what is legally owed to her as a partner in the company. Joan, ultimately, takes the deal rather than fight a corporation with unlimited resources in court.

The acrimonious exchange between Hobart and Harris, as well as the mostly jovial exchange between Pete and Trudy's father, exhibits that the creators of *Mad Men* were poignantly aware that postwar American gender norms were in some ways similar to gender norms in fascist Germany, Italy and Spain. Hobart is particularly depicted as having fascist inclinations, particularly in terms of the rampant sexism and misogyny manifested at his agency in season seven. In the years before World War II, Benito Mussolini instituted policies severely restricting women's access to jobs outside the home. In Germany, the Nazis forbade female party members from giving orders to male members, which is reminiscent of a scene that transpires in the inaugural episode of *Mad Men*; Don Draper first meets with a Jewish woman named Rachel Menken. The meeting ends abruptly with Don angrily declaring, "I'm not going to let a woman talk to me like this," before storming out of the conference room.[148] Don's chauvinist declaration evokes the Nazi policy that forbade women to give men orders.

[147] Season 7 episode 12 "New Horizons" May 3, 2015.

[148] Season 1 episode 1 "Smoke Gets in Your Eyes" July 19, 2007.

This chapter explores *Mad Men's* depiction of sexism and misogyny in 1960s America, which betrays a great deal of masculine anxiety in regard to female sexual empowerment and social mobility in the decades after World War II. The structure of this chapter examines the perils of the whore/Madonna motif depicted in *Mad Men*. Women, most particularly Joan and Peggy (and to a lesser degree Betty), grow to consciously resist the imposition of identity on them by the men in their lives and discover new agency in the process. The whore/Madonna motif in *Mad Men* is depicted to be a product of men's anxieties in reaction to female sexual prowess, social mobility, and quest for economic, as well as political, equality. Peggy and Joan have this imagery imposed on them more than any other characters on the show. They also exploit it and reject it throughout the series, especially in later episodes of the show. Joan and Peggy's resistance to fascistic gender norms is thus central to this chapter. The chapter concludes by pointing readers to the ways in which the gender inequity depicted in 1960s America on *Mad Men* continues to cast an ominous shadow in twenty-first century American society.

The first allusion to the whore/Madonna motif is hinted at in the first episode of the series as Joan explains to Peggy that the men in the office view women as "something between a mother and a waitress, and the rest of the time… well."[149] The blurry conflation of mother and lover is also humorously alluded to in season six when Don asks Kenny Cosgrove where he learned to "dance like that," after both had been shot up with performance enhancing drugs. "My mother," Ken says while flailing his arms

---

[149] Season 1 episode 9 "Shoot" September 13, 2007.

and legs about theatrically as he tap dances, "no -- my first girlfriend," he says.[150] Ken's statement seems to reflect Joan's assertion to Peggy in the first episode of the series that the men see their female subordinates at their Madison Avenue office as something between a mother, waitress and sex object.

In *Mad Men* the Madonna/whore binary is repackaged as the Marilyn Monroe/Jackie Kennedy motif.[151] Jackie is a metaphor for men's libidinal fantasies of the perfect housewife (the private sphere). Marilyn is a metaphor for men's fear of and desire for working women (the public sphere) such as secretaries, waitresses, and prostitutes. Although the notion that all women are either a Jackie or Marilyn (housewife or whore) is a central feature of the show, especially in early seasons, the motif is a kind of straw man designed to critique postwar America's white, masculine gender-supremacy as being akin to fascistic.

The Jackie/Marilyn motif is first explicitly introduced to viewers of *Mad Men* halfway through season one. Platex wants Maidenform's incredibly successful campaign, which centers on women dreaming of "stopping them (men) in their tracks." The bra marketed by Sterling & Cooper is satirically called "the harlequin" -- a mute and costumed character in traditional Greek pantomime. Paul Kinsey earns the acclaim of his male co-workers (misogynists all) when he explains that "women already have a fantasy, and it's

[150] Season 6 episode 8 "The Crash" May 19, 2013.

[151] For more on the virgin/whore motif see Jonathan Gottschall, Elizabeth Allison, Jay De Rosa and Kaia Klockeman, "Can Literary Study Be Scientific?: Results of an Empirical Search for the Virgin/Whore Dichotomy," *Interdisciplinary Literary Studies* Vol. 7, No. 2 (Spring 2006), pp. 1-17.

not sailing the Nile. It's right here. It's Jackie or Marilyn... Every woman is a Jackie or a Marilyn." Peggy, the only woman in attendance at the meeting, respectfully disagrees. Freddy Rumsen qualifies Kinsey's assertion by saying Peggy is more "Irene Dunne" than she is a Marilyn or Jackie. Kenny jokes that Peggy is "Gertrude Stein," a lesbian novelist and playwright (who died of stomach cancer). The irony is that Peggy's identity is still being imposed on her by the men she works with. The more she resists, the more Kinsey persists. "Bras are for men," he says in an attempt to educate Peggy. He adds that, "women want to see themselves the way men do." Don seconds Kinsey's notion by saying, "Because we (men) want both, they (women) want to be both (Marilyn-whore/Jackie-Madonna)."[152]

The Perils of Being Jackie (a housewife)

In the final season of *Mad Men*, Don enters newest wife Megan's Southern California home. Her friend says, "Wilma!" the moment Don enters the room as she washes dishes in the kitchen, which seems to be a private joke between Megan and her friend about Don. The concealed jibe seems to be a critique of Don as a prehistoric husband on par with Fred Flintstone (who actually kind-of looks like Don).[153] The show often makes plain, and at times subliminally, that trying to fulfill men's libidinal fantasy of being a great homemaker is, much like the Affluent Society writ large, not necessarily all it is cracked up to be. At the end of the first episode of the series, for example, the audience is first introduced to Betty Draper, the blond-haired and blue-eyed ideal of Aryan

[152] Season 2 episode 6 "Maidenform" August 31, 2008.

[153] Season 7 episode 5 "The Runaways" May 11, 2014.

domesticity. She pines her days away in the suburbs longing for her husband to come home from the city. She is, however, not introduced to viewers until the very last scene – long after they have become familiar with Don's beatnik mistress, Midge Daniels (Rosemarie DeWitt) – which underscores how peripheral suburban housewives' lives often were to their urbane husband's daily existence in the decades during white-flight suburbanization that followed World War II.[154]

Early in the second episode of season one, Betty alludes to Roger Sterling's wife, Mona, in the ladies room of an upscale French restaurant in Manhattan, that she suffers from the proverbial problem that has no name as a result of her confinement to the comfortable suburban concentration camp, the concepts of which were most famously elucidated by Betty Friedan in the *Feminine Mystique* (1963).[155] Betty then confides to Mona that her hands tend to go numb as a result of the pervasive anxiety, stress, and ennui associated with being a suburban housewife.[156] In the third-to-last episode of season one, Betty's father, Gene Hofstadt, and his new girlfriend, Gloria, visit the Draper's. "Don says, "It's good to have another woman around to give Betty a hand." Gloria flashes an insincere grin as she says, "I live to serve."[157] Later in the

[154] Season 1 episode 1 "Smoke Gets in Your Eyes" July 19, 2007.

[155] For an interesting examination of concentration camp imagery in *Feminine Mystique* see Kirsten Fermaglich, "The Comfortable Concentration Camp": The Significance of Nazi Imagery in Betty Friedan's *The Feminine Mystique*" *American Jewish History*, Vol. 91, No. 2 (June 2003), pp. 205-232.

[156] Season 1 episode 2 "Ladies Room" July 26, 2007.

[157] Season 1 episode 10 "Long Weekend" September 27, 2007.

season Duck Phillips, who is in the process of a contentious divorce, says that, "Dogs are better than wives."[158] In season one, Roger Sterling gives Joan Holloway, his mistress at the time, a bird in a golden cage, which might allude to *Breakfast at Tiffany's* or perhaps to a popular turn-of-the-twentieth-century tune titled, "A Bird in a Gilded Cage," by Arthur J. Lamb and Harry Von Tilzer. The lyrics to the song ad greater depth to the somewhat odd exchange between the wealthy and much older boss gifting his secretary a bird in a cage just prior to coitus:

"There's riches at her command.
But she married for wealth,
not for love,
though she lives in a mansion grand.
She's only a bird in a gilded cage,
a beautiful site to see.
You may think she's happy and free from care
she's not though she seems to be.
Tis sad when you think of her wasted life,
for youth cannot mate with age,
and her beauty was sold for an old man's gold.
She's a bird in a gilded cage."

Roger explicitly tells Joan "I'd like to lock you up for a week,"[159] which foreshadows Don forcing his mistress and neighbor, Sylvia Rosen (Linda Cardellini), to stay in a hotel room for an entire

[158] Season 2 episode 6 "Maidenform" August 31, 2008.

[159] Season 1 episode 6 "Babylon" August 23, 2007.

episode in season six, which ultimately derails their relationship. Also in season six, things come full circle when Roger tells Don, "I want to go to Sunset Strip and watch a girl dance in a cage."[160] The song, "A Bird in a Gilded Cage," actually more accurately describes Betty (whose nickname is Birdie) and Peter Campbell's wife, Trudy (whose nickname is Tweety), and their suburban housewife neighbors' lives more so than Joan, who actually has a modicum more sexual and economic agency than Betty and her neighbors in Dutchess County do.

The notion of women, particularly housewives, as being property caged by men is further broached two episodes after Roger gives Joan the bird in-the-cage as Sterling & Cooper is tasked with marketing the "executive account" on behalf of Liberty Capitol. The "executive account" is a private bank account that permits husbands to steal money away from their suburban housewives without the latter being the wiser.[161] Men of means stealing money away from their wives helps elaborate that countless married women in postwar America were often considered by husbands to be akin to children or property to be tended to, rather than equal partners in an enterprise.

The depiction of women as infantile and childlike creatures in need of masculine guidance and protection is a central aspect of episode seven in season one; Betty's psychologist, Dr. Arnold Wayne (Andy Umberger), and Don have a secret correspondence in which they discuss what they feel is best for Don's increasingly

[160] Season 6 episode 10 "A Tale of Two Cities" June 2, 2013.

[161] Season 1 episode 5 "5G" August 16, 2007.

depressed suburban housewife. Betty has "the emotions of a child," Dr. Wayne explains to Don, "which," he chides, "is common in housewives." Later in the episode, Don is condescending to his wife during an argument by saying, "sometimes I feel like I'm living with a little girl."[162]

Even when middleclass and upper class American women in the decades after World War II were able to find sparse inroads into the public sphere as students, teachers, secretaries, et cetera, it was most often based on the assumption that their forays into the men's world of urban commerce would ultimately be to land a husband (breadwinner) and then settle down to raise a family in the suburbs. In the first episode of the series, Joan, the queen ant of the farm that is Sterling & Cooper, alludes to the fact that playing one's cards right at the office equates to landing a rich man and home in "the country."[163] Joan, however, learns through difficult life experiences in subsequent seasons that the 1960s vision of suburban domestic bliss is not quite what she had envisioned on Peggy's first day at the office.

Even, however, as women made inroads into the public sphere as secretaries, actresses and models – as Bethany Van Nuys' (Anna Camp) role as a courtesan or part of a harem as a supernumerary in Broadway plays points to -- they were still very often cast into roles as either whores or aspiring homemakers.[164] In season four, Pete Campbell explains to Peggy that he can hire two

[162] Season 1 episode 7 "Red in the Face" August 30, 2007.

[163] Season 1 episode 1 "Smoke Gets in Your Eyes" July 19, 2007.

[164] Season 4 episode 1 "Public Relations" July 25, 2010.

women to fight over a ham in order to get free viral publicity for Sugarberry, and charge the cost of the actresses as "whores" to the expense account. Pete later goes to a "Party," which is code for "high-end Manhattan brothel." The prostitute he selects presents herself first as a housewife (Madonna); Pete declines. The prostitute then markets herself as a timid virgin (antithesis of whore); Pete declines. She finally markets herself as a concubine, which finally earns Pete's business.[165]

Quintessential suburban housewife (or so it seems), Betty Draper, likewise learns that her fantasy of being a professional model is fraught with exploitation and emotional peril. Late in season one, for instance, she is cast as a housewife in a Coca-Cola commercial as part of a ploy concocted by Jim Hobart (the guy who told Joan he could have *The New York Times* publish *Mein Kampf* on the front page). Hobart hires Betty to do a bit of modeling for a Coca-Cola spot in an attempt to woo Don to McCann-Erickson from Sterling & Cooper. Even, however, when Betty is able to break out a little from the suburban ennui, she suffers for modeling in Manhattan, as she is still depicted as a happy suburban housewife with an All-American husband (who looks just like Don), two kids (who look just like hers), and family dog, engaged in idle luxury. Betty's lack of genuine agency is likewise illuminated when she is used like a pawn by Hobart in an attempt to woo Don to his agency, and then promptly fired when Don ultimately decides to stay at Sterling & Cooper. The episode concludes with Don trying to console his distressed wife, who is disappointed that she did not land the Coke commercial because the agency supposedly decided

---

[165] Season 5 episode 5 "Signal 30" April 15, 2012.

to go with an "Audrey Hepburn" look rather than "Grace Kelly," which is another concealed wink towards the hollowness of the Jackie and Marilyn motif. Don tries to assuage his disappointed wife's jangled nerves by explaining what a "great mother" she is, and why that is so vital. "I'd have killed to have a mother like you," he concludes. Betty, however, seems terribly dissatisfied.[166]

The notion that the literally manmade motifs imposed on feminine identity by men are designed to serve men's desires and interests grows more evident when Betty grows offended that Don referred to his wife as "the market" to his coworker, Duck Phillips. Betty is later described by Duck as the "perfect wife" – an attractive woman with lots of free time and money to spend. The commoditization of Betty as the "perfect housewife," however, disturbs her.[167] Although women, including arch-conservative and anti-feminist Betty, know themselves to be far more complex than either the Madonna or whore motif, as evidenced by Peggy, Joan, and, at times, Betty's own rejection of the binary, men's anxiety in regard to feminine sexual power and social mobility seems to deeply inform men's objectification of both the Madonna and the whore, which can be internalized by women every bit as much as racism can be internalized by colonized Africans.[168] For instance, Betty confides to her neighbor, Francine, that Dr. Wayne tried to look down the neckline of her dress while she laid on the couch in

[166] Season 1 episode 9 "Shoot" September 13, 2007.

[167] Season 2 episode 8 "A Night to Remember" September 14, 2008.

[168] For more on the internalization of white supremacy see Franz Fanon's *Black Skin, White Masks.* (New York, Grove, 1967).

his office. Rather than feeling disgusted or violated or being offended by her mental health therapist ogling her, Betty feels that as long as men continue to be sexually attracted to her she is "earning her keep."[169] Her statement alludes to the complex ways in which women internalize the objectification imposed on them by men to the point that it shapes their own personal identity and reality. In a later episode, switchboard operator Lois Sadler (Crista Flanagan), for instance, pejoratively refers to herself as a "featherhead," when she is actually being quite coy in finding a reason to meet Salvatore Romano, who she has developed a crush on. Lois's feigned daftness speaks to the performative aspect of femininity in which otherwise smart women act like "featherheads" for fear of their intellect intimidating weak-minded men. Peggy later offers Don a tagline for the "Relaxicizer" in Latin (the language of God in Catholicism). "No Latin," Don demands, "you sound like a valedictorian."[170] Don's comment to Peggy, ironically, illuminates the fear that the client (who sells a vibrator packaged and marketed as an exercise contraption) would be turned off by a female expressing erudition or intellectualism. Don's discouraging Peggy from expressing herself intellectually and Lois's referring to herself as a "featherhead" speaks to the ways in which women, at least those depicted on *Mad Men*, tend to unwittingly perform being the housewife-in-training or empty-headed whore in order to appease men anxious at the prospect of women being something more dynamic than the Jackie/Marilyn/housewife/whore commodified form/product

[169] Season 1 episode 7 "Red in the Face" August 30, 2007.

[170] Season 1 episode 11 "Indian Summer" October 4, 2007.

imposed on feminine identity in order to sell nylons, cold cream, and lipstick to women, concomitant to perpetuating the notion of women as easily understandable and controllable objects readymade for men's consumption.

A pervasive theme throughout the seven seasons of *Mad Men* is that the men on the show seem to think that they really know and understand women at the core of their beings, as evidenced by Don telling Kinsey that women "want a cowboy."[171] Their wives, conversely, feel increasingly estranged from their husbands. The irony is that Don (who is actually Dick Whitman) is always a stranger to his wife, no matter how monumental an effort she makes to truly know and understand her husband and to dutifully fulfill her role as suburban Madonna/Jackie.

In season four, the steno pool is unwittingly exploited in order to conduct a panel for Ponds cold cream, which quickly descends into secretaries crying due to men not being able to really see them for who they are. "It doesn't matter what I see," secretary Allison tearfully tells psychologist Dr. Faye Miller, "it matters what he sees." Freddie, who watches the panel behind a two-way mirror in the adjacent room, says to Peggy, "they (women) just want to get married and they'll buy anything that helps." Dr. Miller later reasserts Freddy's assertion.[172] The satirical irony is that for as much as women in postwar America might have ached to be the Madonna, being a housewife was often as perilous for women as being the Marilyn/whore motif. Being a whore in *Mad Men* is, in

[171] Season 1 episode 2 "ladies Room" July 19, 2007.

[172] Season 4 episode 4 "The Rejected" August 15, 2010.

other words, no better or worse than being a housewife and vice versa.

Protagonist, Don Draper, is as interested in the archetypal whore as much as the Madonna, so long as the lines between the two motifs do not blur or overlap in the form of his wife's identity.[173] But the motifs do, in fact, inevitably overlap, and quite satirically so because the line is, as the women on the show particularly elucidate, imaginary. "You kiss people for money. You know who does that?" Don seethes to his actress wife, Megan (who looks somewhat like Jackie Kennedy), after she had performed a love scene with a male co-star on her hit soap opera in season six. Although he does not explicitly say so, Don unwittingly alludes to Marilyn (whore motif) because he wants his young wife to conform to the Jackie (housewife) motif. A few seasons earlier Don is angered by his wife Betty's itsy–bitsy-teeny-weenie yellow bikini. "Do you want 15-year-old lifeguards, golfers, and millionaire loafers taking summers off staring at you?" he grills his suddenly embarrassed and ashamed wife. In season three, Don learns that Betty had cheated on him with Henry Francis. He calls his future ex-wife a "whore," although he, himself, had previously enjoyed numerous sexual partners before she ever dared to kiss Henry.[174]

Both of Don's wives dutifully tried to fulfill the role of Madonna/happy housewife but were ultimately denigrated when they expressed even the slightest hint of being something more complex. Betty, in particular, went from exuding excitement at the prospect of winning the affection of her increasingly-aloof husband

[173] Season 6 episode 4 "To Have and Hold" August 21, 2013.

[174] Season 3 episode 13 "Shut the Door. Have a Seat" November 8, 2009.

with her toned body stuffed into her new skimpy bikini, to being utterly mortified that he sees her as "desperate" for attention, which underscores how deeply invested her sense of self was entrenched in her husband's perception of her.[175] The point of her identity being subsumed by her husband's is underscored further in an earlier episode when Betty tells Helen Bishop, a volunteer for John Kennedy's 1960 general election campaign, that she is not sure who she is voting for because Don had yet to decide.[176]

Pete Campbell's lust for a concubine in season four echoes Don's pitch to Belle Jolie in season one in which he says that the "Mark Your Man" with one of one hundred shades of lipstick tagline promises women "total ownership" of their man.[177] The irony of women being able to gain total ownership of their man by purchasing products is underscored by the difficulty Betty has of winning a divorce from Don. The notion that the Jackie motif is essentially a product or property owned by her husband grows more prominent in season three as Betty needs to prove adultery in order to win a divorce in the state of New York. Failure to prove infidelity means that Betty is owed nothing by Don, even though her husband has lied to her all along about his actual identity (never mind that he is a serial philanderer). The difficulty in winning a divorce from a husband who has never truly been faithful to his wife underscores the point that women, even the glorified Madonna/housewife, were essentially property owned by their husband, which severely limited female political and

[175] Season 2 episode 6 "Maidenform" August 31, 2008.

[176] Season 1 episode 4 "New Amsterdam" August 9, 2007.

[177] Season 1 episode 8 "The Hobo Code" September 6, 2007.

economic agency in the decades after World War II. Betty's lawyer, who is a well-to-do white man, ultimately urges his client to "go home and give it another try" due to her sparse chances of winning a divorce through legal channels, which underscores the point that divorce laws were designed to protect the interests of men like Jim Hobart and Don Draper.[178]

Two episodes later Betty ultimately breaks the news to Don that she intends to divorce him. Don, the serial philanderer, suggests his wife see her psychiatrist, Dr. Wayne, for proper guidance (and perhaps medication). Betty, to paraphrase, says she is not sick and is no longer conned by her shape-shifting fraud of a husband and demands what she is entitled to. Henry Francis, Betty's new fiancé, urges her to make a clean break from Don and promises to dutifully provide for her and her three young children. Late in the final season of the show Henry, however, becomes angry with Betty after she publicly expresses a political identity slightly askew to his in front of his friends. "Leave the thinking to me," he seethes after the party.[179] Although Betty seems to grow a bit more politically conscious by the end of the series, *Mad Men* depicts her as, ultimately, exchanging a situation in which she is dependent on a man for survival for a comparable state of dependency. It is a glaring paradox that accentuates the fool's gold of a dilemma that trying to play the role of dutiful Madonna, as fantasized by men, creates for housewives, which is ultimately rooted in men's anxiety towards female sexuality and social mobility. As Peggy explains to Roger close to the end of the series,

[178] Season 3 episode 11 "The Gypsy and the Hobo" October 25, 2009.

[179] Season 7 episode 5 "The Runaways" May 11, 2014.

"you know I have to make men feel at ease," which had never occurred to him.[180]

Men's Anxiety

Gender discrimination becomes an even more prominent feature on the show as evidenced by Peggy and Joan's character arcs, but more subliminally so by Bert Cooper's ant farm in what was previously Burt Peterson's (Michael Gaston) office. Lane Pryce's personal assistant (secretary), John Hooker, stares bewilderedly at the ant farm, which is a metaphor for men's fear of feminine power, as he laments, "This place is a gynocracy."[181] Two episodes later Don inadvertently slings a jai alai pelota through the glass façade of the ant farm, thereby destroying the metaphorical gynocracy. Joan, who is the queen ant of the office, ironically sprays the insects dead with bug killer later in the episode.[182]

Anxiety towards female sexual power and social mobility is, as *Mad Men* elaborates, the greatest source of sexism and misogyny in the show. In season five, for instance, Herb Rennet (Gary Basaraba) of the Auto Dealers' Association, aches to enjoy an evening of sexual pleasure provided by Joan in exchange for the Jaguar XKE account, which the agency desperately needs to stay in business. "You're talking about prostitution," Joan seethes to Pete, who is a partner at Sterling & Cooper, as she is presented with the idea. "I'm talking about business at a very high level," Pete says,

[180] Season 7 episode 12 "Lost Horizon" May 3, 2015.

[181] Season 3, Episode 1 "Out of Town" August 16, 2009.

[182] Season 3 episode 4 "The Arrangements" September 6, 2009.

which again speaks to the pervasive theme on *Mad Men* that everyone, including the men, are whores. "Do you think of Cleopatra as a prostitute?" Pete continues, "She was a queen. What would it take to make you a queen?" Joan ultimately takes Lane's advice and demands a five percent stake in the company in exchange for spending a nauseating night of soul stealing displeasure with Herb, an unrepentant misogynist who seems to think that women are objects to be consumed and then discarded. Joan is likewise depicted as a metaphor of the car during Don's pitch to Jaguar executives, which is interspersed with scenes of Joan spending the evening with Herb. The tagline of the campaign, as crafted by wunderkind Michael Ginsberg, is "Jaguar: At Last Something Beautiful (Joan, Marilyn, Jackie, et cetera) You Can Truly Own." The tagline particularly speaks to men's anxiety related to not actually being able to really understand or truly control women because women are not actually the hollow Marilyn/Jackie motif used to market products such as Jaguars to men suffering status anxiety, which is depicted to be an impetus for men making objects of women.[183]

The objectification of women, as the paragraph above speaks to, is a pervasive theme in *Mad Men*. In season two, for instance, some young creatives craft a jingle for Martinson Coffee with the line, "exotic girl, exotic brew" in the interest of marketing coffee to kids. The notion that women are objects owned by men is alluded to many times in *Mad Men*, especially the conflation of women with cars. Early in the series Betty compares herself to a car in need of repair during an appointment with Dr. Wayne not long after Don

---

[183] Season 5 episode 11 "The Other Woman" May 27, 2017.

compares a psychiatrist to a mechanic who "pops the hood and has a look around."[184] Four episodes later Joan assures Roger that he will land a "newer model" as a mistress. "The '61s are coming out," she says seductively, "I hear the fins are bigger."[185] An episode later Roger apologizes to Don for getting so drunk that he made a pass at Betty the previous evening by sheepishly admitting, "we've all parked in the wrong garage."[186] In season five, Megan Draper's friend, Julia (Meghan Bradley), pretends to be a Jaguar as she crawls across a conference table in a short skirt, which titillates the creatives (except for Ginsberg) tasked with crafting taglines.[187] An episode later Don explains the sales pitch in which Jaguar is made synonymous with a mistress to his wife Megan. She seems offended, as evidenced by her rhetorical question aimed at her husband: "so, a wife is a Buick in a garage?"[188]

Men's status anxiety and fear of being whored is depicted as often being rechanneled into flagrant sexism towards and objectification of women. Late in season one, for example, Roger and Don have drinks afterhours at the office with two twenty-year-old twins who had auditioned for the double-sided aluminum campaign earlier in the episode. Roger makes persistent sexual advances towards Mirabelle Ames (Alexis Stier), who seems more

[184] Season 1 episode 2 "Ladies Room" July 26, 2007.

[185] Season 1 episode 6 "Babylon" August 23, 2007.

[186] Season 1 episode 7 "Red in the Face" August 30, 2007.

[187] Season 5 episode 10 "The Other Woman" May 27, 2012.

[188] Season 5 episode 11 "The "Other Woman" May 27, 2010.

like a Jackie than a Marilyn. Roger is later seen riding on her back in the office as if she was a pony. He later suffers a heart attack during coitus.[189] Two episodes later Kenny tackles and sexually assaults a secretary (Allison) who he confirms wears "blue panties," before leading her towards a secluded office, presumably for sex.[190]

Men's status anxiety and fear of being made a whore is depicted in *Mad Men* as being rechanneled into sexism towards women, but also into sexist marketing of products. A Few episodes after Kenny tackles Allison during an office party, the business of selling Mohawk Airlines ensues. Don advocates objectifying stewardesses in miniskirts as a means of marketing air travel to businessmen. In season four, Stan Rizzo seems distracted from his work as he plumbs the newest edition of *Playboy Magazine*. "Are you going to stare at girls who can't stare back, or get some work done," Peggy says, seemingly evoking Walter Benjamin's notion of a flâneur as she grills Stan about what she perceives to be his anxiety towards women. Peggy later insinuates that Stan has a tiny penis, which seems to both embarrass and emasculate him. Lane and his father later visit the Playboy club, which further underscores the centrality of women (such as cocktail waitresses) as sexualized objects readymade for anxious men's consumption.[191]

Masculine anxiety is further elaborated in season five when Stan laments to Peggy that "just because you are a boob-carrying

[189] Season 1 episode 10 "Long Weekend" September 27, 2007.

[190] Season 1 episode 12 "Nixon vs. Kennedy" October 11, 2007.

[191] Season 4 episode 10 "Hands and Knees" September 26, 2010.

consumer does not mean your opinion should matter more" in regards to the Playtex (a woman's product) ad campaign.[192] An episode later Pete, who has been stood up by reluctant mistress Beth Dawes (Alexis Bledel), sorrowfully asks Harry Crane, "Why do they (women) get to decide what happens?" Harry laments, "They just do."[193] The angst-ridden exchange between Pete and Harry underscores the power of female sexuality, which creates a great deal of anxiety in the men on the show. Kinsey, the man who crafted the Jackie/Marilyn campaign, seems particularly angst ridden. An irony of the Madonna/Whore/Jackie/Marilyn paradigm and the conflation of women with cars and various other objects is that all were, according to *Mad Men*, ultimately products of men's libidinal desires and anxiety. The point is particularly underscored when Kinsey masturbates in a secluded office afterhours to the Marilyn/Jackie ad that had earlier won him so much acclaim from his male coworkers, which likewise highlights the sexual objectification of both the Jackie and Marilyn motif. Close to the end of the series Kinsey is lured into being a Hare Krishna, though he does not believe in the dogma, because Lakshmi Bennett (Anna Wood) has sexual power over him.[194]

In *Mad Men* masculine anxiety, as Kinsey's character especially elaborates, is central to the codification of women as either the whore and/or Madonna. The point is especially underscored in season one when Don goes to the Village in

[192] Season 5 episode 7 "At the Codfish Ball" April 29, 2012.

[193] Season 5 episode 8 "Lady Lazarus" May 6, 2012.

[194] Season 3 episode 10 "The Color Blue" October 18, 2010.

downtown Manhattan and smokes marijuana with Midge, his mistress, and some of her beatnik buddies. Midge emasculates the seemingly effeminate beatniks compared to uber-masculine Don by explaining how she met the alpha-male ad man: "you know you gotta leave the Village for a good screw," she says. Don then goes into the bathroom on a head full of marijuana and slips into a childhood memory in which a transient hobo (Paul Schulze) says to the young Dick Whitman (Brandon Killham) "Don't be scared, kid; you ain't a man yet," thereby implying that becoming a man is a process of becoming afraid.[195] The scene ends with Midge – Betty's antithesis -- refusing to go to Paris with Don, which illuminates that she refuses to be his possession or pet, which seems to emasculate the glib ad man, who ultimately diverts the angst into more fervent philandering in subsequent episodes.

The reduction of the Madonna/whore motif down to a sex slave (such as Bethany Van Nuys as a member of a harem or Pete buying a prostitute after she markets herself as a concubine) underscores the anxiety associated with feminine power and social mobility that grows more central to the show as it entered the fourth and fifth season. Later episodes of the show particularly elaborate that the social movements of the 1960s included second-wave feminism – women's quest for equal pay and reproductive rights and thus genuine political equality. In other words, *Mad Men* does not merely depict women as passive victims to men's oppression. Identity is, in *Mad Men*, depicted to be much more complex than the man/woman binary, never mind the Jackie/Marilyn motif. In short, every one of the main characters on

[195] Season 1 episode 8 "The Hobo Code" September 6, 2007.

Mad Men is depicted as a whore at times. But most also resist the imposition of others' power, particularly in terms of who has the agency to decide one's true self.

Sometimes a Hammer, Sometimes a Nail, But Never Really Jackie or Marilyn

Simone de Beauvoir's now famous argument in *The Second Sex* (1949) that gender is as much an imposition by others and performance as it is a biological fact is a recurring theme throughout *Mad Men*. In fact, everyone is essentially depicted as whores – women to men, men to more powerful men, Sterling & Cooper to Lucky Strike Cigarettes, GM, and Jaguar – each ultimately in service of the capitalist system, which is peculiarly fueled by conspicuous consumption of products marketed by ad agencies. Close to the end of season four the notion that everyone (regardless of their gender) is both hammer and nail at various points in their lives is further elaborated when a psychologist hired by Sterling & Cooper in the interest of "better serving clients' needs" describes Don as "a certain kind of girl," and tobacco as "the boy that suits him best." The wider context of the assertion is that Phillip-Morris is starting a cigarette brand (Virginia Slims) marketed exclusively to women. "We will listen more than we will speak," Bert Cooper says to the room full of men (and Joan and Dr. Miller). "Like a good girlfriend," the psychologist qualifies.[196]

In season one, young Dick Whitman tells an itinerant hobo "I'm a whore child."[197] In the final season of the show Don's inter-

[196] Season 4 episode 12 "Blowing Smoke" October 10, 2010.

[197] Season 1 episode 8 "The Hobo Code" September 6, 2007.

office rival, Jim Cutler (Harry Hamlin), refers to Don (who is on leave after drunkenly telling Hershey executives that he grew up in a whorehouse) as "our collective ex-wife who we still owe alimony" to.[198] In season two, the viewer learns that Kinsey used to dress like a girl at Princeton because that's "how Shakespeare" performed.[199] The fluidity of gender is cheekily winked at close to the end of the series when a room full of drunken American Veterans of Foreign Wars hoots, hollers, whistles, and cheers wildly for a drag queen (that they don't seem to notice is a drag queen) as she climbs out of a Mache cake and performs burlesque.[200]

Identity, especially gender, is, in short, incredibly fluid in *Mad Men*. The difference is, however, the men impose identity on women as an expression of fear and anxiety associated with ascendant feminine sexual power and social mobility. This seemingly duplicitous theme surfaces again and again in the series. Women are often perceived by the men on the show to be either the archetypal Madonna or a whore, or more explicitly – Jackie Kennedy or Marilyn Monroe. The women, especially Peggy and Joan, however, grow to resist the imposition of identity, which seems to further exacerbate anxiety amongst the men in their lives.

A good example of the spuriousness of the Jackie/Marilyn binary can especially be detected in season one when Rachel Menken, who knows nothing of the Jackie/Marilyn ad campaign concocted for Playtex by her lover, Don Draper, tells him, "I'm

[198] Season 7 episode 2 "A Day's Work" April 20, 2014.

[199] Season 2 episode 2 "Flight 1" August 3, 2008.

[200] Season 7 episode 13 "Milk and Honey Route" May 10, 2015.

really more American than Jewish… I could have had another mother and been a Marilyn instead of Rachel."[201] The following season, comic Jimmy Barrett, who likewise knows nothing of the motif marketed by Sterling & Cooper, tells housewife Betty Draper, "You're not Marilyn, but you're definitely his (President John F. Kennedy) type, believe me I've met him."[202] In other words, women, as *Mad Men* elucidates, are in fact neither of the fantasized commodified forms that men's anxieties on the show compel them to erroneously believe. Joan, Peggy, and even Betty to some degree, as such, all grow to resist the imposition of identity on them throughout the course of the show.

The notion that all women want to ultimately settle down and be dutiful suburban housewives is especially complicated by the lesbians -- Joyce and Carol -- on the show, and by Joan and Peggy as the series evolves. Late in season one, Joan's closeted lesbian roommate, Carol (Lauren Hackman), professes her longtime but secret romantic love for Joan. "Just think of me as a boy," Carol pleads. But Joan dismisses her roommate's advances as a result of stress from a "hard day" and convinces her to come along for a night out on the town as she "empties some bachelors' pockets." Joan later unwittingly forces Carol into a situation with a sleazy and sweaty bachelor. Carol seems to have reconciled herself to a life of loveless misery, as evidenced by her checking out emotionally and spiritually as her date ostensibly rapes her, though she reluctantly verbally consents to his sexual advances. The fact that Carol resigns herself to having sex with a man she finds

[201] Season 1 episode 6 "Babylon" August 23, 2007.

[202] Season 2 episode 3 "The Benefactor" August 10, 2008.

reptilian because it is what is expected of her seems to underscore her lack of agency in a homophobic social system that forces some, like Carol and Salvatore Romano, to pretend to be something they are not in order to avoid being ostracized from the hegemonic heteronormative society.

Joyce (Zosia Mamet), although also lesbian, is depicted to be Carol's antithesis. She represents the idea that being men's dutiful support system is stultifying, if not also soul stealing. This theme is a subtext of the show. "These men," Joan says to Carol in season one, "we're constantly building them up, and for what?"[203] In season four, Joyce explains to Peggy that "women are the pot, we heat them (men) up, hold them, contain them. Who wants to be a pot?"[204] Joyce's line speaks to the growing desire of both lesbian and heterosexual women in the 1960s to break out of the limited supporting roles of homemaker/secretary-whore/Madonna-Marilyn/Jackie paradigm perpetually rebranded and imposed upon women by powerful men in places like fascist Italy, Spain, Germany, and especially by ad men on Madison Avenue.

Peggy's Empowerment

No one woman on *Mad Men* represents feminine empowerment and social mobility more than the intrepid Peggy Olson. She is first introduced to viewers of *Mad Men* in an elevator surrounded by young male co-workers. Moments later Kenny Cosgrove says, "You have to show them (young women such as

[203] Season 1 episode 10 "Long Weekend" September 27, 2007.

[204] Season 4 episode 9 "The Beautiful Girls" September 19, 2010.

Peggy) what kind of man you are so they know what kind of girl to be." Later in the episode Pete and Joan both viciously critique Peggy's appearance and offer her unsolicited advice on how to better attract men. "Put a bag on your head," Joan suggests, in order to figure out what men might find most desirable about her. Towards the end of the episode, Kinsey steals a kiss from Peggy, but she nervously resists his advances. "Do you belong to someone else?" He asks, thereby underscoring the notion that men in postwar America as depicted in *Mad Men,* much like the men in fascist Italy, Spain and Germany, were often inclined to think of women as objects playing supporting roles and that their "value" was in being desired, possessed, and consumed by more powerful men.[205]

Close to the end of season one Peggy somewhat diffidently explains to Don her value to the company and why she deserves a raise. Don says, "You presented like a man, now act like one."[206] Six episodes later Bobbie Barrett, who is depicted as a husky voiced, black wearing and heavily backlit femme fatale, explains to Peggy, "You have to start living the life of the person you want to be. You can't be a man. Don't even try… It's (female sexuality) a powerful business when you know what you're doing."[207] In season three, Peggy asks Don for the raise he had refused to give her earlier; she also mentions the equal pay amendment.[208]

[205] Season 1 episode 2 "Ladies Room" July 26, 2007.

[206] Season 1 episode 11, "Indian Summer" October 4, 2007.

[207] Season 2 episode 5 "The New Girl" August 24, 2008.

[208] Season 3 episode 5 "The Fog" September 13, 2009.

In the first episode of the series Dr. Emerson (Remy Auberjonais), who was recommended to Peggy by Joan, lectures her about birth control and tells her the pills are not a license for licentiousness. He threatens to take her off the medication if he senses she is becoming a "strumpet" or "the town pump."[209] Dr. Emerson's anxiety towards female sexuality underscores men's anxiety towards the fact that the more women were able to take control of their sexuality and reproduction the more progressive-minded women were empowered to demand full economic and political equality.

In a late episode of season one female sexuality and empowerment is a central theme. Peggy is sexually stimulated by the exercise contraption (the "Relaxicizer") she is tasked with marketing. Betty later masturbates as Astrud Gilberto's "Aqua de Beber" plays in the background whilst fantasizing of the air conditioning salesman who dropped by the house earlier in the episode. Don later scolds Betty for letting the salesman in the house. Francine, Betty's friend from the neighborhood, tells Betty that her husband, Carlton, would "break her arm" if she ever let a man in the house whilst he was at work.[210] Don's anger at his wife letting a man in the house whilst he was away underscores the notion that men often considered housewife's to be every bit as much their property as was the house or sedan. The instance is also interesting because it elaborates that women have a secret internal life, including sexuality, transcendent of the men that supposedly

[209] Season 1 episode 1 "Smoke Gets in Your Eyes" July 19, 2007.

[210] Season 1 episode 11 "Indian Summer" October 4, 2007.

own them. Both instances of women (in this case Peggy and Betty) taking ownership of their sexuality alludes to the legalization of the birth control pill in 1960, and women increasingly taking control over both their sexuality and reproductive rights, which was considered a great threat to traditional masculine institutions and cultural mores rooted in Abrahamic religions.

In season four, Peggy goes to a party in downtown Manhattan with Joyce, a lesbian photo editor for *Time Life*, who serves as a symbol of the young, hip, exciting, 1960s New York City art scene. Joyce unabashedly makes a pass at Peggy, who politely explains that she has a boyfriend. "He doesn't own your vagina," Joyce says. "No," Peggy jokes, "but he's renting it."[211] The next episode sardonically concludes with Roger Hammerstein's incredibly sexist antithesis of feminism, "I Enjoy Being a Girl," as performed by Peggy Lee.[212] The lyrics are as follows:

I'm a girl and by me that's only great
I am proud that my silhouette is curvy
that I walk with a sweet and girlish gait
With my hips kind of swivelly and swervey

I adore being dressed in something frilly
When my date comes to get me at my place
Out I go with my Joe or John or Billy
Like a filly who is ready for the race

---

[211] Season 4 episode 4 "The Rejected" August 15, 2010.

[212] Season 4 episode 5 "The Chrysanthemum and the Sword" August 22, 2010.

When I have a brand new hairdo
With my eyelashes all in curls
I float as the clouds on air do
I enjoy being a girl

When men say I'm cute and funny
And my teeth aren't teeth but pearls
I just lap it up like honey
I enjoy being a girl

I flip when a fellow sends me flowers
I drool over dresses made of lace
I talk on the telephone for hours
with a pound and a half of cream upon my face

I'm strictly a female female
And my future I hope will be
In the home of a brave and free male
who'll enjoy being a guy, having a girl like me

When men say I'm sweet as candy
As around in a dance we whirl
It goes to my head like brandy
I enjoy being a girl

With someone with eyes that smolder
Says he loves every silken curl
That falls on my ivory shoulder
I enjoy being a girl

When I hear a complementary whistle
That greets my bikini by the sea

I turn and I glower and I gristle
But I'm happy to know the whistles meant for me[213]

The deeply entrenched and often unabashed Cold War objectification of women in mass marketing and popular culture writ large is further elaborated an episode later as some of the girls in the secretarial pool at the agency are used like lab rats in a Belle Joli lipstick-testing panel. The scene, much like "I Enjoy Being a Girl," helps to illuminate the performative aspect of gender. Salvatore Romano, a closeted homosexual, dissects the women comprising the panel through the two-way mirror. Harry is meanwhile titillated as he compares the girls to "pouting blowfish." The secretaries seem, for the most part, excited at the prospect of having the opportunity to try so many shades of lipstick, which seems to inspire the ire of the resident drunk, Freddy Rumsen. "We should have put a man in there so they take it seriously," he laments. Close to the conclusion of the episode Peggy foreshadows the arc of her character over seven seasons when she says, "I don't think anyone wants to be one of a hundred in a box."[214]

In the Belle Joli campaign, the men, especially Don, pitch the product with the tagline, "Mark Your Man," which is interesting for two reasons: first, the notion that men and women are property that belongs to their love interest; second, men imposing masculine identity onto female identity. Closer to the end of the episode the men celebrate selling the idea to Belle Joli. Peggy's newly

---

[213] Oscar Hammerstein II, Richard Rodgers, Peggy Lee, "I Enjoy Being a Girl," New York, 1958.

[214] Season 1 episode 6 "Babylon" August 23, 2007.

discovered talent was essential to selling the campaign. Freddy, who "discovered" Peggy after her insightful remark about women wanting to be cherished for their individualism and not "one of a hundred in a box," congratulates her by saying, "homerun ballerina."[215] Seven episodes later Ken says Peggy is "like Kinsey (the creator of the Marilyn/Jackie campaign) but with balls."[216] Freddy and Kenny's conflation of masculine and feminine gender norms illuminates that Peggy is just beginning to discover a modicum of agency with which to cultivate her own identity at the agency, rather than have it imposed on her by the men in the office.

In season three, Peggy chafes at the Patio (Diet Pepsi) campaign speaking to men and not to women, who actually drink diet soda. "Shouldn't it (the ad) be a woman's fantasy?" Peggy asks Don. "Men want her (Anne Margaret)," Don explains to Peggy, "women want to be her."[217] The irony is that Peggy has to "speak the boys' language" and "go to their country" to gain social mobility, which Bobbie Barrett urges her to do in an earlier episode. Peggy is desperate to be included in the boys' club because she does not want to be left out of the idea making and decision-making process, and is especially fearful of her voice being further marginalized on account of her gender. Peggy is constantly, whether conscious of it or not, having to fight against the notion that she is either Marilyn or Jackie (or Irene Dunne or Gertrud Stein). In fact, most of the women centrally depicted on the show, particularly Joan and Peggy, are both Jackie and Marilyn at various

[215] Season 1 episode 6 "Babylon" August 23, 2007.

[216] Season 1 episode 13 "The Wheel" October 18, 2007.

[217] Season 3 episode 2 "Love Among the Ruins" August 23, 2009.

points during the seven seasons on the show, all the while resisting the reductionist binary imposed on them by the men in their lives. In other words, the fact that both Peggy and Joan appear to be both sides of the binary underscores the point that the whore/Madonna motif is merely a hollow sign of men's anxiety and a means of marketing products.

Joan: Bought but Unbossed

No character arc on *Mad Men* is more dynamic than Joan's. Marilyn Monroe's sudden death by drug overdose in season two seems to underscore the silent sorrow so many women suffered during the Cold War. "She was a movie star, she had everything, and she threw it away," Roger callously says to his mistress, Joan, who is as distressed by Monroe's overdose as she was earlier by the shoddy treatment Shirley MacLaine's character suffered in *The Apartment* (1960).[218] Early in the show's existence Joan references Billy Wilder's movie, *The Apartment*," which is about a young elevator operator (played by Shirley MacLaine) who works in an office that has a similar hyper-masculine frat house dynamic and gender segregation to Sterling & Cooper's. Insurance worker C.C. Baxter (Jack Lemmon) lends his Upper West Side apartment to company bosses to use for extramarital affairs. When his manager, Mr. Sheldrake (Fred MacMurray), begins using Baxter's apartment in exchange for promoting him, Baxter is upset to find out that Sheldrake's mistress is Fran Kubelik, the elevator girl at work whom Baxter has a crush on. Baxter must ultimately decide between the girl he loves and the advancement of his career.

[218] Season 2 episode 9 "Six-Month Leave" September 28, 2008.

Joan begins the series as being comparable to Shirley MacLaine's character in *The Apartment*. Shortly after Roger suffers a heart attack, Cooper urges Joan, who is heartbroken, not to "waste her youth on age" as they step onto the elevator. He then motions for her to press the down button, which speaks to the fact that the creators of *Mad Men* surreptitiously encourage viewers to make the connection between Joan's character and Fran Kubelik early in the series.[219] By the end of the series' run, however, Joan has worked, hustled, and exploited every asset she has into a partnership at the agency, only to be forced out for half of what she is owed close to the end of the series by fascist Jim Hobart.

The power of female sexuality and threat of social mobility is, in short, personified most of all by Joan. In season two, she does well proofreading scripts in the interest of helping the agency's clients avoid potential conflicts of interest in regards to shows' controversial contents, such as abortion. Though Joan does an outstanding job with the assignment she is still grossly objectified by peers in the process. Men are, according to the depiction of well-to-do white men in postwar America on *Mad Men*, culturally conditioned to think that women such as Joan ache to be objectified as sexual objects and potential housewives. Joan is later disappointed to be passed over for the new television operations position at Sterling & Cooper so that a younger and woefully less experienced and less qualified man could be hired for the job. She is particularly upset and let down because she did such a good job and enjoyed the process. But Harry, who was told to hire a man by Roger Sterling (Joan's lover and boss), is completely oblivious to the fact that Joan would even want to be something other than a

---

[219] Season 1 episode 10 "Long Weekend" September 27, 2007.

housewife or secretary, which is denigrated as women's work, especially by John Hooker, who fancies himself as a masculine brainworker -- "Mr. Pryce's right arm" and not merely "a typist." But, ironically, Hooker is ultimately proven to be as replaceable as a common secretary or divorced housewife. Joan, conversely, proves herself to be indispensable to the company as it wages a July Fourth-weekend coup against Putnam, Powell, and Lowe, and then especially in season five as she saves the agency from bankruptcy by spending a nauseating night with the lecherous Herb Rennet.[220]

Joan begins the series as the quintessential Marilyn who actually wants to be Jackie but gradually evolves into a quasi-feminist as a result of being raped by her fiancé, Greg, in season two and generally treated by men such as Harry Crane, and even the otherwise gentlemanly Lane Pryce as a sexual object. Joan begins the series as the personification of the proverbial "pot" that holds men, as alluded to by Joyce in season four. For example, in season three a scene begins with Joan trying to soothe Greg, her husband (a season after he raped her). Greg, a young doctor, has recently suffered disappointment at work by being passed over for a promotion after he botched a surgery. He throws a fit. "You don't know what it's like to work your whole life for something and not get it," he whines. Joan, who earlier in the series did a great job proofreading scripts only to be passed over for a woefully less qualified and younger man, smashes Greg over the head with a flower vase (the tangible symbol of the pot Joyce references in season four).[221]

[220] Season 2 episode 8 "A Night to Remember" September 14, 2008.

[221] Season 3 episode 11 "The Gypsy and the Hobo" October 25, 2009.

Despite men's desires to force women into a proverbial box of identity, which the box of Belle Jolie lipstick on the show is a metaphor for, Joan and Peggy are conversely depicted to be infinitely more complex and dynamic. For instance, Joan seems to be obviously a "Marilyn," at least to Kinsey, in early seasons of the show. But in season four, after learning she is pregnant with Roger Sterling's child, Joan's reflection in a fogged commuter train window looks like a Renaissance portrait of Mother Mary (the Madonna). The fact that Joan, who becomes a partner at the agency after becoming a mother, speaks to her evolution from Marilyn to a boss and mother who ultimately ends the series as the sole proprietor of her own production company.[222]

The power of female sexuality and threat of social mobility is, in short, most prominently depicted in Joan's character arc. But her power and agency, as Hobart's power over her illuminates, remains limited throughout the series. The fact that Joan is forced out of McCann-Erickson for half the money owed to her betrays the fact that although Joan and Peggy both have more power and agency by 1970 when the show concludes than they did in 1960 when the show begins, full gender equality in twenty-first century America is as unfulfilled a dream at it was at the beginning of World War II, which speaks to how entrenched fascistic gender norms in American society were during the waning decades of the twentieth century and beyond.

In *Mad Men*, sexism and misogyny are, however, depicted to be as much the products of progressive and liberal minded men's anxieties and privileges as they are with wealthy white men's fears

---

[222] Season 4 episode 10 "Hands and Knees" September 26, 2010.

of losing power and control. In season five, for instance, Peggy and her new boyfriend, Abe Drexler, get into a heated debate in which Abe defends African-Americans' quest for civil rights, but seems oblivious to the plight of women. "They're not shooting women to keep them from voting," Abe chastises Peggy for not taking a harder line against Fillmore Auto Parts, an unabashedly racist client the agency she works for represents. "Civil rights isn't something to be fixed with a public relations campaign," he says. Peggy then tries to enlighten Abe by explaining that:

> "Most of the things Negroes can't do, I can't do either. And nobody seems to care… Half of the meetings take place over golf, tennis, and a bunch of clubs where I'm not allowed to be a member, or even enter. The University Club said the only way I could eat dinner there was if I arrive in a cake. I'm sure they (African Americans) can fight their way in (at an ad agency) like I did. Believe me, nobody wanted me there.

Abe condescendingly retorts, "Alright Peggy, we'll have a civil rights march for women." [223]

The tense exchange between Abe and Peggy harkens back to a conflict between Frederick Douglass and Susan B. Anthony in the nineteenth century. Douglass, an ardent advocate of women's rights, spoke eloquently at the first Women's Rights Convention, which was held in Seneca Falls in 1848, and gladly signed the Declaration of Sentiments. The relationship between Douglass and Anthony, however, soured after the American Civil War due to the

[223] "The Beautiful Girls," *Mad Men*, Episode 9, AMC, September 19, 2010.

passage of the Fourteenth and Fifteenth Amendments, which excluded women. "When women, because they are women, are dragged from their homes and hung upon lamp-posts," Douglass said, "then they will have an urgency to obtain the ballot."[224]

The exchange between Peggy and Abe, which mirrors the conflict between Anthony and Douglass, is an example of the trouble oppressed men and women have in connecting the dots that inevitably lead to confronting the harsh reality that African Americans and women of all races are victims of the same brand economic and political exploitation and oppression rooted in a white masculine supremacy that has existed since the United States was first founded. The exchange between Abe and Peggy is likewise a metaphor for the diminished power of the New Left in the 1960s, due to the pervasive sexism and misogyny amongst otherwise progressive-minded men personified in *Mad Men* by Abe. White middleclass otherwise progressive men like Abe, as well as the millions of suburban housewives and evangelical Christian women who supported Ronald Reagan due to their inveterate misogyny towards women such Geraldine Ferraro (neither Marilyn or Jackie), underscores the point that both liberal men and conservative women are culprits in the pervasive gender (and racial) discrimination that persists in the United States in the twenty-first century. This point is alluded to in season one when Don remarks that if women find out that John Kennedy is a

---

[224] David B. Chesebrough, *Frederick Douglass: Oratory from Slavery*. (Westport, CT: Greenwood Press, 1998), p. 67.

womanizer, it'll "put him over the top" with undecided women voters.[225]

Though Joan begins the series tutoring Peggy on how to score a man and house in the country, by the end of the series, after leaving McCann-Erickson with only half the assets rightfully owed to her, the single mother asks Peggy to be her business partner. "You won't answer to anyone," Joan promises her. "It'll be ours with our name on it."[226] But Peggy, who had always seemed to be more progressive than Joan, is not terribly dissatisfied at the new and unabashedly chauvinist agency where she works, which is owned by Jim Hobart. Two episodes earlier the women already employed at Hobart's agency are depicted as devoutly not "women's lib" as they describe their unofficial women's club that boasts of being "strictly conscious lowering."[227]

Mad Men ultimately helps illuminate that in terms of civil rights in postwar America, the trajectory was often one step forward and another step back for women such as Peggy and Joan. There was, in fact, a lawsuit going on in 1968 in which the federal government investigated a glaring lack of cultural diversity in the advertising industry. In 2013 there was another study published about the lack of equality in American advertising agencies. The study illuminates that things have not changed much on Madison Avenue since the 1960s in terms of workplace diversity. As FastCompany reported, while eighty

[225] Season 1 episode 10 "Long Weekend" September 27, 2009.

[226] Season 7 episode 14 "Person to Person" May 17, 2015.

[227] Season 7 episode 12 "Lost Horizon" May 3, 2015.

percent of American women control consumer spending, just three percent of creative directors at American advertising agencies are women.[228] And so despite Peggy and Joan's social mobility as depicted on *Mad Men*, their success both highlights and obscures the fascistic gender discrimination and inequity that that remains deeply entrenched in American society in the twenty-first century.

Chapter Three

"Neoliberalism, *Mad Men,* and American Opposition to Marxism"

In the 1920s Benito Mussolini ordered heavily armed squads of Blackshirts to viciously attack striking workers and peasants as he sought to purge Italy of Bolshevism. In the 1930s Adolf Hitler's stormtroopers served a similar function to that as the Blackshirts, and Nazi concentration camps first swelled with Marxists and then Jews. And though important distinctions exist amongst fascist groups in terms of ideology and rituals, there are also distinct commonalities. Racism and sexism can be synonymous with fascist movements. But perhaps the darkest shade in the overlapping circles in the Venn diagram comparing fascist groups scattered in disparate parts of the world in the twentieth century is, according to Richard Beyler, Alexei Kojevnikov and Jessica Wang, vitriol towards Marxism, which was often perceived to be a threat towards nationalism.[229] Political opposition to Marxism helped

---

[228] Lenika Cruz, "With Brands, What Exactly is *Mad Men* Selling?" *The Atlantic*, May 5, 2015.

[229] See Richard Beyler, Alexei Kojevnikov and Jessica Wang, "Purges in Comparative Perspective: Rules for Exclusion and Inclusion in the Scientific

facilitate consent to a culture industry rooted in nationalism, consumer capitalism, and increased militarism in the United States in the decades after World War II, much as it had in Interwar Europe.[230]

The "American century," as it were, witnessed two Red Scares in the wake of the world wars. Both McCarthyism and the execution of Jewish-Americans Julius and Ethel Rosenberg, who seemed to be the typical American family, particularly underscore elements of fascism deeply embedded in postwar American society. The Second Red Scare in particular unleashed America's tendency towards fascism that had long existed in the nation's identity to seep to the surface during the Cold War. Fear of communism spreading from Eastern and then Western Europe and then to the rest of the world (particularly the postcolonial world) helped trigger the Second Red Scare, which lasted in the United States from roughly 1947 – 1956. The Second Red Scare likewise alludes to the First Red Scare after World War I, and the subsequent xenophobic political violence associated with the Federal Bureau of Investigation's Palmer Raids in the wake of the 1920 bombing of the J.P. Morgan building on Wall Street in lower Manhattan. Both Red Scares ultimately exposed elements of

---

Community under Political Pressure," *Osiris*, 2nd Series, Vol. 20, Politics and Science in Wartime: Comparative International Perspectives on the Kaiser Wilhelm Institute (2005), pp. 23-48. For a comparison between fascist purges in comparative perspective see Alex Goodall, "The Battle of Detroit and Anti-Communism in the Depression Era," *The Historical Journal* Vol. 51, No. 2 (Jun., 2008), pp. 457-480.

[230] For more on the concept off the "Culture Industry" and Adorno see R.W. Witkin, *Adorno on Popular Culture*, (New York, Routledge, 2003).

political fascism deeply embedded in twentieth century American society. The same can be said of the execution of the Rosenbergs who, like Sacco and Vanzetti a generation earlier, were convicted on the strength of flimsy evidence and executed as enemies of the state during times of heightened national hysteria.

In the years immediately following World War II empires such as the United States, Great Brittan and France had a kind of branding problem in disparate parts of the globe that had been colonized by those empires. Part of the reason Marxism and communism seemed such healthier alternatives to capitalism in so many parts of the postcolonial world in the decades after World War II is that industrialism and capitalism were driving forces in Europe's invasion of Asia and Africa all through the nineteenth century, which was one of the primary causes of the twentieth century's world wars. Since Marxists were one of the prime targets of European fascists in Nazi Germany and Il Duce's Italy in the decades before World War II, leftists often appeared to emerge from World War II seeming to possess greater moral authority than the fascists and imperialists who were largely responsible for the world wars. The notion that leftists had a kind of moral high ground in the Cold War contest between the Soviet Union and United States to win economic, political, and thus ideological allies helped justify the authoritarian impulses and purges that seeped to the surface of the American experience during McCarthyism and the sensationalized Rosenberg trial of the early 1950s.

Opposition to Marxism is thus also evident in *Mad Men's* depiction of 1960s America. The Second Red Scare especially casts a long and ominous shadow over early seasons of the show. In season one, for instance, Betty admits to Don that she kissed a

Jewish boy named "Rosenberg" when she was in high school. Salvatore Romano, in the following scene, jokingly refers to a shade of Belle Jolie lipstick as "Ethel Rosenberg pink." Freddy Rumsen then callously quips a faux tagline: "wear it to the (electric) chair."[231] The following season an attendee at a party hosted by Betty says that the long and hot summer reminds her of the Rosenberg execution.[232] In season five, an executive from Manischewitz, whose last name is Rosenberg, frets that people might mistakenly think he is related to Ethel and Julius.[233]

Joseph McCarthy is also referenced during an episode titled "Nixon vs. Kennedy" set during the 1960 general election.[234] Bert Cooper is said to have spent the night of the 1960 general election at the Waldorf Astoria in Manhattan with "every Republican luminary save Jesus and Joseph McCarthy."[235] Early in season two, a network censor admits to Harry Crane, the head of television operations at Sterling & Cooper, that he "misses the blacklist," which purged leftist artists from the Hollywood System.[236] Early in the Cold War the House Un-American Activities Committee show trials targeted artists, intellectuals, and homosexuals as supposedly pernicious champions of Marxist ideology. The rise of social

[231] Season 1 episode 6 "Babylon" August 23, 2007.

[232] Season 2 episode 6 "Maidenform" August 31, 2008.

[233] Season 5 episode 9 "Dark Shadows" May 13, 2012.

[234] Season 2 episode 8 "Six Month Leave" September 28, 2008.

[235] Season 1 episode 12 "Nixon vs. Kennedy" October 11, 2007.

[236] Season 2 episode 3 "The Benefactor" August 10, 2008.

documentary photography at the end of the nineteenth century in the United States by the likes of Jacob Riis deeply informed photographers a generation later, such as Dorothea Lange, that made visible the poverty and struggles of tenant farmers, urban slum dwellers, and African Americans fighting for basic civil rights. After World War II, however, as communism became America's collective enemy number one, Cold War conformity caused formerly activist photographers to increasingly fix their lens on subjects not considered "subversive" in order to preserve themselves from blacklists in the interest of saving their careers.[237] In other words, the purge of leftism is Cold War American society is evidence of fascism comparable to the brand that existed in Interwar Europe.

Mad Men depicts opposition to Marxism as a central feature of postwar American life. The postwar American purge of leftism is particularly alluded to in *Mad Men* in the form of Èmile Calvet (Ronald Guttman), Megan Draper's father. He is a Marxist scholar who has terrible difficulty publishing his latest treatise due presumably in part to the fact that leftism is by the 1960s so far outside the mainstream of the "Affluent Society's" postwar economic boom that a leftist text would likely be of little value as a consumer product in a culture defined most peculiarly by consumer capitalism in opposition to communism, a sentiment especially fostered by the American advertising industry.

---

[237] For an account of the political pressures faced by the Photo League, which was blacklisted by the U.S. Attorney General in the postwar period see Bezner in Lili Corbus. Photography and Politics in Amedea: From the New Deal into the Cold War. Baltimore: Johns Hopkins UP, 1999).

Mad Men rightly, as Èmile's difficulty getting published underscores, depicts the 1960s as a time of conformity to consumer capitalism, imperial militarism, and increased violence in the American experience than ever before. In season three, Suzanne Farrell, Sally's teacher and Don's newest love interest, expresses distrust in him because all the dads, including Don, are wearing "the same shirt" as they watch the solar eclipse.[238] The gray suit that Don is usually seen wearing throughout the series in particular came to be emblematic of Cold War conformity. It signaled the emergence of a de-individuated style of dress, which signaled and performed an extended franchise of power: the power not of families and individuals but of corporate men.[239] In season two shock-comic Jimmy Barrett, the personification of the banality of evil, quips that Don is the "Man in the Gray Flannel Suit."[240] Barrett's joke alludes to a number of classic novels that came out in the decades after World War II that critiqued stultifying American conformity in the context of the Affluent Society, including Sloan Wilson's *The Man in the Gray Flannel Suit* (1955), William H. Whyte's *The Organization Man* (1956), and Paul Goodman's *Growing Up Absurd* (1956); Allen Ginsberg's poem, *Howl* (1955), likewise critiqued postwar American conformity as being inherently conformist and soul stealing.

[238] Season 3 episode 7 "Seven Twenty Three" September 27, 2009.

[239] See Katherine Gantz "*Mad Men's* Color Schemes: A Changing Palette of Working Women," *Studies in Popular Culture*, Vol. 33, No. 2 (Spring 2011), pp. 43-58, p. 45. See also Simon During, Cultural Studies: A Critical Introduction, (New York: Routledge, 2005), p. 180.

[240] Season 2 episode 9 "Six-Month Leave" September 28, 2008.

Opposition to Marxism casts a long though sometimes subliminal shadow over *Mad Men's* depiction of postwar America. In season three, Lane Pryce, for example, notes that London Fog's name is a bit of a misnomer because "there is no fog in London," he says. "It was all the coal dust," thereby alluding to the horrendous working conditions in England's mines and factories that inspired Friedrich Engel's critique of mid-nineteenth century industrialization and capitalism in his seminal *The Condition of the Working Class in England* (1845).[241] As Egalitarian as Marx and Engels hoped to be, they were widely vilified as naïvely utopian by fascists in the decades prior to World War II and equally so by American conservatives, particularly Darwinist "political realists" such as Bert Cooper, during the Cold War.

Mad Men rightly depicts leftism as widely vilified and either purged or driven underground in American society both before and after World War II, even amongst the poor. In season one, for instance, Don has a childhood memory set during the Great Depression in which his family is visited by a transient hobo (a victim of capitalism). Don's poverty-stricken and bedraggled stepmother remarks that, "Communists are souls but can't be saved." The hobo reluctantly concurs.[242] The exchange underscores the point that even those who might logically be inclined to Marxist ideology -- in this case marginalized working-class Americans -- tend to eschew leftism like a pariah as a result of fear of reprisal.

[241] Season 3 episode 1 "Out of Town" August 16, 2009.

[242] Season 1 episode 8 "The Hobo Code" September 6, 2007.

In season one, the viewer of *Mad Men* is apprised by Roger Sterling that the main issues in the 1960 general election between Vice President Richard Nixon and Massachusetts Senator John Kennedy are "communism, healthcare, and taxes."[243] An episode later Bert Cooper, who has a portrait of J.D. Rockefeller on the bureau in his office,[244] gives Don a $2,500 bonus as a thanks for the agency's many contented clients and urges him to read Ayn Rand's dystopian *Atlas Shrugged* (1957) -- a libertarian tome that postulates that love is not romantic but rather based solely on self-interest. "I believe we are alike," Cooper tells Don. "By that," he qualifies, a "productive and reasonable man and in the end, completely self-interested. He considers self-interest to be evidence of moral strength. "We are different," he concludes, "unsentimental about all the people who depend on our hard work." Cooper later urges Pete Campbell to read Rand's classic, too. In Don and Pete, Cooper sees men like him, completely unsentimental and unapologetic Social Darwinists, much like Hitler and Mussolini were so proud to be. On the surface, the creators of *Mad Men* do not appear to make a moral judgment on Cooper's worldview. In the subtext of the episode, however, Dick Whitman's father exhibits the same cold and calculating Darwinist characteristics Cooper champions, namely utter lack of sentimentality for the people that work for him, as evidenced by Archie Whitman's (Joseph Culp) refusal to pay a hobo for services rendered.[245] Archie also double-crosses the farming co-operative he belonged to late in season three as the

[243] Season 1 episode 7 "Red in the Face" August 30, 2007.

[244] Season 1 episode 12 "Nixon vs. Kennedy" October 11, 2007.

[245] Season 1 episode 8 "The Hobo Code" September 6, 2007.

price of crops drops and he decides to go it alone, which undermines their ability to collectively bargain.[246] What is particularly interesting about Cooper and Whitman acting in such a manner is that it is seen a good business when Cooper acts so callously, but depicted as deplorable when the working class man acts in a similar manner.

In season one of *Mad Men,* both Richard Nixon's "Checker's Speech" and his highly publicized red baiting of Helen Gahagan Douglass as the "Pink Lady" are alluded to, which hint at Nixon and postwar American popular culture as being highly inclined to opposition to Marxism comparable to the vilification of leftists in 1930s Europe.[247] Late in season four, government agents ask Betty Draper if Don has any leftist inclinations as her ex-husband tries to gain security clearance in order to do business with weapon's manufacturers.[248] Being a leftist would disqualify Don. This speaks to the lack of genuine political plurality and purge of leftism in postwar American society as the nation's economic and political power was more systemically concentrated in Sunbelt states, which, particularly Nixon and Reagan's California, were home to the ever-entrenched military industrial complex.

It should thus come as no great shock, then, that anti-leftist sentiment, some might say paranoid hysteria, was central to American mass marketing (soft power propaganda) and is thus likewise prominent in *Mad Men's* depiction of postwar American

[246] Season 3 episode 13 "Shut the Door. Have a Seat" November 8, 2009.

[247] Season 1 episode 7 "Red in the Face" August 30, 2007.

[248] Season 4 episode 10 "Hands and Knees" September 26, 2010.

society. "Madison Square Garden is the beginning of a new city on a hill," Don seems to foreshadow Reagan's first inaugural address as he pitches an idea to a real estate developer who plans to tear down Pennsylvania Station in order to build the sports arena and concert venue. "If I come to you," the developer stipulates to Don, "I don't want that communist (Paul Kinsey) on my account -- the radical."[249] Paul, who two seasons earlier cheered when Nixon won Ohio in the 1960 general election, is by no means a genuine leftist. But the developer considers him a "communist radical" because he had the sentimental temerity to refer to Penn Station as a masterpiece work of art and thus thought it a shame that it was to be torn down to build what would ultimately become a symbol of American consumerism.

Mad Men also does well to connect the Second Red Scare to the Lavender Scare, which was the systemic persecution of homosexuals in the 1950s in the United States and United Kingdom, which paralleled McCarthyism. Gay men and lesbians were often scapegoats and considered fellow travelers of communists, which justified the purge of known and alleged homosexuals. In season one, for instance, Kenny Cosgrove describes Postwar American society as, "America's Military-Industrial-Boyfriend-Girlfriend Complex," which alludes to postwar American militarism and subsequent reassertion of heteronormativity in American politics and popular culture.[250] Cold War conformity, as *Mad Men* helps to illuminate, played a large role in criminalizing homosexuality and driving the lifestyle

[249] Season 3 episode 2 "Love Among the Ruins" August 23, 2009.

[250] Season 1 episode 2 "Ladies Room" July 26, 2007.

deeper into the shadows of mainstream American society -- such as into the men's room at Bloomingdale's Department Store.[251] Prior to the Cold War homosexuality was not as overtly vilified in many major multicultural cities such as New York.[252] In postwar America homosexuality was, however, much like it was in fascist Germany and Italy, widely perceived to be a sign of mental illness and/or moral depravity. "You're sick," Pete Campbell chastises homosexual Bob Benson (James Wolk) in season six.[253] A season later Bob bails Bill Hartley (Matthew Glave), a colleague at General Motors, out of jail after he had been severely beaten by police for trying to fellate an undercover officer in the men's room of a Manhattan department store; an ageing white police officer tells Bob to take his "friend to a head shrinker."[254]

Communism and homosexuality, as the Lavender Scare helps illuminate, were often conflated by Cold War conservatives. But this continued a practice formerly associated with European fascists. Dagmar Herzog's "Hubris and Hypocrisy, Incitement and Disavowal: Sexuality and German Fascism"[255] and Sandra

[251] Season 6, episode 1 "The Doorway" April 7, 2013.

[252] See George Chauncey, *Gay New York: Gender, Urban Culture, and the Making of the Gay Male World, 1890-1940* (New York, Basic Books, 1995).

[253] Season 6 episode 12 "The Quality of Mercy" June 16, 2003.

[254] Season 7 episode 6 "The Strategy" May 18, 2014.

[255] Dagmar Herzog's "Hubris and Hypocrisy, Incitement and Disavowal: Sexuality and German Fascism" *Journal of the History of Sexuality* Vol. 11, No. 1/2, Special Issue: Sexuality and German Fascism (Jan. - Apr., 2002), pp. 3-21 and Sandra Ponzanesi's "Queering European Sexualities Through Italy's Fascist Past: Colonialism, Homosexuality, and Masculinities" in Mireille Rosello, Sudeep

Ponzanesi's "Queering European Sexualities Through Italy's Fascist Past: Colonialism, Homosexuality, and Masculinities" both examine the centrality of homophobia and violence to manufacturing consent to fascist regimes in Germany and Italy concomitant to stifling rational dissent.

The homophobia depicted in Herzog's and Ponzanesi's respective articles is in many ways similar to *Mad Men's* depiction of homophobia in 1960s America. The epithet "homo" is often used by several characters on the show, most notably Ken and Pete, and Michael Ginsberg, who grows certifiably paranoid that the IBM360 supercomputer in the office during season seven is making him gay.[256] Duck Phillips refers to Kurt and Smitty as a "couple of homos" in season three when Peggy says she is having lunch with them.[257] In season five, Pete tells Lane Pryce that he is jeopardizing the account because an executive at Jaguar thinks he is "a homo."[258] The following season Michael Ginsberg, who suffers from repressed homosexuality, says to Bob Benson, a closeted homosexual, "Tell me the truth, are you a homo?" Bob, however, refuses to admit the truth out of fear of reprisal.[259] There are also several overtly disparaging remarks flippantly made about homosexuality by characters on *Mad Men*. In season three, for

Dasgupta, Eds. *What's Queer about Europe?: Productive Encounters and Re-enchanting Paradigms, New York,* Fordham University, 2014.

[256] Season 7 episode 5 "The Runaways" May 11, 2014.

[257] Season 3 episode 2 "Love Among the Ruins" August 23, 2009.

[258] Season 5 episode 5 "Far Away Places" April 22, 2012.

[259] Season 6 episode 10 "A Tale of Two Cities" June 2, 2013.

instance, Betty says that her daughter Sally has taken to Don's tools "like a little lesbian."[260] In season four, a standup comic jokes that Lane and Don are homosexuals, which draws a number of laughs from the audience.[261] "My god is he queer," Kenny Cosgrove says of Megan Draper's friend at Don's fortieth birthday party.[262] In the final season of the show Roger says, "when we (Sterling & Cooper) grow up we're going to murder you (McCann-Erickson) and marry your wife" to Jim Hobart in the sauna at the New York City Athletic Club, before announcing to the other men in the steam-filled room that Hobart is a "live one," as if to indicate that Hobart is a homosexual making a pass at him.[263]

Mad Men depicts postwar American society as so culturally stultifying and violent that many homosexual Americans feel forced into the proverbial closet for their own protection. Some homosexuals, such as Salvatore Romano and Lee Garner, Jr., are married to women and "passing" as straight, which seems to particularly torture Sal's wife, Kitty (Sarah Drew). Elliot Lawrence (Paul Keeley) of Belle Joli is also gay. And Sal seems genuinely attracted to him, but resists his advances in season one for fear of ruining his life. "What are you afraid of?" Elliot cajoles Sal during a late-night drink at a hotel bar. "Are you joking?" Sal bemusedly asks as if Elliot is criminally naïve.[264] The awkward and tense

[260] Season 3 episode 1 "Out of Town" August 16, 2009.

[261] Season 4 episode 3 "The Good News" August 8, 2010.

[262] Season 5 episode 1 "A Little Kiss" March 25, 2012.

[263] Season 7 episode 6 "The Strategy" May 18, 2014.

[264] Season 1 episode 8 "The Hobo Code" September 6, 2007.

exchange between Elliot and Sal happens just moments after McCarthy's blacklist is mentioned by a secretary in the agency's steno break room, as if the creators of *Mad Men* want the viewer to connect the Red Scare to the Lavender Scare, both of which underscores the inveterate fascism that existed in postwar American society. Two seasons later Lee Garner, Jr. of Lucky Strike Cigarettes makes a pass at Sal late one night in the editing room of the agency. Sal, however, resists his advances. "I'm married," Sal pleads. "So am I," Lee persists. "There's been a misunderstanding," Sal fulminates. "I know what I know," Lee declares before Sal finally escapes from the sadistic cigarette baron. Later in the episode Don expresses anger at Sal for refusing Lee's advance. "You (homosexual) people," Don grunts; "Lucky Strike can shut off our lights," he adds while firing Sal for jeopardizing Sterling & Cooper's relationship with the company's biggest account.[265] But Garner and Lucky Strike ultimately cuts ties with Sterling & Cooper in season four anyway.

    The banality of postwar American evil is especially alluded to by the execution of the Rosenbergs, the blacklists, and rampant homophobia of postwar American society. *Mad Men* makes this plain with the Smiths. Kurt Smith (Edin Gali) is a designer from Germany who, along with his creative partner, Smitty Smith (Patrick Cavanaugh), is hired by the agency to market Martinson Coffee to teenagers. Kurt is the first out and proud gay character to exist on the series. He and Peggy become friends. Some of their coworkers tease them after they make plans to attend a Bob Dylan concert together. Kurt, however, matter-of-factly informs the jokesters that he is homosexual and "has sex with the man [sic],"

[265] Season 3 episode 9 "Wee Small Hours" October 11, 2009.

which elicits the nauseated bewilderment of Pete, Ken, and Harry. "I don't think that means what you think it means," Ken condescendingly says. "I knew queers existed," he later adds, "I just don't want to work with them." The fact that Kurt (a German) and Smitty (an American) share the same last name seems to indicate that they may be more than merely creative partners. This point is alluded to two episodes before Kurt admits he is gay when Sal, a closeted homosexual, asks if Kurt and Smitty count as "one person."[266] Smitty defends his partner's unrepentant homosexuality to Kenny. "It's different in Europe," he half-heartedly explains. "More for me," Smitty diffidently adds as he looks lustily at Joan, who seems to detect his dissembled insincerity. "You think Smitty is in love?" Kenny says snidely in reaction to Smitty's defense of his partner after the former leaves the room.[267]

    The depiction of homophobia in *Mad Men* is not merely anecdotal. It is – as the Smiths particularly illuminate -- meant to critique the fascism deeply embedded in postwar American society. "We have the biggest porn consumption in the world and yet at the same time we're fighting for gay rights and gay marriage," *Mad Men* executive producer Matthew Weiner told *Time* in 2014, thereby underscoring the point that he perceived homophobia to be deeply rooted in American society in the half-century since the end of the 1960s. Altogether, *Mad Men* makes evident that postwar American fascism couched in a language of "family values" was fueled in part by a conformity violently imposed as an anecdote to the spread of communism.

[266] Season 2 episode 9 "Six Month Leave" September 28, 2008.

[267] Season 2 episode 11 "The Jet Set" October 12, 2008.

The postwar American opposition to Marxism is especially prevalent in season three. Walter Cronkite, for instance, anecdotally notes Lee Harvey Oswald's alleged ties to "Fair Play for Cuba, Marxism, and Communism," thereby insinuating that communism killed the president of the United States as much Oswald did.[268] A season later, at the company Christmas Party, an embittered freelance psychologist hired by Sterling & Cooper bemoans leftists to Lane Pryce. "They are children and they can't accept the fact that others have to make decisions for them," the psychologist laments to Lane. "You're from Great Brittan; I thought you'd be familiar with the perils of socialism." Cooper then adds, "Civil Rights is the beginning of a slippery slope." The psychologist further frets, "if they pass Medicare they won't stop until they ban private property." Dr. Miller, another freelance psychologist hired by the agency who seems somewhat tipsy, bored, and sympathetic towards civil rights activists, sneers, "Storm their houses and rape their wives," while smiling wryly.[269]

The utopian notion of a society free of social stratification is likewise alluded to by Paul Kinsey as he tells freedom riders aboard a bus south to Mississippi in season two, "If anything, advertising helps bring on change. The market -- and I'm talking about in a purely Marxist sense -- dictates that we must include everyone. The consumer has no color."[270] Kinsey, however, ignores the fact that race has always been a quasi-class in the United States,

[268] Season 3 episode 12 "The Grown Ups" November 1, 2009.

[269] Season 4 episode 2 "Christmas Comes But Once a Year" April 1, 2010.

[270] Season 2 Episode 10 "The Inheritance" October 5, 2008.

from slavery all the way through Jim Crow, and that American real estate values and wealth were largely defined along racial lines long after the end of World War II. In season three Lane Pryce bemoans a stolen credenza and office supplies during a partners' meeting. The scene then slides into Paul Kinsey -- who had stolen a typewriter from the office in an earlier episode -- saying, "People forget that Karl Marx was the greatest economist who ever lived," in a failed attempt to console Pete Campbell, who is befuddled that the company's client, Admiral Television, is so much more popular amongst African-American consumers than white consumers. "And whatever you think of his solution," Kinsey adds, "the question he (Marx) posed was about the catastrophic up and down of the market." Pete grumbles, "Well then, I'll tell the folks at Admiral that Karl Marx says everything is okay."[271]

In season one, Sterling & Cooper is tasked with convincing American consumers that Israel is a "glamorous" tourist destination. Pete, a proud New Yorker and Dartmouth College graduate, is perplexed by the concept of kibbutz. "The whole thing is pretty red," he says suspiciously, "these communes – Kibbutzes [sic]. It's positively Soviet." He later notes to Don that Israel has a "commie government."[272] In season five and six,, which is set sometime around the Seven Days War, the viewer is taken inside the bedroom of Stan Rizzo, a progressive artist. A poster of Moshe Dayan hangs over Stan's bed. Dayan, an Israeli war hero who lost an eye in a battle with Palestinians, was born on the first Kibbutz in 1915, which seems to illuminate that Rizzo, and by proxy the

[271] Season 3 episode 5 "The Fog" September 13, 2009.

[272] Season 1 episode 6 "Babylon" April 23, 2007.

creators of *Mad Men*, are perhaps sympathetic to communal living, or at least the state of Israel, which Pete views as "Soviet" due to Israeli's traditional agrarian sense of communal living.273 In the final season of the show Roger Sterling's daughter, Margaret – who is as much a native New Yorker as Pete is -- leaves her young son and husband in Manhattan to join a commune in upstate New York.274

In season five, several employees of Sterling & Cooper attend a raucous and Gatsby-esque Kentucky Derby soiree hosted by Roger Sterling. Bert Cooper and Abe Drexler -- Peggy's newest love interest -- debate the merits of what history (in hindsight) has proven to be an awfully misguided and arguably paranoid justification of the United States' postwar imperial foreign policy, "Domino Theory" – the idea that if a country such as Korea or Vietnam were to fall to the communists, that all of Asia, followed by the rest of the planet, would too. Abe rightly argues that, "Vietnam is a civil war" and that monolithic communism is "a myth." Stan backs Abe by saying, "Come on Bert, it (the Vietnam War) is for profit… Bombs are the perfect product. They cost a fortune and are only used once." Bert motions towards Stan's cousin, who is on shore leave and dressed in his crisp Navy whites; "So you're saying this man here is coming home in a bag for nothing?" Bert asks. Stan's cousin does ultimately die in Vietnam in season six.275 *Mad Men* depicts Stan's cousin as giving his life not to

---

273 A kibbutz is a collective community in Israel that was traditionally based on agriculture. The first kibbutz, established in 1909, was Degania.

274 Season 7 episode 4 "The Monolith" May 4, 2014.

275 Season 6 episode 7 "The Crash" May 19, 2013.

protect the United States from any communist menace, but rather to serve the interests of the capitalist system, which, as Stan indicates, is fueled by advertising and warfare.

In season one, Roy Hazelitt (Ian Bohen), a beatnik, denigrates ad man Don for making "the lie" and creating "want." Darwinist Don coldly replies, "There is no lie. There is no system. The universe is indifferent."[276] One of Midge's stoned beatnik buddies later remarks that, "Love is bourgeois… a bunch of ants going to a hive." The line indicates that, even when Marx is not explicitly a topic on *Mad Men*, the concept he coined – social class – is as central to the show's depiction of postwar American consumerism as racism and sexism are.

Betty alludes to being a higher class than Don's in season three. "All this time I thought you were some football hero who hated his father," blue-blooded Betty denigrates Don soon after discovering he is a fraud. "I knew you were poor. I knew you were ashamed of it. I see how you are with money. You don't understand it."[277] And though Don tells Roy that the "system" is an imaginary product concocted in the minds of the weak, Lane Pryce, the chief financial officer at Sterling & Cooper, is painfully aware of the "very real system of money coming in and money going out (of the company)."[278] Roger Sterling's haughty profligacy puts him at

[276] Season 1 episode 8 "The Hobo Code" September 6, 2007.

[277] Season 3 episode 11 "The Gypsy and the Hobo" October 25, 2009.

[278] Season 4 episode 2 "Christmas Comes But Once a Year" August 1, 2010.

odds with Lane in season four as the former insists on throwing a lavish Christmas party comparable to a "Roman orgy" in order to dazzle Lucky Strike's Lee Garner, Jr. into keeping the cigarette company's business with Sterling & Cooper. "I know you are accustomed to living out of a bottomless pocket," Lane vents his frustration as he alludes to Roger being a spoiled child.[279]

The system Don references as "indifferent" and that Lane considers terribly real is capitalism, which is depicted in *Mad Men* to be as real as cancer. The system is also depicted to be as fertile field for authoritarianism as any other ideology. As Hannah Arendt notes in *The Origins of Totalitarianism* (1951), the ideal breeding ground for totalitarianism is a free and liberal consumer society.[280] And while class distinctions could be smoothed over to a degree by granting the working classes greater access to consumer credit and consumer goods such as suburban homes, luxury sedans, and vacations to places like Spain and Rome they could never be fully abolished, which creates tension between workers and their bosses, especially since workers' livelihoods tend to be much more precarious than managers'.

Class tension and capitalist contempt for workers is especially expressed by Roger Sterling in season five when he says, "boo hoo, they (striking airline mechanics) need more wrenches."[281] A fascistic contempt for workers and a free press is further alluded

[279] Ibid.

[280] Hannah Arendt, *The Origins of Totalitarianism*, (Orlando: Harcourt, 1976), p. 317.

[281] Season 5 episode 4 "Mystery Date" April 8, 2012.

to in season three when a Manhattan real estate developer laments that, "We should have torn Penn Station down during the newspaper strike, nobody would have noticed."[282] A season earlier Harry Crane says, "They don't care about us," of Putnam, Powell, and Lowe shortly after the British firm buys Sterling & Cooper. "We're just salaries on a ledger. They will draw a line and get rid of everything below it."[283] In season seven, Jim Cutler says, "we (the agency) don't owe you anything, you're a hired hand," to Lou Avery, who suffers status anxiety soon after Don returns from his leave of absence.[284]

Status anxiety is, in fact, commonly depicted on the show. Early in season two, for instance, Harry Crane grows furious that Kenny Cosgrove makes more money than he does.[285] Four episodes later Don buys a Cadillac Coup de Ville (the quintessential symbol of having made it in postwar America) a scene after being invited to be a partner by Cooper. A few scenes later, during a picnic, Don reminisces to his family a story of having to find the outhouse with a rope during darks nights on the farm when he was a kid. Sally, Don's daughter, asks if they (the Drapers) are rich.[286] Class stratification and unabashed materialism is likewise alluded to by both Betty and her son Bobby during Thanksgiving Dinner in

[282] Season 3 episode 2 "Love Among the Ruins" August 23, 2009.

[283] Season 2 episode 13 "Meditations in Times of Crisis" October 26, 2008.

[284] Season 7 episode 7 "Waterloo" May 25, 2014.

[285] Season 2 episode 3 "The Benefactor" August 10, 2008.

[286] Season 2 episode 7 "The Gold Violin" September 7, 2008.

season five when the son says, "I'm thankful that I've got two houses and they're both really big and I got a new sled." Betty adds, "I'm thankful that I have everything I want and nobody has anything better."[287]

The myth of America being a true meritocracy where class does not matter much is also critiqued in season two as Salvatore Romano asks Harry Crane, "Isn't media a meritocracy?" Harry retorts, "Do you think that?" as if he had never noticed any semblance of equality of opportunity in the industry. The centrality of class in postwar American society as being inherently unfair is further elaborated by the creators of *Mad Men* in an episode titled "Favors," in which Don pulls strings to save Sylvia Rosen's son from being sent to Vietnam. The man who taught Don's partner, Ted Shaw, to fly, pulls strings to get Mitchell (Hudson Thames) into the Air National Guard, which seems to allude to the way George W. Bush's, Bill Clinton's, Donald Trump's, and countless others' connections allowed them to dodge Vietnam, a war fought primarily by working class men who had been drafted into the service.[288]

The inherently unequal American class system is alluded to again in season three when Burt Peterson is fired as head of accounts at Sterling & Cooper. Harry Crane is seen lamenting the tax rate just before the scene slides into Peterson being fired from the agency shortly after his wife's death (from cancer). "Fellow comrades in mediocrity," Peterson seethes to his former co-

[287] Season 5 episode 9 "Dark Shadows" May 13, 2012.

[288] Season 6 episode 10 "Favors" June 2, 2013.

workers, "you can all go straight to hell!" He then looks squarely at Don as he says, "see you on the bread lines," as if to remind the viewer that Don (actually Dick Whitman) grew up mired in poverty in the midst of the Great Depression.[289]

Social anxiety and mobility are particularly central features of Don Draper's character. "You've got a $5 haircut," Don, who fraudulently stole a higher rank (from private to lieutenant) by assuming Don Draper's identity after his superior officer dies in Korea, says to Pete in season one, "you've been given everything."[290] The following season Don (Dick Whitman) has a flashback to the time he asked Anna Draper (the real Don Draper's widow) for a divorce soon after falling in love with Betty. He promises to take financial care of Anna forever and acknowledges how different his life would be if not for assuming the social class of a dead man.[291] "In another lifetime I'd be your chauffer," Don says to Roger close to the end of the final episode of the show, thereby demonstrating that he is acutely aware of how precarious his inclusion on the highest rung of America's postwar social pyramid is.[292]

Anti-hero Don's character arc is in some ways a critique of the commoditization of the American Dream. In season three, for example, Don's (actually Dick Whitman's) humble beginnings

[289] Season 3 episode 1 "Out of Town" August 16, 2009.

[290] Season 1 episode 12 "Nixon vs. Kennedy" October 11, 2007.

[291] Season 2 episode 12 "The Mountain King" October 19, 2008.

[292] Season 7 episode 1 "Time Zones" April 13, 2014.

seem to endear him to Goldwater Republican Connie Hilton, who remarks that Don is "like a son, more than a son because" Don "didn't have what they have, and" he "understands."[293] Hilton's sentiment seems to touch the normally unsentimental and neoliberal ad man.[294] In season two, Cooper explains to Don the significance of inclusion in New York City aristocracy. "Philanthropy is the gateway to power," Cooper says as he tells Don that the glib ad man has been asked to sit on the board of directors at the Museum of Early American Folk Art, which is considered a great honor. "There are a few people who get to decide what happens in this world," Cooper enlightens his underling; "You have been invited to join them. Pull back the curtain and take your seat."[295] In season five, Don moves from an apartment on Waverly and Sixth in Downtown Manhattan to Seventy-Seventh and Park Avenue, which is a tangible symbol of his social mobility and ascendance into New York City high society.[296]

The specter of New York City high society is as central to the show as Don's social mobility is. Pete Campbell and his wife, Trudy, Roger Sterling, Bert Cooper, and Henry Francis all personify postwar New York City aristocracy. In season two, Freddy Rumsen, whose father was a traveling salesman, refers to Roger as

[293] Season 3 episode 9 "Wee Small Hours" October 11, 2009.

[294] Ibid.

[295] Season 2 episode 7: "Gold Violin" September 7, 2008.

[296] Season 5 episode 6 "At the Codfish Ball" April 29, 2012.

"Bonnie Prince Sterling."[297] In season four, in an episode titled "New Amsterdam," which alludes to Dutch imperialism, Cooper explains to Don the importance of appeasing Pete, his subordinate, because his mother's side of the family, the Dykmans, once owned everything north of 125th Street, and who continue to have deep connections with other Manhattan aristocrats, who the agency would like to pursue as clients.[298] In season three, Betty says that "the Rockefellers own half the land in Ossining (a wealthy suburb north of New York City)."[299] Betty later marries Henry Francis, who works for Nelson Rockefeller. In other words, even housewife Betty is socially mobile, considering Don is nouveau riche compared to her second husband, Henry, who works for American royalty.

Mad Men, as the paragraph above highlights, often depicts wealth as begetting more wealth. Pete, who begins his life rich, gets even more help from his wife's father, who is an executive at Vicks Chemical, to buy an apartment in Manhattan, which would have proven to be a very good investment.[300] In season four, Jane's incompetent and plagiarist cousin, Danny Siegel, gets a job at the agency because of his relation to Jane's husband, Roger Sterling.[301] Danny ultimately becomes a successful movie producer in Hollywood.

[297] Season 2 episode 9 "Six Month Leave" September 28, 2008.

[298] Season 1 Episode 4 "New Amsterdam" April 9, 2007.

[299] Season 3 episode 7 "Seven Twenty Three" September 27, 2009.

[300] Season 1 episode 13 "The Wheel" October 18, 2007.

[301] Season 4 episode 6 "Waldorf Stories" August 29, 2010.

In the twentieth century celebrity also became a kind of royalty in American society. Megan Draper, an aspiring actress, yearns to be a celebrity. Her Marxist professor father, however, does not seem to approve of Megan's newfound affluence as Don's wife. "Why do you look so sad?" Èmile asks Megan shortly after she receives an award for her work crafting an advertisement for Heinz Baked Beans.

> "Is this your passion? I always thought you were very single-minded about your dreams and this would help. But now I see you skipped the struggle and went right to the end. This apartment, this wealth that someone handed to you, this is what Karl Marx was talking about, and it's not because someone else deserves it, it is bad for your soul."[302]

An episode later, Megan runs lines with her pal, Julia (Meghan Bradley), a waitress and aspiring actress in her acting class, who has landed an audition for *Dark Shadows*, an odd and hokey soap opera. Megan teases her classmate due to how ridiculous the lines in the script are. Megan's classmate, echoing Èmile an episode earlier, notes how easy Megan's life is compared to every other aspiring artist she knows.[303] She refers to Megan's apartment, which her father earlier referred to as "exquisitely decadent," as Megan's "throne on Seventy-Fifth and Park." The comment offends Megan. "Hey," she says, "that's not fair." Julia responds quite matter-of-factly, "no… it's not," as if critiquing the capitalist system

---

[302] Season 5 episode 7 "At the Codfish Ball" April 29, 2012.

[303] Season 5 episode 9 "Dark Shadows" May 13, 2012.

as inherently unfair by criticizing Megan.304 Megan later lands a Butler Footwear commercial thanks to Don's nepotistic intervention, which later leads to Megan landing a steady role on a daytime soap opera.

In season four, Don laments to his lawyer that the capital gains tax (in the midst of Lyndon Johnson's Great Society and the escalation of the Vietnam War) is a whopping forty-eight percent. A season later Don seems unnerved that "Megan's father is a communist, or a socialist, or Maoist… or some ideology that makes him hate" what his son-in-law does for a living.305 Don, however, is actually and oddly much more like Èmile than he might like to believe. On his first visit to Don's and Megan's luxury midtown Manhattan apartment Èmile refers to the space as "exquisitely decadent." Marie, Èmile's wife, says, "his eyes and his politics are in a fight."306 Though Èmile describes Don and Megan's apartment as "decadent," he also wonders why Don carried the luggage up to the apartment rather than having the doorman carry the suitcases, thereby underscoring that Èmile has subconsciously grown accustomed to class and division of labor and is in practice arguably less leftist than Don (who carries the luggage) is ideologically neoliberal. Plus, although Don is the consummate consumer (most notably of tobacco, booze and real estate), and Èmile is ideologically Marxist, both ultimately shill utopianism for a living. The similarity between neoliberal ad man Don and Marxist

304 Ibid.

305 Season 5 episode 7 "At the Codfish Ball" April 29, 2012.

306 Season 5 episode 8 "Lady Lazarus" May 6, 2012.

Èmile is alluded to by Megan in season six; she eviscerates her father to Don in the wake of Martin Luther King Jr's assassination. She is appalled that Èmile applauds "the escalation of decay," which alludes to Karl Marx's assertion that civilization would one day decay to the point that the setting for an epic battle between capital and labor would inevitably present itself and the proletariat would ultimately take over the means of production and a social utopia would flourish.[307] "I'm so sick of that Marxist bullshit," Megan vents to Don. "My father hides behind his intellect. He doesn't want to feel any emotions," she says. "You don't have Marx, you've got a bottle."[308]

In season five, Don seems to personify the nature of capitalism when he undermines Michael Ginsberg's idea to win the Snoball Ice Cream account. "What do I care?" Ginsberg fumes to Don on an awkward and tense elevator ride up to the office, "I've got a million of them (ideas)." Don snidely replies, "I guess I'm lucky you work for me then."[309] Don's smug line speaks volumes because it indicates the split in his personality between being an unabashed capitalist and also simultaneously a proletariat who aches to have agency and ownership of his labor and unique genius to make people spend money on things they do not need. Though at times seeming to be a neoliberal libertarian Don also sometimes seems to exude Marxist inclinations. In season five, for instance, he

[307] See Karl Marx, *The Communist Manifesto*, (London and Chicago, Ill. Pluto Press, 1996).

[308] Season 7 episode 4 "The Monolith" May 4, 2014.

[309] Season 5 episode 8 "Lady Lazarus" May 6, 2012.

urges the workers at the agency to "prepare to take a great leap forward," which echoes Mao Zedong's efforts to transform China from an agrarian backwater to an industrial superpower.310 The biggest clue that Don's identity is defined by a tension between his service to the capitalist system as an ad man-in-conflict-with his desire to own his own labor, talent, and energy and to live on his own terms is especially illuminated by his obdurate refusal to sign a contract with the agency.311 Don's desire to own his own labor and creativity was undoubtedly informed by his visceral confrontation with grinding poverty as a child. But Sterling and Cooper, the guys signing the paychecks that pay for Don's mortgage and Cadillac, demand ownership of his energy, talent and labor. In season three, Conrad Hilton (the consummate neoliberal capitalist), who "comes and goes as he pleases,"312 is the president of the international corporation that Sterling & Cooper is desperate to do business with. Hilton demands that "all the principles be secure" before he agrees to sign with the agency. That means Don has to be under contract at Sterling & Cooper. Bert Cooper provides Don with a parable about Sacagawea (the capitalist) carrying a baby (the proletariat) on her back and the baby thinking it, rather than Sacagawea, discovered America. You've been standing on other people's shoulders and now it's time to pay us back," Cooper says to Don. "Would you say I know something about you?" Cooper adds. "I would" Don regretfully

---

310 Season 5 episode 10 "Christmas Waltz" May 20, 2012.

311 Season 1 episode 11 "Indian Summer" October 4, 2007.

312 Season 3 episode 13 "Shut the Door. Have a Seat" November 8, 2009.

concedes. "After all," Cooper concludes, "who is *really* signing the contract anyway?"[313]

Marx's theory of alienation describes the estrangement of people from aspects of their *Gattungswesen* ("species-essence") as a consequence of living in a society stratified by social classes, which is exactly what Megan's father tries to explain to his daughter at the American Cancer Society Codfish Ball in season five (see above). The alienation from the self is, according to Marx, a consequence of being a mechanistic part of a social class, the condition of which estranges a person from their humanity. And though the contract offered to Don is very generous he instinctively eschews it because he intuitively knows that the contract equates to selling his soul to the company and ultimately to being owned.

Don is ultimately given an ultimatum by Cooper and granted the weekend to think the offer over. Roger Sterling meanwhile phones Betty in the interest of getting her to apply pressure to her recalcitrant husband. She, however, informs Roger that "Don is going to do whatever he wants." She does, however, broach the subject with Don over the weekend. He explains to her that, "no contract means I have all the power. They want me but can't have me." Don is finally coerced into signing the contract as "Don Draper" (though he is as much Dick Whitman). The episode ends quite satirically as the song "Sixteen Tons" by Tennessee Ernie Ford plays over the credits.[314] The lyrics, which are presumably a metaphor for Don, are as follows:

[313] Season 3 episode 7 "Seven Twenty Three" September 27, 2009.
[314] Season 3 Episode 7 "Seven Twenty Three" September 29, 2009.

"Some people say a man is made outta mud
A poor man's made outta muscle and blood
Muscle and blood and skin and bones
A mind that's a-weak and a back that's strong

I was born one mornin' when the sun didn't shine
I picked up my shovel and I walked to the mine
I loaded sixteen tons of number nine coal
And the straw boss said "Well, a-bless my soul"

I was born one mornin', it was drizzlin' rain
Fightin' and trouble are my middle name
I was raised in the canebrake by an ol' mama lion
Cain't no-a high-toned woman make me walk the line

If you see me comin', better step aside
A lotta men didn't, a lotta men died
One fist of iron, the other of steel
If the right one don't a-get you
Then the left one will

You load sixteen tons, what do you get
Another day older and deeper in debt
Saint Peter don't you call me 'cause I can't go
I owe my soul to the company store."[315]

[315] Meryl Travis and Tennessee Ernie Ford, "Sixteen Tons," (New York, Capital Records, 1955).

Hilton, of course, ends up firing the agency in a subsequent episode. The sad irony, for Don anyway, is that he sold his soul to Sterling & Cooper, which has lasting consequences for the protagonist in subsequent seasons of the show. In the final season of the series, for example, Don is placed on indefinite leave after telling Hershey's executives about how much he loved the candy bar as a dirt-poor kid living in a whorehouse during the Great Depression.

Don's contract especially seems to be a metaphor for the specter of fascism in postwar American society. Harry Crane, for example, tells Don that the agency plans to sign Commander Tobacco while Don is on leave. In season four, Don penned an open letter to *The New York Times* in which he "slit" the tobacco industry's "throat." The agency signing Big Tobacco thus signals, as Harry eloquently puts it, the "final solution" for Don at the company.[316] Roger later refers to Jim Cutler's scheme to force Don out of the company by signing Commander as his "secret plan to win the war," which is an allusion to Richard Nixon's 1968 presidential campaign in which he refused to tell the public of his secret plan of how he would get America out of Vietnam.[317] Nixon's plan was ultimately the "Madman" theory of relentless carpet-bombing, which ultimately did not compel the Vietcong to surrender.

The larger context of *Mad Men's* depiction of opposition to Marxism in 1960s America is the creators of the show's own battles

[316] Season 7 episode 5 "The Runaways" May 11, 2014.

[317] Season 7 episode 6 "The Strategy" May 18, 2014.

with *AMC* during production of the series. This point seems alluded to in season two when Marilyn Monroe's voice can be heard saying in the background, "We're what's okay with the business, management is what's wrong with the business," shortly after her death as Betty turns the radio on.[318] This seems to allude to the creators of *Mad Men's* own labor strife with *AMC*. Production of the show between seasons four and five was, in fact, halted due to a stalemate in negotiations between the network and the creators of the show.

Turmoil between workers and management, in fact, seeps into the series in season five. Mohawk Airlines, for instance, which had been dropped by Sterling & Cooper in season two so that the upstart ad agency could pursue American Airlines after Flight 1 crashes into Jamaica Bay, returns to do business with the revamped agency. Mohawk is desperate to avoid bankruptcy and is deep in debt due to planes needing to be overhauled as a mechanic strike looms. An episode later the mechanic strike throughout the airline industry cripples most airlines, but proves to be a boon for Mohawk, whose mechanics cut a side deal with the company's management to keep planes in the sky and the company afloat. "Fly over the picket line with Mohawk… and Mohawk, breaking the strike one flight at a time," Peggy jokes to Roger as he solicits her to spend the weekend crafting taglines for Mohawk's corporate image campaign. "Hey Trotsky," he says while exhaling a lung full of tobacco smoke, "you're in advertising." The labor strife in the airline industry is the backdrop of a negotiation between Roger (the capitalist) and Peggy (the proletariat). Peggy ultimately crushes

[318] Season 2 episode 9 "Six Month Leave" September 28, 2008.

Roger, who due to time constraints, is desperate and thereby at a severe disadvantage at the bargaining table. The viewer later learns that President Lyndon Johnson "is afraid of losing the labor vote and so won't force arbitration" in the Airline industry.[319]

The fact that there is no longer any unified labor vote in the United States in the twenty-first century speaks to the fact that globalized capitalism, especially consumerism, has become hegemonic in the decades since the end of the Cold War. Don's unwillingness to acknowledge the intractable reality of America's deeply embedded class system concomitant to his own bitter struggle to own his labor speaks to the labor strife between *AMC* and creators of *Mad Men* that stalled production prior to the publication of season five. But the show also speaks to the purge of liberalism in postwar American society, including the assault on organized labor, and the neoliberalism fostered by corporate conformity and America's longtime duality between being associated with freedom and liberty concomitant to having authoritarian impulses embedded in the nature of the capitalist system, which is inherently unequal and not at all designed to be egalitarian. And so *Mad Men*, although serving consumer capitalism by selling ad space for seven seasons to some of the very companies the show critiques, is as unbound by orthodox ideology as the scholars in the Frankfurt School tended to be. The Frankfurt School, especially Theodor Adorno, like the creators of *Mad Men* and Hannah Arendt, identified totalitarian impulses and tendencies as much in America's postwar militarized consumer society as in Stalin's, Hitler's, Mussolini's authoritarian regimes.

[319] Season 5 episode 4 "Mystery Date" April 8, 2012.

Chapter Four

"*Mad Men*, Violence, and the Banality of Evil in 1960s America"

The racism, sexism, and militant opposition to communism in Cold War America underscores the violence central to American society in the decades after World War II, especially during the Vietnam War. Violence was, as Richard Slotkin's *Gunfighter Nation: The Myth of the Frontier in Twentieth Century America* (1992), illuminates, is often considered regenerative, especially at borderlands.[320] Violence was also championed by both the Nazis and Italian Blackshirts in the Interwar Era as being redeeming.

Implied and overt violence are also central components of *Mad Men*, which is particularly evident in the show's fascination with self-harm – and not just cigarettes and booze, but suicide. The show is, for example, set during the Atomic Age, a time in which it seemed to many that humans had developed an inveterate death wish as primal as the urge to procreate.[321] This ethos is most

---

[320] In *Gunfighter Nation* Slotkin examines fiction, Hollywood westerns, and the writings of Hollywood figures and Washington leaders to elaborate the racialist theory of Anglo-Saxon ascendance and superiority. This countered Frederick Jackson Turner's thesis proffered at the turn-of-the-twentieth century in which he argued that the closing of the frontier exerted the most influence in popular culture and government policymaking in the twentieth century. Slotkin argues that Theodore Roosevelt's view of the frontier myth provided the justification for most of America's expansionist policies, from Roosevelt's own Rough Riders to Kennedy's counterinsurgency and Johnson's war in Vietnam. Slotkin, it is interesting to note, was, as of 2018, a longtime professor of English and American Studies at Matthew Weiner's alma mater, Wesleyan.

[321] Season 1 episode 1 "Smoke Gets in Your Eyes" July 19, 2007.

notably personified in *Mad Men* by Dr. Greta Gutman (Gordana Rashovich), the German-speaking consumer researcher hired by Sterling & Cooper in the first episode of season one. The primal human death wish, Dr. Gutman argues, might be used to sell cigarettes in the wake of the surgeon general placing warnings on tobacco packages.

The chapter that follows here is divided into three parts, all of which probe the violence depicted in *Mad Men* as a means of exploring the reality of violence in 1960s America. The first part of the chapter examines *Mad Men's* use of implied violence and examines how the show depicts a kind of dehumanization and desensitization to violence – a banality of evil -- in postwar America. Part two examines overt violence in *Mad Men*, including the show's depiction of political violence. Part three pays particularly close attention to *Mad Men's* treatment of violence towards children and women in the 1960s. The global backdrop of *Mad Men's* depiction of implied and overt violence in 1960s America is the specter of nuclear holocaust, the Cold War, anti-colonialism, the American war in Indochina, and conformity to consumer capitalism, which grows increasingly conflated with politics in the decades after World War II.

Death particularly casts a dark and ominous shadow over the show, especially in the form of cancer and suicide. Adam Whitman and Lane Pryce hang themselves. Don feels responsible for both. In season one, Roger mentions that one of Margaret's boyfriends committed suicide, which foreshadows his daughter's own nervous breakdown in season seven.[322] The first episode of

[322] Season 1 episode 6 "Babylon" August 23, 2007.

season two Don doodles a noose during a meeting. He is seen doing the same thing during a meeting in season five when Lane gushes that he has a lead with Jaguar, which ultimately contributes to his suicide by hanging later in the season.[323] Eight episodes later Joan is deeply distraught by Marilyn Monroe's drug overdose and subsequent death.[324] "I'm going to go to my favorite restaurant and have a glass of cyanide," Roger says in season four, "I'm going to commit suicide."[325] In season five, Don responds to Megan wanting to have dinner with Pete Campbell and his wife, Trudy, at their new suburban home by saying, "Saturday night in the suburbs, that's when you really want to blow your brains out,"[326] which echoes Paul Kinsey's rhetorical assertion in season one that he would kill himself if *The Twilight Zone* was cancelled. Moments earlier Kinsey nonchalantly apologizes for being late to the meeting because "someone threw them self in front of a train."[327] Four episodes later Harry Crane says that John. F. Kennedy's campaign jingle makes him "want to blow his brains out."[328] Early in season six Don crafts and ad campaign for a hotel in Hawaii in which he

[323] Season 2 episode 1 "For Those Who Think Young" July 27, 2008.

[324] Season 2 episode 9 "Six Month Leave" September 29, 2008.

[325] Season 4 episode 9 "The Beautiful Girls" September 9, 2010.

[326] Season 5 episode 5 "Signal 30" April 15, 2012.

[327] Season 1 episode 6 "Babylon" August 23, 2007.

[328] Season 1 episode 10 "Long Weekend" September 27, 2007.

seems obsessed by suicide.329 Later in the season Roger makes light of Hemingway's suicide.330

In addition to several references to suicide, *Mad Men* poignantly critiques postwar America's ever-evolving fascination with and titillation for violence, which grew especially prominent in the 1960s. In season one, for instance, Francine Hanson's son, Ernie (Josiah Polhemus), dons an Army helmet on his head and a cowboy holster with two guns around his hips. In season three Don's son, Bobby, wears a German helmet from World War I that had been placed on his head by Betty's increasingly senile father, Gene. Bobby seems to delight in the fantasy as he pretends to shoot people with an imaginary rifle.331 In later episodes of the show both Roger's grandson, Ellery (Jordan Fiderio), as well as Bobby Draper are seen running through a room firing toy machineguns.332 Ellery is particularly interesting because he is dressed in overalls and a blue plaid shirt very similar to the outfit worn by Danny (Danny Lloyd) in Stanley Kubrick's *The Shining* (1980).

The American fetish for violence in the 1960s surfaces especially in the third episode of season six when Joan and her sister go to the Electric Circus, a psychedelic gathering place reminiscent of the Milk Bar in Kubrick's cinematic depiction of

---

329 Season 6 episode 1 "The Doorway" April 7, 2013.

330 Season 6 episode 11 "Favors" June 9, 2013.

331 Season 3 episode 4 "The Arrangements" September 6, 2009.

332 Season 7 episode 4 "The Monolith" May 4, 2014; and Season 7 episode 10 "The Forecast" April 19, 2015.

Anthony Burgess' novel, *A Clockwork Orange* (1971). The song playing over the loud speakers at the Electric Circus is "The Ballad of Bonnie and Clyde" by Serge Gainsbourg; a young hipster leans over the couch and introduces himself to Joan by saying, "Johnny and Joan... Bonnie and Clyde," then engages her in a passionate kiss, which she earnestly reciprocates.[333] Inspired by the film of the same title, Gainsbourg composed the song around "The Trail's End," a poem written by Bonnie Parker shortly before she and Clyde Barrow were shot to death in a police ambush, which foreshadows the "police riot" at the 1968 Democratic National Convention at a Hilton Hotel in downtown Chicago six episodes later. Both *Bonnie and Clyde* (1967) as well as *A Clockwork Orange* both critiqued the growing fetish for commodified violence in the decades after World War II.[334]

In season five, company partners Pete Campbell and Lane Pryce get into a fistfight in a conference room at the agency. "This is barbaric," Bert Cooper pleads. Roger also intuitively knows that it is highly unprofessional for two of his partners to duke it out at work, but neither he nor Don bothers to stop the fight because they look forward to the existential pleasure provided by two men punching each other in the face.[335] It is also important to point out that the vast majority of the backdrop of the series is the Vietnam War. In that sense Pete and Lane's fight might be a metaphor for

[333] Season 6 episode 4 "To Have and Hold" April 21, 2013.

[334] See Steven M. Cahn's "*A Clockwork Orange* is Not About Violence," *Metaphilosophy*, Vol. 5, No. 2 (April 1974), pp. 155-157.

[335] Season 5 episode 5 "Signal 30" April 15, 2012.

men's barbaric interest in watching other -- often younger -- men wage violence against other men. The same could be said of the interest surrounding the Sonny Liston and Cassius Clay (Muhammad Ali) prizefight in season four.[336]

In season three, Joan jokes to Don in the waiting room of a hospital, "That's life, one day you're on top of the world, the next day a secretary is running you over with a lawnmower," after an executive at Putnam, Powell, and Lowe's foot is lost as a result of a drunken secretary driving over it on a John Deere riding lawnmower during a raucous company party.[337] *Mad Men*, as the incidents above indicate, depicts a nation of people who have grown dehumanized concomitant to growing desensitized to violence in a manner comparable to the German pencil pushers and taskmasters depicted in Hannah Arendt's *Eichmann in Jerusalem: A Report on the Banality of Evil* (1963). The notion of the banality of evil famously elucidated by Arendt is particularly evident in *Mad Men's* depiction of 1960s America.[338] In season one, for example, Dick Whitman's half-brother, Adam, tells Don that his father's wife had died of stomach cancer. "Good," Don says coldly.[339] In season three, Roger makes a crass joke about Yetta Wallenda falling to her death during a high-wire walk and later being removed from the

[336] Season 4 episode 7 "The Suitcase" September 5, 2010.

[337] Season 3 episode 6 "Guy Walks Into an Advertising Agency" September 20, 2009.

[338] For more on the banality of evil see Hannah Arendt's classic E*ichmann in Jerusalem*, (New York, Viking, 1963).

[339] Season 1 episode 5 "5G" August 16, 2007.

sidewalk "with a hose."340 In season five, Megan Draper seems to allude to the agency employees' dark hearts when she asks, "what's wrong with you people? You're all so cynical. You don't smile. You smirk."341 Late in season four, Roger learns that David Montgomery, a rival ad executive, has died. "Here's your silver lining," he says, as he hopes to win some of the recently deceased's clients.342 In season six, Pete tells the agency's creatives that Frank Gleason has died of cancer. "Dreams do come true," Johnny Mathis (the copywriter not the pop star) callously gushes. In season seven, Sally learns that one of her classmates is going to miss school until Easter due to the recent death of her mother, who died of cancer. "I wish my mom would die," Sally's friend, Caroline, remarks. "I'd stay here (at school) until 1975 if I could get Betty in the ground," Sally retorts, foreshadowing her mother's own diagnosis of stage-four lung cancer in season seven.343

Tough there is a great deal of overt violence depicted throughout *Mad Men*, implied violence is perhaps even more pernicious. There is particularly couched violence directed towards liberalism that runs through the series. In the inaugural episode of *Mad Men*, Lee Garner, Jr., for example, says, "we might as well be living in Russia" in response to the federal government regulating that cigarettes can no longer be marketed as healthy. Moments later Pete compares the danger of cigarettes to the danger of riding in

---

340 Season 3 episode 2 "Love Among The Ruins" August 23, 2009.

341 Season 5 episode 1 "A Little Kiss" March 25, 2012.

342 Season 4 episode 11 "Chinese Wall" October 3, 2010.

343 Season 7 episode 14 "Person to Person" May 17, 2015.

cars sans seatbelts. "You still have to get where you're going," Pete says, "smoke your cigarettes."[344] A General Motors executive in season six, who has taken Kenny Cosgrove duck hunting in rural Michigan, says, "See that tree, pretend it's Ralph Nader," which speaks to the auto industry's staunch unwillingness to add seatbelts to cars until ultimately being forced to by the federal government, which was influenced in part by Ralph Nader's consumer activism in *Unsafe at Any Speed* (1965).[345] Rachel Carson's classic, *Silent Spring* (1962), like Nader's *Unsafe At Any Speed*, and *Mad Men*, all depict corporate America as knowingly doing harm to people but caring far more for profits than humanity and basic human decency. *Mad Men's* allusions to the federal government's regulating of the tobacco industry in season one and the auto industry in season five seems to allude to a kind of banality of evil deeply embedded in corporate America, especially considering that executives for both big tobacco and automobile companies knew

---

[344] Season 1 episode 1 "Smoke Gets in Your Eyes" July 19, 2007.

[345] Season 6 episode 12 "The Quality of Mercy" June 16, 2013. Supreme Court Justice Lewis Powell wrote a famous memorandum to American business leaders in 1971 in reaction to the federal government's increased regulation of big business. Powell alleged that entities such as the Environmental Protection Agency as supposed evidence that the federal government had waged warfare on free market capitalism and thus the very fabric of American society. The wider cultural context and critique made by the creators of *Mad Men* in which a GM executive fantasizes of shooting Ralph Nader is that the episode was produced shortly after the federal government (i.e. American taxpayer) bailed GM out after the 2008 collapse of the global financial system. The series is, in short, as much a critique of twenty-first century America as it is a critique of the United States in the 1960s. For more on the impact of the Powell Memorandum in American History see Jacob S. Hacker *and* Paul Pierson's *Winner-Take-All Politics: How Washington Made the Rich Richer---and Turned Its Back on the Middle Class (New York, Simon & Schuster, 2011).*

their products were harming and at times killing consumers, yet cared far more about profits than human life. The same could be said of American politicians such as Lyndon Johnson and Richard Nixon knowing that the North Vietnamese were not actually evidence of a global communist conspiracy and that a military and political victory was impossible in Indochina but continuing to draft Americans into the military and to carpet-bomb dykes, dams and civilians.

In season seven, the show stretches into the early 1970s, a point in American history when the Cold War was on the wane and the War on Terror was inchoate. This allusion to political violence seeps into the show. Joan, for example, mentions "radicals blowing up department stores on a daily basis," which seems to allude to the Weather Underground and the subsequent unraveling of the American New Left.[346] Later in the episode Kenny criticizes his father-in-law, who had recently retired as executive at Dow Chemical. "Your father was a cog in a giant machine that made weapons and poison," Kenny grills Cynthia (Larisa Oleynik), his bemused wife. "And you sold them!" she says defiantly in an effort to defend her father's honor and profession. Though Kenny seems to find Dow reprehensible for its responsibility in causing irreparable carnage in Vietnam, he later becomes head of advertising at the international conglomerate that makes napalm as a means of vengefully turning the tables on Roger Sterling, who had recently fired him from the ad agency. Dow becomes a

---

[346] Season 7 episode 8 "Severance" April 5, 2015.

prominent client of Roger's company, which gives Kenny the power in the relationship.[347]

The specter of implied violence is further alluded to in the form of the grim horror caused by the Manson Family, which is mentioned in consecutive episodes late in season seven.[348] In the final episode of the series Don is desperate to leave the New Age retreat that Stephanie (Caity Lotz) has abandoned him at. "You can try to hitch," the affable girl at the front desk of the retreat explains to Don, "but you'll be standing there all day. You can thank Charlie Manson for that," she adds.[349] As benign as the comment may seem, it is actually evidence that the creators of *Mad Men* were acutely aware of the heightened level and scope of violence at the center of the American experience in the 1960s and 1970s, and how the nature of the nation had changed as a result.

Aside from the sadistic callousness expressed towards death in several instances on the show, *Mad Men* likewise – as alluded to by its depiction of car and cigarette manufacturers – evokes a widespread callousness and crass care for cash more than human life amongst American businesspeople. Early in the second season of the series, for example, American Airlines Flight 1 crashes into Jamaica Bay, which inspires a few tasteless jokes by Paul Kinsey and Freddy Rumsen. "Idlewild (airport) to Jamaica Bay in eight minutes," Freddy, an alcoholic, drunkenly jokes. But the most notable quip is authored by Pete Campbell who jokes that the

[347] Ibid.

[348] Season 7 episode 9 "New Business" April 12, 2015.

[349] Season 7 episode 14 "Person to Person" May 17, 2015.

passengers aboard the doomed flight were on their way to a golf function, and the bay "turned plaid on impact." The satirical irony is that, as Pete and viewers later learn in the episode, his father had perished in the crash. Later in the episode an American Airlines executive seems to be much more concerned about the company's stock price and fear of investors unloading their shares in the wake of the tragedy than he is with the departed lost in the crash and the emotional state of the loved ones left behind.[350]

    This crass care for cash more than human life is a particularly prominent feature in *Mad Men*. In season one, for instance, Bert Cooper cajoles Roger, who is recovering from a massive heart attack, to risk his recovery in order to appease Lucky Strike, who is considering firing the agency due to Roger's recent incapacitation. Roger suffers a second heart attack during the meeting. In season two Peggy seems glad that Playtex turned down the Marilyn/Jackie ad campaign because Marilyn Monroe's sudden death by drug overdose, which would have caused the company to pull the ads from magazines, costing the agency untold profits.[351] In season three, shortly after the death of her grandfather, Sally watches news coverage about a Buddhist monk's self-immolation in Saigon, Vietnam, in protest of the Ngo Diem's oppressive Catholic regime. The news of the burning monk is followed immediately by information about the stock market, followed by a Winston Cigarette commercial.[352] In season six, an insurance

[350] Season 2 episode 2 "Flight 1" July 27, 2008.

[351] Season 2 episode 9 "Six Month Leave" September 28, 2008.

[352] Season 3 episode 4 "The Arrangements" September 6, 2009.

salesman meets with Don, Roger, Stan Rizzo, and Michael Ginsberg in the hopes of capitalizing on the hysteria surrounding the assassination of Martin Luther King, Jr. and the urban riots that followed all across the country.[353] An episode later Pete and Harry get into a heated argument – which seems a metaphor for the tension between neoliberals and humanists in the 1960s -- due to Harry lamenting the financial cost to the company due to program preemptions in the wake of King's assassination. "They might cancel the Stanley Cup," Harry bemoans. Pete calls Harry a "bona fide racist," and snidely adds that, "you'll make your money back next fall on some TV movie about the death of a great man."[354] In season seven, Pete and Peggy voice concern at the prospect of the Apollo 11 crashing on the moon. "We won't be able to present (to Burger Chef) for a year," Peggy frets, echoing a similar statement made by Pete.[355]

In addition to a crass care for cash more than humanity, there is also callousness directed towards alcoholics in *Mad Men*. Freddy, a somewhat affable drunk who gets sober later in the series, gets so inebriated in season two that he wets his pants just prior to a scheduled presentation to clients. Sal thinks Freddy's imbroglio is hilarious. Pete, however, is disgusted and later engineers Freddy's ouster from the company. Pete justifies his calculated underhandedness by defending himself to Peggy by explaining, "He (Freddy) did it to his self. Those people (alcoholics)

[353] Season 6 episode 5 "The Flood" April 28, 2013.

[354] Ibid.

[355] Season 7 episode 7 "Waterloo" May 25, 2014.

have no self-control. I refuse to feel bad. We're all going to get raises. You could have his office."[356] Pete ultimately sees Freddy as weak and degenerate rather than as a sick man who is traumatized by World War II (later in the episode Roger tells Don that Freddy killed fifteen Germans). Duck Phillips, who is also a World War II veteran and who killed seventeen men in Okinawa, Japan, is (in season two), a recovering alcoholic in the midst of a bitter divorce. But Duck backs Pete rather than Freddy, who suffers the same disease. Don, who is also an alcoholic, defends Freddy as Kenny, Kinsey, and Sal gleefully "dine on the misery" of Freddy's demise.[357] Alcoholism was in the early 1960s, as alluded to by *Mad Men*, widely perceived to be a moral failure rather than a sickness, which speaks to a pervasive lack of empathy in postwar American society, as personified by Duck and Pete in season two.

Close to the end of season two Don steals away to Palm Springs with Joy, a young girl he meets while on business in California. Don passes out on the pool deck outside of a mansion. "I thought you were going to break your neck," Joy's libertine mother giggles at the thought of Don dying.[358] This kind of callousness towards human suffering – this banality of evil -- is a prominent feature on *Mad Men*. For instance, when news of John Kennedy being shot first breaks on television, the people working at Sterling & Cooper are, like the taskmasters depicted in *Eichmann in Jerusalem*, too wrapped up in their monotonous tasks such as

[356] Season 2 episode 9 "Six-Month Leave" September 28, 2008.

[357] Ibid.

[358] Season 2 episode 11 "The Jet Set" October 12, 2008.

typing, filing papers, and bothering about their own social status and standing to even notice the tragedy unfolding right in front of them. Later in the episode Duck, who at first seems transfixed by Walter Cronkite's coverage of the shooting, pulls the power chord of the television from the wall and ignores the tragedy for a while in order to enjoy a sexual tryst with Peggy, who is many years his junior.[359] Two seasons later a 14-year-old girl backstage at a Rolling Stones concert in Queens tells Don, "I'm going to jump on Brian Jones like Jack Ruby,"[360] thereby indicating that she was in some way subconsciously effected by watching the murder of Lee Harvey Oswald live on daytime television a few years earlier, which likewise speaks to how prevalent violence in the home was, both in terms of entertainment (Vietnam is often referred to as the "Television War") and domestic violence, which is likewise prominently featured in later seasons of *Mad Men*.[361]

Dehumanization as a result of desensitization to violence is especially central to season five of the series. It is particularly interesting to note that there are several nurses depicted throughout *Mad Men*. Most of the time nurses are benignly present at births, hospitals, or doctor appointments. In season three, a girl auditioning for a commercial tells Harry and Peggy that she had

---

[359] Season 3 episode 12 "The Grown Ups" November 1, 2009.

[360] Season 5 episode 3 "The Tea Leaves" April 1, 2012.

[361] See Michael Mandelbaum, "Vietnam: The Television War," *Daedalus* Vol. 111, No. 4, Print Culture and Video Culture (Fall, 1982), pp. 157-169. See also Michael Anderegg, *Inventing Vietnam: The War in Film and Television*, (Philadelphia, Temple University Press, 1991).

been cast as a waitress and a nurse before.[362] Sally and Bobby's babysitter -- Don's neighbor across the hall from his lower Manhattan apartment -- is a nurse, as is Stan Rizzo's girlfriend.[363] The number of nurses seems important because in the third episode of season five Peggy's new friend, Joyce, who is a photo editor at *Time Life*, shows the agency's creatives pictures of the Chicago nurse massacre that were "not suitable for publication." Joyce describes what happened to the victims in gory detail. "You're excited by it," Ginsberg, who amputates his own nipple in season seven, expresses disgust, "those girls are trussed up like a cut of meat. It's disgusting. It's one of those things I wish I didn't see." Joyce seems inspired by Ginsberg's sense of empathy and humanity and continues to indulge Peggy and Stan, both of whom are titillated by the gore and horror. "There was nine" Joyce theatrically jokes of the slain nurses, "one survived. I only alone escaped to tell thee." Peggy eggs Joan on by asking, "How did she do that?" Stan explains matter-of-factly, "She hid under the bed. He lost count." Ginsberg, who is depicted as certifiably insane in season seven, is actually depicted in this particular scene in season five, as the most morally sane character in a dark wilderness in what many critics of the era, such as Allen Ginsberg, who had worked at an advertising agency in Manhattan in the 1950s, perceived to be an increasingly manic world. "You know what," Michael impugns Joyce, Peggy, and Stan, "You're sickos," he says before storming out of the creative lounge. Peggy, as if suddenly coming to a humanistic epiphany as a result of Ginsberg's disgust

[362] Season 3 episode 3 "My Old Kentucky Home" August 30, 2009.

[363] Ibid.

and horror, reluctantly admits that Michael is right to be so disturbed. Peggy thereby acknowledges the banality of evil and desensitization to violence she had not previously noticed existed in her.364

Later in the series Pete, who has lived in Manhattan his entire life and thus does not know how to drive a car, has to take a driver's education course to get his license so that he can commute from his new home in the suburbs into the city. He is by far the eldest in the course. He ogles a recent high school graduate bound for Ohio State University as a film depicts the danger and horrors of reckless driving. During an intermission, the young woman tells Pete, "Those videos (of car accidents) are gruesome. I think we should go back to riding horses." The video seems to allude to and underscore the auto industry's resistance to implementing seatbelts in cars and GM's acrimony towards Nader's *Unsafe at Any Speed*. The young woman also mentions ex-Marine Charles Whitman, the sniper at the University of Texas, who murdered fourteen and wounded thirty-two people from a bell tower. She notes that the UT massacre happened just two weeks after the Chicago nurses were butchered. "Things seem so random all of a sudden and times feels like it's speeding up," she confides. Pete replies while smiling wryly, "We should go back in (to the classroom). We don't want to miss the mayhem." Later in the episode Cynthia Cosgrove likewise mentions Whitman to Megan at Trudy's suburban soirée. "They say he had a brain tumor," Megan says. Cynthia, Kenny's wife, explains that her husband wrote a short story that seemed to foreshow the murders. In the story a rogue robot undoes a bolt on a

---

364 Ibid.

bridge connecting planets, which collapses, and kills many people, which seems to allude to later seasons when the agency buys a supercomputer reminiscent of HAL9000 in Stanley Kubrick's *Space Odyssey 2001* (1968). "Without his gun would he be able to kill twenty people?" Kenny asks in what seems to be the Matthew Weiner's thinly veiled critique of American gun violence, which had grown epidemic in the twenty-first century. Later in the episode Pete discusses how the plane his father died on (in season two) is the same as ten planes Mohawk, which is a client of the agency, likewise has in its fleet. Roger responds, "there was seven plane crashes in Vietnam yesterday alone. It's Braniff's problem," he says; "let them eat their award winning work," which again underscores the crass care for cash more than human life, and the inherent banality of evil embedded in corporate America as depicted in *Mad Men*.[365] That point is underscored further late in season six when Pete and his brother, Bud (Rich Hutchman), decide not to search for their mother, who had either been pushed or fallen from a ship into the sea off the coast of Panama, because the operation would be too costly. "She loved the sea," Pete says as he rationalizes his decision not to pursue recovering his mother's remains, thus illuminating that he values money more than her.[366]

    In season five, Betty finds a drawing of a whale riddled with arrows made by her preadolescent son, Bobby. Later in the episode Don, Peggy, and Michael Ginsberg work on a campaign for Snoball Ice Cream in which storyboards depict a police officer, Sitting Bull, and a lady that looks a lot like environmentalist Rachel Carson

[365] Season 5 episode 4 "Signal 30" April 15, 2012.

[366] Season 6 episode 13 "In Care Of" June 23, 2013.

about to be smashed in the face with snowballs.[367] It is especially important to note the woman who appears to be Carson in the storyboard mentioned above because violence towards the environment is likewise prominently depicted in *Mad Men*. Violence towards the environment and also towards Native Americans, for example, is suggested when Jimmy Barrett body-shames Edith Schilling (Jan Hoag) of Utz Potato Chips by insensitively joking, "call Sitting Bull. We found the last buffalo."[368] America's buffalo population was, of course, wiped out as a result of railroads (which are symbolic of industrialization) and white "settlement" of large swaths of the Transcontinental West. In season two, the Draper family thinks nothing of leaving their trash scattered on the lawn of a roadside park after their picnic, which seems to be lifted from Jon Kenneth Galbraith's *The Affluent Society* (1958), and evokes "Iron Eyes Cody," the famous crying Indian (actually an Italian) in the "Keep America Beautiful" public service announcement (1970). In the same episode that the Draper's leave their trash behind, Duck Phillips mentions seeing a refrigerator in a pond while "birding" with a client.[369] Three episodes later Betty seems to gain existential satisfaction by shooting her neighbor's pigeons out of the sky.[370] In season five, Don wants to open the terrace door of his midtown Manhattan apartment during the Macy's Thanksgiving Day Parade. Megan, however, prevents him

---

[367] Season 5 episode 7 "At the Codfish Ball" April 29, 2012.

[368] Season 2 episode 3 "The Benefactor" August 10, 2008.

[369] Season 2 episode 7 "The Gold Violin" September 7, 2008.

[370] Season 1 episode 9 "Shoot" September 13, 2007.

from doing so because "the radio says there is a smog emergency," and "the air is toxic."[371] The wanton violence directed towards nature in the service of heavy industry is also alluded to in season six, as a GM executive tells Don that, "my dad used to take me down to Lake Erie when I was a kid. But now the water is bad," which might allude to the Cuyahoga River fire in 1969, or more literally to the actual rampant pollution of the Great Lakes while the Midwest was still an industrial juggernaut.[372]

Overt violence is as central a feature on *Mad Men* as is implied violence. In season three, for example, Don and Betty are called into a conference in which Sally's teacher, Suzanne Farrell, apprises the parents that their daughter has grown increasingly violent of late and had recently asked a lot of questions about the murder of civil rights activist Medgar Evers. Miss Farrell tells Sally's parents that the kid Sally fought is "a big girl" often tormented by students who "stick pencils in her sides because they think she can't feel it." Later in the episode Betty has a hallucination while in childbirth; she sees her mother having little success staunching blood from the gaping and gushing cavity in Medgar Evers' head as she warns, "you see what happens to people when they speak up?"[373] A season later Sally seems transfixed by a news story on television about James Reed, a Unitarian Minister clubbed to death by a mob of angry white men. Later in the episode she is caught touching herself in a sexual

[371] Season 5 episode 9 "Dark Shadows" May 13, 2012.

[372] Season 6 episode 11 "Favors" June 9, 2013.

[373] Season 3 episode 5 "The Fog" September 13, 2009.

manner by her friend's mother at a slumber party. When Sally denies that she was masturbating, her mother threatens, "Don't you dare lie to me or I'll cut your fingers off."[374] The following season concludes with Lane Pryce, a partner at the agency, hanging himself in his office after being caught by Don committing check fraud. The suicide hits Don especially hard, since his half-brother, Adam, had also committed suicide by hanging earlier in the series.[375] The episode concludes with Beth Dawes (Alexis Bledel), the woman Pete cheated on Trudy with, in hospital to receive electroshock therapy.[376]

    The banality of evil depicted in overt and implied violence on *Mad Men* is particularly underscored by America's war in Indochina. In the first episode of season six, for example, Peggy confronts a crisis in the form of the "Lend Me Your Ear" Super Bowl advertisement for Koss Speakers and Headphones due to a recent report of American soldiers sadistically amputating and wearing Vietcong ears as jewelry. A comedian on *The Johnny Carson Show* makes a crass joke about an Army General saying that the necklaces made of ears worn by American soldiers were "not regulation." The offending soldier responds by saying to the General, "I'm sorry, I couldn't hear you. Can you speak into my necklace?" This factually based incident seems to underscore the banality of evil in 1960s America as a result of the centrality of

    [374] Season 4 episode 5 "The Chrysanthemum and the Sword" August 22, 2010.

    [375] Season 1 episode 11 "Indian Summer" October 4, 2007.

    [376] Season 5 episode 12 "Commissions and Fees" June 3, 2012.

violence associated with the Vietnam War.377 Three episodes after the Koss incident, Martin Luther King, Jr. is assassinated, which sends a shockwave of violent anger reverberating across the nation, especially in the country's inner-city communities.378 "They didn't catch him," Abe says to Peggy of King's assassin, "but you know who it was." Here, Abe seems to allude to the entrenched white fascism and political violence, such as lynching, that has long existed in the nation's history and collective identity. Though the news of King's murder causes a short intermission during the Clio's advertising award show, it continues after a ten minute hiatus, which likewise seems to underscore the crass care-for-business more than human life.379 Two episodes later, Robert F. Kennedy, the frontrunner to win the nomination as the Democratic Party's presidential candidate in the 1968 general election, is murdered. Stan's cousin is also reportedly killed in action in Vietnam an episode later.380

Also in season six, Peggy mistakes Abe for a burglar and inadvertently stabs him in the chest. He fights for life in the back of a speeding ambulance as he breaks up with her. "You're a scared person who hides behind complacency," he wheezes. "I don't know why I thought you were braver; you're in advertising. Your

---

377 Season 6 episode 1 "The Doorway" April 7, 2013.

378 Season 6 episode 5 "The Flood" April 28, 2013.

379 Ibid.

380 Season 6 episode 6 "For Immediate Release" May 5, 2013.

activities are offensive to my every waking moment. I'm sorry. But you'll always be the enemy."[381]

The following episode opens at the 1968 Democratic National Convention in Chicago. "They can debate the war," Don explains to his young and somewhat naïve wife, Megan, "they just can't come out against it. They'll start debating thirty seconds after primetime."[382] She calls him cynical, but later realizes he was right. The fact that Cold War American conformity – in opposition to communism – was so pervasive in 1968 that it stifled rational political dissent and did not precluded anti-war politicians from openly opposing the war just six months after the Tet Offensive without risking their careers illuminates the fascistic lack of genuine political plurality in Cold War American society, which was a time in American history when the military and weapons industries became the preeminent political powerbrokers in the context of the United States' Sunbelt economic boom. Later in the episode, the Peace Plank is rejected by the Democratic National Committee, sparking outrage amongst the mostly liberal creatives at the agency that mirrored the anger on the streets of Chicago during the convention, which culminated in an incredibly violent "police riot." Megan, who is upset by what seemed to be clear and present evidence of fascism as it unfolded on her television screen in Manhattan, worriedly calls Don, who is in California on business. "They [the protesters] are throwing rocks," Don states as a defense for the actions of the marauding police officers, whose boss, Chicago Mayor Richard Daley, was accused of employing

[381] Season 6 episode 9 "The Better Half" May 26, 2013.

[382] Season 6 episode 10 "A Tale of Two Cities" June 2, 2013.

"Gestapo tactics" by Abraham Ribicoff, the Democratic Senator from Connecticut.[383]

Mad Men, as the show's depiction of the 1968 DNC helps to evince, also puts political violence at the center of the drama, especially season six, which is set in the extraordinarily tumultuous year of 1968. The massacre at Kent State in 1970, and numerous other riots, are likewise alluded to, as are the assassinations of Medgar Evers, President Kennedy, his younger brother, Robert Kennedy, and Martin Luther King, Jr. King and the Kennedy's murders, in particular, are treated by the show's creators as shared national traumas comparable to that collectively experienced by Americans on September 11, 2001. Betty and her maid, Carla, for example, cry together as they watch the early reports of John Kennedy's death in Dallas in November of 1963. Sally and Bobby also seem traumatized as they watch their mother and Carla, their primary caregivers, weep.

Roger's daughter, Margaret, however, is far more upset that her wedding will be ruined by the national mourning associated with John Kennedy's death than she is saddened by the national tragedy that, in hindsight, ultimately transformed the character of the nation. Some Americans, according to Mad Men's depiction, also exhibited callous disregard for the value of the president's life in the wake of the murder. "They'll never cancel" (Margaret's wedding), Pete grumbles to his wife, Trudy; "You know why? Because they're happy. You should have heard some of the things people (at the agency) said yesterday," such as "he made a lot of enemies." Later in the episode Peggy suffers a crisis of conscience

[383] Season 6 episode 9 "A Tale of Two Cities" June 2, 2013.

because the Aqua Net storyboards that were made for a television spot she crafted are eerily similar to the Zapruder film of Kennedy being killed in the motorcade in Dallas, which seems to be the show's creators tongue-in-cheek way of critiquing the crass care-for-profit-more-than-human-life philosophy that is so commonly exhibited by public relations-obsessed corporations.[384]

The Rachel Carson-looking woman, depicted in the Snoball Ice Cream storyboard mentioned above, who appears to be smashed in the face with a snowball is, in addition to alluding to violence towards the environment, also important because it speaks to the implied and overt violence towards women prominently featured on *Mad Men*. In addition to implied and overt violence chronicled above, *Mad Men* forces viewers to confront the horror of overt violence directed towards women and children in 1960s America, a time in which violent crime at home seemed to mirror America's growing violence abroad in places like Vietnam. In season five, for instance, Don defends Dow-Corning Chemical for making napalm. The mention of napalm and Don's defense of the weaponized defoliant might evoke in viewers' and readers' minds the famous Pulitzer Prize-winning image of Phan Thi Kim Phuc, the naked Vietnamese girl running up the street as her skin melts off her body as a result of napalm, which further underscores the centrality of violence, particularly violence towards females and children, which Americans seemed increasingly desensitized to, if not titillated by, in the 1960s.[385]

[384] Season 3 episode 10 "The Color Blue" October 18, 2009.

[385] Season 5 episode 7 "At the Codfish Ball" April 29, 2012.

In season one, Pete exchanges a chip-and-dip set given to Trudy and him as a wedding gift for a .22-calber rifle. Pete later takes the gun to the office and aims it at women as they pass by. He then proudly displays the weapon above his head as if it was a trophy he had won.[386] A season earlier, Pete watches a Belle Joli lipstick panel, comprised of secretaries, being conducted at the agency and jokingly asks, "At what point do we start running electricity through their chairs?"[387] This references what Freddy said moments earlier in the episode about Ethel Rosenberg, a mother of two young boys, who wore lipstick to her execution, and also foreshadows the increasingly violent 1960s, including the Vietnam War, especially violence towards women, which becomes a particularly central theme in the show in later seasons.[388]

The theme of female sexuality being powerful is broached at the end of season one and persists at the start of season two when Betty's car breaks down. She ultimately flexes her sexuality to pay only $3 for parts and labor after the mechanic says, "the part alone is $9." Betty deploys her sexuality to gain concessions, which empowers her and seems to slightly emasculate the mechanic. But there is also an underlying threat of sexual assault in the dynamic between the mechanic and Betty, who are out on a dark and secluded street in a rural section of the suburb.

The theme of violence, especially sexual assault, grows more central to the story as the series persists.[389] The specter of rape

---

[386] Season 1 episode 7 "Red in the Face" August 30, 2007.

[387] Season 1 episode 6 "Babylon" August 23, 2007.

[388] Season 1 episode 7 "Red in the Face" August 30, 2007.

[389] Season 2 episode 1 "For Those Who Think Young" July 27, 2008.

looms particularly large in the show. In season three, for example, Ada Louise Huxtable, a critic for *The New York Times*, writes a column in which she refers to the plan to demolish Pennsylvania Station in order to build Madison Square Garden as a "Rape on Thirty-Fourth Street."[390] In season one, Don says to his underlings after a meeting, "at some point seduction ends and force is being requested."[391] The third episode of season two begins with the shock-comic Jimmy Barrett body-shaming Ms. Schilling as "the Hindenburg," the Nazi zeppelin famous for a fiery disaster in which the radio announcer cried out, "oh the humanity!" Near the end of the episode, Jimmy's wife and manager, Bobbi, tries to extort $25,000 from Don and the agency because the company would violate Jimmy's contract if the agency terminated his sponsorship on the basis of his verbal assault on Mr. Schilling's obese wife, which, Bobbi asserts, should be considered a "compliment" and "honor." Don proceeds to sexually assault Bobbi outside the restroom at an upscale Manhattan restaurant, which causes her to quickly capitulate to his demands.[392] Six episodes later, Pete forces himself sexually on his neighbor's German nanny. She seems petrified and does not consent nor specifically reject his sexual advance.[393] In season three, Don drives from the suburbs to Manhattan early one morning as a soundbyte from Martin Luther King Jr's "I Have a Dream" speech is followed immediately by a

[390] Season 3 episode 2 "Love Among The Ruins" August 23, 2009.

[391] Season 1 episode 8 "Hobo Code" September 6, 2007.

[392] Season 2 episode 3 "The Benefactor" August 10, 2008.

[393] Season 3 episode 8 "The Souvenir" October 4, 2009.

story about the murder of an anonymous woman.[394] When Peggy informs her mother of her plans to move from Bay Ridge, Brooklyn to Manhattan in season three, her mother replies, "You'll get raped, you know that?"[395] A season later, a freelance artist named Joey Baird (Matt Long) draws a crude and cartoonish picture of Joan fellating Lane Pryce, which he then tapes up in the window of her office. "What do you do around here except for walk around like you're trying to be raped?" Joey snidely asks Joan as she confronts him after finding the suggestive drawing depicting her as a whore. Joey later lets slip to Peggy that Joan reminds him of his mother.[396]

In season five, Sally watches *Mystery Date*, a hokey television game show; Pauline (Pamela Dunlap), Henry Francis' mother, is on the phone in the background detailing the brutal Chicago nurse murders and is clearly titillated by the carnage she describes. Pauline later explains to Sally that her father kicked her when she was a child. "'That's for nothing, so look out,'" she paraphrased her obviously abusive father. "It was valuable advice," she concedes. Later in the episode, Sally reads in the newspaper tucked under her covers about the gruesome slaying of the nurses in Chicago. She later asks Pauline, "Why did he (the killer) do that?" Pauline replies, "Probably because he hates his mother… He probably watched them from afar, in their short uniforms, stirring his desire." Sally asks, "Why didn't they run away?" Ms. Frances retorts, "Because they were scared. They probably thought, 'he can't rape nine of us.' They didn't know it was going to be worse

---

[394] Season 3 episode 9 "Wee Small Hours" October 11, 2009.

[395] Season 3 episode 4 "The Arrangements" September 6, 2009.

[396] Season 4 Episode 8 "The Summer Man" September 12, 2008.

than that." Sally frets, "How am I going to sleep?" Ms. Frances ultimately gives the terrified child a barbiturate (which Marilyn Monroe overdosed on), which seems to speak to the increased medication of children in the waning decades of the twentieth century.[397]

The following episode, Butler Footwear visits the agency. Michael Ginsberg tells the executives from Butler about a discarded ad campaign the creatives at the agency decided not to present because it was "too dark." The Butler executives cajole him into explaining the discarded idea. "We were going to go with Cinderella," Michael says as he elaborates that she was stalked outside a dark and forbidding castle. "She is wounded prey," he explains, "but she wants to be caught." Butler ultimately picks the darker campaign, thereby evoking the fetish for sensationalized violence, especially towards women, in the 1960s.[398]

An episode later, Sally's father, Don, is very ill and has a recurring hallucination of a former tryst named Andrea Rhodes (Mädchen Amick) who he and his wife Megan had run into in a midtown elevator earlier in the episode. "You're a sick, sick man," Andrea tells Don in the midst of a nightmare. He ultimately imagines murdering her and stuffing her corpse under Megan and his California king-size bed. The episode acerbically concludes with a popular song performed by the Crystals titled, "He Hit Me (And

[397] Season 5 episode 4 "Mystery Date" April 8, 2012.

[398] Ibid.

It Felt Like a Kiss)," which was produced in 1962 by none other than serial woman abuser Phil Spector. The lyrics are as follows:

"He hit me
And it felt like a kiss.
He hit me
But it didn't hurt me.
He couldn't stand to hear me say
That I'd been with someone new,
And when I told him I had been untrue
He hit me
And it felt like a kiss.
He hit me
And I knew he loved me.

If he didn't care for me
I could have never made him mad
But he hit me,
And I was glad.
He hit me
And it felt like a kiss."[399]

    In season six, Sally's friend, Sandy (whose mother had recently died of cancer), spends the night at the Francis Mansion. Young Bobby has a crush on Sandy, who is a very talented violinist. He seems especially glad that she plans to spend the night. Henry later compliments Sandy's playing to his wife, Betty,

---

[399] Gerry Goffin, Carole King, and Phil Spector, "He Hit Me (And It Felt Like a Kiss)" 1962, New York City, Phillies Records.

as he climbs into bed. "Why don't you go in there and rape her,'" Betty says, "I'll hold her arms down," which seems to mortify Henry.[400] Also in season six, Glen Bishop shows up at Sally's new boarding school with booze, marijuana, and an army jacket heavily adorned with protest pins. He ends up fighting Rolo (Liam Aiken), the boy who gave him a ride, after Rolo forces himself on Sally, which, likewise, underscores the centrality of violence towards women prominently depicted on the show.[401]

Domestic violence, as the lyrics of the Crystals hit song above alludes to, is also prominently depicted on the show. Domestic violence, for the purposes of this chapter, includes battered wives and neglected children. In the second episode of the series, Sally runs into the kitchen with a plastic dry-cleaning bag over her head. "The clothes that were in that bag better not be on the floor of that closet," Betty scolds her daughter, thereby indicating that Betty is far more concerned about her material goods than with the health, wellbeing, and safety of her young child.[402] In the following episode, an attendee (a World War II veteran) at Betty's party smacks Francine's young son, Ernie, who is dressed like a cowboy, in his face. Ernie's father, Carlton (Kristoffer Polaha), chastises his son -- who was running in the house -- rather than confronting the man that slapped his child.[403]

[400] Season 6 episode 1 "The Doorway" April 7, 2013.

[401] Season 6 episode 11 "The Quality of Mercy" June 16, 2013.

[402] Season 1 episode 2 "Ladies Room" July 19, 2007.

[403] Season 1 episode 3 "Marriage of Figaro" August 2, 2007.

Early in season two, Don smashes Bobby's toy robot, not because he is particularly angry with his son, but rather because he is frustrated with his wife's persistent demands that he be more of a disciplinarian. Don later explains to Betty that his father beat him relentlessly when he was a child and all it did was inspire Don to fantasize about murdering his father.[404] Six episodes later, senile Gene Hofstadt gropes his daughter, Betty, who he confuses for his recently deceased wife. Moments later, Gene thinks Betty is a small child and promises to take her for ice cream. The implication is that Gene may have sexually assaulted his daughter.[405] The following season Sally, who has just entered puberty, is found riding between the cars of a commuter train into Manhattan because she does not have enough money for the fare. "You're lucky I found her... the types on those trains," Vivian Winters (Sarah Benoit), the woman who finds Sally on the train ominously says to Don, as if to indicate that she could have been raped.[406] In season six, the viewer learns that Don was molested by a prostitute when he was a boy and beaten savagely by his stepmother with a wooden spoon as a result.[407] In season four, Lane Pryce is waylaid by his father, which seems to send Lane into a state of arrested development, indicating that when he was a child he had likely been beaten often and severely by his father.[408]

[404] Season 2 episode 4 "Three Sundays" August 17, 2008.

[405] Season 2 episode 10 "The Inheritance" October 5, 2008.

[406] Season 4 episode 9 "The Beautiful Girls" September 19, 2010.

[407] Season 6 episode 8 "The Crash" May 19, 2013.

[408] Season 4 episode 10 "Hands and Knees" September 26, 2010.

Domestic violence directed towards wives is nearly as prominently depicted in *Mad Men* as is violence towards children. In season one, for example, Pete white knuckles his rifle as he glares at Trudy as if fanaticizing about killing her as she scolds him for exchanging a chip-and-dip given to the couple as a wedding present in exchange for the gun.[409] Four episodes later Betty's friend, Francine, says that her husband would "break [her] arm" if she ever let a salesman in the house without him being home.[410] The following season, Don and Betty have a violent shoving match.[411] Also in season three, Roger and his twenty-year old wife feud in their luxury Manhattan apartment. "Go away," Jane demands. Roger then viciously seethes, "Or what, you'll kill yourself?" which speaks to what an abusive husband he is.[412] Two seasons later, Don tackles Megan during a bitter fight that begins with her not liking sherbet at a Howard Johnson in upstate New York; Don abandons her at the restaurant (this after an entire episode seemingly devoted to forcing viewers to seriously contemplate violence towards women).[413] In season seven, Roger tackles his adult daughter, Margaret, as he attempts to take her away from a commune in upstate New York.[414] In season six, a

---

[409] Season 1 episode 7 "Red in the Face" August 30, 2007.

[410] Season 1 episode 11 "Indian Summer" October 4, 2007.

[411] Season 2 episode 4 "Three Sundays" August 17, 2008.

[412] Season 3 episode 12 "The Grown Ups" November 1, 2009.

[413] Season 5 episode 6 "Far Away Places" April 22, 2012.

[414] Season 7 episode 4 "The Monolith" May 4, 2014.

woman who lives down the street from Pete and Trudy's suburban home, who he had earlier enjoyed a tryst with at his Manhattan apartment, arrives at their doorstep in the middle of the night. Her face is bruised and bloody as a result of being beaten by her jealous and enraged husband. Pete is, however, far less consumed with feelings of guilt regarding his infidelity to his wife or sympathy for his battered mistress than he is with fear of being exposed as a philanderer. He is, instead, angrily accusatory of the battered wife. "What did you tell him (her husband)?" Pete demands a moment after Trudy leaves the room to get the abused woman ice to quell the swelling of her swollen face. Trudy, later in the episode, instinctively knows something happened between her husband and the woman from down the street, especially since the husband yells, "She's your problem now, Campbell!"[415] The backdrop of the episode is the January 1968 Tet Offensive, which was an especially bloody assault by the North Vietnamese Army, that briefly occupied the American Embassy in Saigon. Tet was a watershed moment in turning public opinion against the war because it exposed the fact that President Johnson, the Pentagon, and network news had long been lying to the American public by perpetuating the profound untruth that the Vietcong and National Liberation Front were losing the war due to a gross imbalance in "body count" figures. The term "body count" likewise speaks to a dehumanization and desensitization to violence and the banality of evil in Cold War American society. New Orleans district attorney, Jim Garrison, is also anecdotally a guest on *The Johnny Carson Show*, which alludes to John and Robert Kennedy's murder, and the country's growing distrust of traditional institutions such as its

---

[415] Season 6 episode 3 "The Collaborators" April 14, 2013.

government, which *Mad Men* often depicts as serving the interests of corporations such as Lucky Strike, GM and Dow to the detriment of average Americans (consumers).[416]

All of the real and stylized, implied and overt violence depicted on *Mad Men* could possibly be chocked up as sensationalism concocted for consumption by the creators of the show to sell ad space to transnational corporations, such as GM, Dow, Jaguar, Coca-Cola, and dozens of other products overtly and stealthily marketed throughout seven seasons of the series. But the show's depiction of violence, both real and stylized, is more than mere sensationalism designed to titillate consumers, as so much of the graphic content, including the references to degradation of the environment, depicted in seven seasons of *Mad Men* was not merely dreamt up in some writers' room in the Hollywood Hills. The disturbing fact of American GIs wearing the ears of slain enemies; network news gushing to Americans about astronomical body counts as viewers dined on TV dinners; millions of lives lost in the Vietnam War; the murder of the Kennedy brothers, Evers, and King; the brutally and fascistic repression of non-violent protesters at the 1968 Democratic National Convention; the slaying of college students at Kent State and Jackson State; the brutal murders of nurses in Chicago (the site of the 1968 DNC convention and murder of Fred Hampton); followed just weeks later by the massacre at the University of Texas; and the violent reprisals by opponents of totalitarianism in Prague, Paris, and Mexico City; and then the horrific Manson Family murders, are all part of the actual historical record and are glaring evidence of an increased normalization and desensitization to war, graphic violence (both

[416] Ibid.

implied and overt), and a distinct banality of evil deeply embedded in American consumer/militaristic society in the decades after World War II. The fact that many avid fans of *Mad Men* likely overlooked the numerous allusions to the implied and overt violence chronicled in the pages above likewise speaks to the pervasive desensitization to violence in twenty-first century America, which is as defined by militarism, warfare, violence, racism and sexism as was 1960s America.

Chapter Five

"The New Man, Nationalism, Militarism, and the Menacing Fetish for Youth"

In both Interwar and Postwar Europe and the United States mass media often conspicuously, and sometimes unwittingly, glorified concepts such as the New Man, which couches military values as it compels young people to risk their lives to fight for the glory of the nation (and the elder statesmen who run it). Adolf Hitler and Benito Mussolini in particular fetishized the New Man, which was characteristically depicted to be relentless, physically strong, morally hard, and youthfully exuberant about the nation.[417] In addition to the glorification of the New Man motif serving as a commercial for warfare, youth was subsequently fetishized as a means of selling products and ideology. These themes are also

---

[417] For more on the celebration of the New Man in the context of fascist regimes in interwar Europe see Thomas J. Saunders, "A 'New Man:' Fascism, Cinema and Image Creation," *International Journal of Politics, Culture, and Society* Vol. 12, No. 2 (Winter, 1998), pp. 227-246; see also David D. Roberts, "Myth, Style, Substance and the Totalitarian Dynamic in Fascist Italy," *Contemporary European History* Vol. 16, No. 1 (Feb., 2007), pp. 1-36.

prominent in *Mad Men's* depiction of American society during the 1960s.

The commodified New Man championed by fascists in the Interwar Era was also, like Bert Cooper, an unabashed Social Darwinist contemptuous of delicate and sentimental souls. In season one, for instance, Cooper gives Don Draper a $2,500 bonus, in part due to his underling seemingly exuding the same libertarian streak and utter lack of sentimentality that exists in him.[418] Earlier in the season, Cooper chides Roger for smoking cigarettes, which he sees as a sign of turpitude and weakness. "[Neville] Chamberlain would have given Hitler his mother," Cooper exclaims while deriding the disgraced English Prime Minister's addiction to tobacco at the 1938 Munich Conference held between France, Germany, and Great Brittan in which Chamberlain promised to not intervene in the event that the Nazis occupied the Sudetenland, which ostensibly led to World War II. Later in the episode, effete Pete Campbell exchanges a serving dish, given to his wife and himself as a wedding present, for a shotgun. He later tells Peggy of his masculine fantasy of being a rugged hunter who kills his own food.[419]

Postwar American manufacturers of products such a Gillette's Right Guard deodorant and Jaguar automobiles (an English company) and the advertising agencies in league with them as depicted in *Mad Men* aimed to convince consumers that products such as Pete's trusty shotgun could empower and transform the

[418] Season 1 episode 13 "The Wheel" October 18, 2007.

[419] Season 1 episode 7 "Red in the Face" August 30, 2007.

mundane man into the tough and rugged "New Man" by buying products.[420] Don Draper is, as much as the ads designed to seduce men into being better versions of their former selves by consuming products, an example of the fascistic' fetish with the New Man. The notion of Don being a self-made New Man is a prominent theme throughout the series. "I want to work," Don says to Cooper in season three, "I want to build something of my own," he states, thereby evoking the New Man ethos that is, like Don's hailing of Madison Square Garden in season three as proof of Manhattan being a "shiny city on a hill," evidence of the Protestant Work Ethic that helps to correlate interwar German history with postwar American history.[421]

Don is likewise, at least on the surface, synonymous with modernists' fetish for progress. In season one, for example, Dick Whitman (Don Draper) says to his half-brother, Adam, shortly before the latter's suicide, "there's only one direction in life – forward."[422] Don reiterates the phrase the following season to Peggy after she gives birth to Pete's son. Also in season two, in an attempt to win American Airlines' business shortly after one of the company's jets crashes into Jamaica Bay, Don tells executives, "America has no history; only horizons," which evokes John F. Kennedy's inaugural address in 1961. The line in particular seems to speak to the Nazis' desire to transcend the humiliation and

[420] Season 2 episode 11 "The Jet Set" October 12, 2008.

[421] Season 3 episode 13 "Shut the Door. Have a Seat" November 8, 2009.

[422] Season 1 episode 5 "5G" August 16, 2007.

economic calamity associated with World War I.[423] In the finale of season four, Megan Draper tells Don, her future husband, that she knows who he truly is at the core of his being – a man always trying to "improve" himself.[424]

Though the duplicitous New Man that was so popular amongst fascist in the Interwar Era represented the transcendence of past traumas and new horizons, the concept also nostalgically glorifies the past as a golden bygone era. Italian fascists, for example, hailed the soldiers of ancient Rome as models to be emulated, much like Americans today view World War II as America's greatest generation. French fascists praised the brutal barons of the Middle Ages and the original conquerors of Europe, the Franks. Don, as also alluded to in Pete's fantasy of being a rugged hunter, embodies American nostalgia for a more perceived-masculine and maverick past lost to the annals of history – the image of which is ardently consumed in American westerns, cop dramas, and populist American politics, which Ronald Reagan, in particular, shrewdly capitalized on as governor of California and later as President of the United States. The New Man was, however, also quite duplicitous as the concept simultaneously represents tradition and modernity. In season two, Don's voice is heard quoting an excerpt from Frank O'Hara's *Meditations in Times of Crisis*: "I am waiting for the catastrophe of my personality to seem beautiful again and interesting and modern."[425] But Don's

[423] Season 2 episode 4 "Three Sundays" April 17, 2008.

[424] Season 4 episode 13 "Tomorrow and" October 17, 2010.

[425] Season 2 episode 1 "For Those Who Think Young" July 27, 2008.

character also expresses a duplicitous nostalgic yearning for the past concurrent to a complete ease with the trappings of modernity. "I'm new and different," Don admits to his new lover, Suzanne Farrell, in season three, "or maybe I'm exactly the same."[426]

Don, in short, is vintage, which is quintessentially modern. And he alludes to this particular point in season four when he tells executives at Life Cereal that, "nostalgia feels good, but is a little bit painful." Two episodes later he confides in his diary, "we're flawed because we want so much more. We're ruined because we get these things and wish for what we had," thereby underscoring the inherent psychosis associated with being abstracted into two identities in tension, such as the traditional (agrarian and populist) and modern (urban and industrialist), a duality that can be detected in both the New Man championed by fascists, as well as Don, and even in the very nature of consumerism, which is a system in which people are defined more by the products they purchase and vacations they take than by the daily labor they perform. This tension between the authoritarian and militarist New Man, in tandem with the urge for freedom and mobility, is also very much embedded in American identity.

Mad Men tends to depict the 1960s American experience as increasingly consumerist, conformist, militaristic, violent and voyeuristic. Though the fascist New Man was both a mythological and duplicitous commoditization used to lure young people into consuming products concomitant to risking their lives for the nation, it was most always designed to celebrate and inculcate a sense of seemingly natural (Darwinist) nationalistic military values

[426] Season 3 episode 9 "Wee Small Hours" October 11, 2009.

in the hearts and minds of young men. *Mad Men* thus rightly draws many correlations between postwar American consumer culture and the military industrial complex, often depicting them as two sides of the same coin.

At the forefront of naturalizing military values in postwar American consumer society was the shilling of patriotism in the context of a Cold War that coerced conformity amongst consumers. In season one, Lee Garner, Sr. likens cigarettes to America. "It's from the Indians," he explains to Don and Roger as the agency struggles to market the brand in the wake of the surgeon general's regulation of the tobacco industry's ability to market cigarettes as healthy. In season three, the American Revolution is explicitly alluded to as Sterling & Cooper wage a July Fourth-weekend coup to win its independence from Putnam, Powell, and Lowe – a British firm.[427] One of Don's many one-night stands hums the *Star Spangled Banner* as she fellates him the following season.[428] "This is America," femme fatale Bobbi Barrett, another of Don's many trysts, says in season two, "pick a job and become the person who does it," which speaks to conservative discourse in postwar American society, most notably the "pull yourself up by the bootstraps" reductionism of poverty to an individual's own moral or intellectual failure, rather than a consequence of structural inequity rooted in the nature of the American economic and political system.[429]

---

[427] Season 3 episode 6 "Guy Walks Into an Advertising Agency" September 20, 2009.

[428] Season 4 episode 6 "Waldorf Stories" August 29, 2010.

[429] Season 2 episode 5 "The New Girl" August 24, 2008.

In the early 1940s, President Franklin Roosevelt and Henry Wallace envisioned social mobility for all Americans without having to join the military. In 1944, Roosevelt proposed passing a second bill of rights that would make the American Dream far more attainable for far more Americans. Roosevelt's argument was that the political rights guaranteed by the Constitution and the original Bill of Rights had proved inadequate to assure each American true equality in the pursuit of happiness in the United States. His solution to stem the tide of pervasive poverty and world wars was an "economic bill of rights" to guarantee each and every American a job, regular access to food, clothing and leisure, good housing, adequate medical care, social security, and education. Roosevelt, in short, imagined a nation free from fear. He envisioned in the United Nations an entity that could help foster an economic bill of rights for all the world's citizens, which he believed would make future world wars unthinkable. But by the time Roosevelt's bill made its way through the Republican-majority Congress, the president had died and his dream of a second bill of rights for all Americans had been chiseled by a Republican-majority congress into the G.I. Bill of Rights, which increasingly incentivized joining the military as a means of poor Americans finding mobility into the middle class, which helped transform the United States into the most militarist nation on the planet in the decades after World War II. The G.I. Bill, along with the related Second Red Scare, helped stoke the fetish for American militarized nationalism in a manner not seen in U.S. history since the Civil War. As a result of the failure to pass a second bill of rights in lieu of the G.I. Bill one of the few ways poverty-stricken Americans in the decades after World War II were able to "pull themselves up by the bootstraps" was by donning combat boots and joining the ever-growing United States military.

The conformist hyper-nationalism and militarism of postwar America evokes the nationalism and militarism of Third Reich Germany in the years preceding World War II. In the 1930s, a German was said to become a Nazi when a Hitler Youth from a rich family and a Hitler Youth from a poor family became brothers in arms; no redistribution of wealth had to happen to palliate class conflict thanks to the nationalistic fraternity fostered by the military. In war it did not matter if the soldier next to another came from a poor or a wealthy background as long as he fought bravely for the glory of the nation. Much like European fascists, Hollywood producers during World War II and in the decades after, including very many Jewish Americans during the Cold War purges of the McCarthy Era, increasingly downplayed class differences in postwar American society as largely subjective and unimportant in a place like the United States, where joining the ever-growing military provided wide and newly paved avenues out of the lower class for both black northerners and white southerners willing to fight and die for the nation.

The United States subsequently went from being isolationist in the Interwar Era to an unabashed warrior culture and preeminent global empire by mid-century. The specter of communism as a widely perceived evil and threat to America's neoliberal values in the decades after World War II, which supposedly demanded strangling in its cradle, concomitant to the flowering of new military towns all across the Deep South and Transcontinental West, helped absorb millions of poor people --

both black and white – who were desperate for class mobility, into the Armed Forces in the decades after World War II, which helped perpetuate Americans' fervent sense of patriotism. The absorption of millions of poor Americans into the military also stoked a brand of nationalism that seemed to increasingly diminish white Americans' ethnic markers, which was subsequent to a seemingly diminished sense of empathy for and affinity towards poor peoples of the world, particularly in places such as Russia, Cuba, Vietnam, Iraq and Afghanistan. The postwar American military industrial complex and consumerism, in short, acted as a kind of counter-revolutionary institution that (much like the American prison industry today) perpetuated the racial, political, and economic status quo (wealthy white men predominately in charge of the economic and political system), which is ultimately rooted in the nation's founding as a slave state.

The postwar glorification of war and gore in Hollywood movies and network television, like westerns (which are metaphors for nineteenth century industrialization and capitalism), was enjoyed by millions of American kids who increasingly put aside toy trains and cars in order to enjoy the existential pleasure and imagined empowerment experienced by donning military garb and firing plastic weapons that go ratt-a-tatt-tat. Mass media, in short, played an especially prominent role in the glorification of violence and militarism in Cold War America. The popularization of war in the decades after World War II is alluded to in season one of *Mad Men* when Lieutenant Don Draper (Troy Ruptash) says to Dick Whitman, "what misconception traveled down the road to convince you to be here (the Korean War), a movie?"[430] In season

---

[430] Season 1 episode 12 "Nixon vs. Kennedy" October 18, 2007.

one, Francine's son, Ernie, wears a military helmet and a cowboy holster with two pistols on his hips.[431] In season six, Roger's grandson, Ellery, dressed in a blue plaid shirt and red overalls like Danny in Stanley Kubrick's *The Shining* (1980), storms through the agency offices firing a toy machinegun. Roger's secretary, Caroline (Beth Hall), pretends to be shot dead.[432] A season later Betty and Don's son, Bobby, runs through the Francis mansion firing a toy machinegun.[433] These incidents, all of which are set during America's war in Indochina, seem to critique the sinister fetish for gun violence that has grown epidemic in the United States since the Cold War.

In *Mad Men,* gunplay and war is by no means trivial, which makes it incredibly anomalistic in the context of the late-twentieth and early twenty-first century American infotainment that especially perpetuates hero worship of America's warrior class. War in *Mad Men* is mostly depicted as a terrible menace that leaves men terribly traumatized and, in some cases, caught in a state of arrested development, which adds greater poignancy to the little boys depicted in the show dressed in military garb and firing toy assault rifles.

The war vets in *Mad Men* are especially depicted to be deeply traumatized. In season one, for example, Roger seems terribly spooked by the memory of his father telling him of the

---

[431] Season 1 episode 2 "Ladies' Room" July 26, 2007.

[432] Season 7 episode 4 "The Monolith" May 4, 2014.

[433] Season 7 episode 10 "The Forecast" April 19, 2015.

times he killed Germans with a bayonet in World War I. Roger later has to be prodded by patriotic Betty to reminisce about World War II.[434] In season two, viewers learn that Freddy's alcoholism is rooted in the trauma he experienced killing several Germans in World War II.[435] Two seasons later viewers learn that Roger is also deeply traumatized by his wartime memories of the South Pacific. He is, for example, terribly crass during a meeting with representatives of Honda Motorcycles, a Japanese company. "They are not the same people," Pete pleads with Roger after the calamity of a meeting is crashed by the traumatized war vet. "How can they not be the same?" Roger seethes, "I am!" He later asks Joan Holloway, "Since when is forgiveness a better quality than loyalty?" Joan attempts to sooth his jangled nerves by assuring him, "You fought to make the world a safer place, you won, and it is." He glares accusatorily at her as he asks, "You really believe that?" Her reply speaks volumes about the centrality of the American military during the Cold War and pervasiveness of military conflict in American society in the decades after World War II; "I have to?" she says flatly, as if to indicate, 'what choice do I have?'[436] Two episodes later, Duck Phillips' wartime trauma is broached when he finds Peggy, his young lover, drunk late at night in the office with Don (his former rival at Sterling & Cooper). "I killed seventeen men in Okinawa! You still think you're better than me?" Duck

[434] Season 1 episode 7 "Red in the Face" August 30, 2007.

[435] Season 2 episode 9 "Six-Month Leave" September 28 2008.

[436] Season 4 episode 5 "The Chrysanthemum and the Sword" August 22, 2010.

drunkenly slurs as he struggles to pin Don, who is even drunker, to the floor.[437]

Close to the end of the series a drunken World War II vet in attendance at a Veterans of Foreign Wars fundraiser struggles to tell the story of a harrowing and soul crushing experience he endured as a young man fighting in the Hürtgen Forest in Germany, which left him deeply traumatized. The scene provides the clearest example of an entire generation of men self-medicating their posttraumatic stress disorder (PTSD) with booze; the depiction of which is starkly contrasted to Ted Brokaw's gushing glorification of the "greatest generation."[438] In season five, World War II veteran Roger Sterling says, "bombs away," before dumping a glass of vodka into his mouth.[439] "Over here," the traumatized vets at the VFW fundraiser belt out, but change the lyrics from "Over There," as they tell guttural war stories, to "Over here! Over Here! Get that kid with the booze over here, because the Yanks are coming, the Yanks are coming…" In the proceeding scene, Pete and his brother discuss that they are how they are (self-interested and inclined to philandering) because that is how their father was, which, in light of the trauma their father's generation suffered, as depicted in *Mad Men*, speaks volumes about the mangled state of American masculinity in the decades after World War II. [440]

[437] Season 4 episode 7 "The Suitcase" September 5, 2010.

[438] Tom Brokaw, *The Greatest Generation* (New York, Random House, 1998).

[439] Season 5 episode 3 "Tea Leaves" April 1, 2012.

[440] Season 7 episode 13 "The Milk and Honey Route" May 10, 2015.

Mad Men thus depicts the trauma experienced by Americans sent to fight in the Korean War and America's war in Vietnam to be as soul shattering as it was in World War II. In the premier episode of season four, Don, for instance, is interviewed by a Korean War vet who lost his leg in combat.[441] In the next-to-last episode of the show, Don heads west to escape the corporatist conformity at McCann-Erickson, the agency that acquired his company. Don's Cadillac blows a rod and breaks down somewhere west of Wisconsin, and he is stranded in a small rural town while waiting for his car to be repaired. He is later cajoled by a World War II veteran, who owns the motel Don is staying in while his car is in the shop, into attending a fundraiser with some members of the local branch of the VFW. One of the drunken World War II vets at the gathering reminisces that he did not "break any of the real commandments until" he "was in Europe." The motel owner comforts his buddy by saying, "You do what you have to do to come home." For only the second time in the entire series the viewer gets a profound sense of the trauma Dick Whitman experienced in the Korean War and why he was so desperate to assume Don Draper's identity in order to get back home as soon as possible, even if it meant committing identity theft followed by a lifetime of fraud.[442] Don's trauma is also alluded to in season four when he confides in his diary, "I hope it [Vietnam] is not another Korea." [443] In season six, he flatly declares to his neighbor, Dr.

---

[441] Season 4 episode 1 "Public Relations" July 25, 2010.

[442] Season 7 episode 13 "The Milk and Honey Route" May 10, 2013.

[443] Season 4 episode 8 "The Summer Man" September 12, 2010. See Also Season 7 episode 14 "Person to Person" May 17, 2015.

Arnold Rosen, that the "war (in Vietnam) is wrong," which is evidence that Don is beginning to shed his duplicitous identity as the authoritarian New Man, which culminates in the final season of the series as he meditates and envisions Coca-Cola's utopian and globalist classic, "I'd Like to Teach The World to Sing" television commercial.[444] Don's character arc, in short, by the series finale seems to be more aligned with Abe Drexler's (critical theorist) who says to Peggy in season six, "This unjust war is finally having an effect on commerce," than he is like neoliberal Bert Cooper, who adores Ayn Rand.[445]

Ironically, the New Man motif that young Dick Whitman is alluded to having been seduced into becoming as a result of movies by Donald Draper early in the series while both were in Korea was affected by the terror of warfare. This is likewise personified by Private First-Class Dinkins in the premiere episode of season six. Don chats with Dinkins, a drunken Marine on rest and relaxation duty in Hawaii. Dinkins is meant to personify the fact that many of the American boys sent to Vietnam in the 1960s and 1970s were coming home as emotionally and psychologically (if not also physically) scarred as the men in World War II and the Korean War. Dinkins, an extremely inebriated Marine, explains to Don that an M2 fifty-caliber machinegun could decimate a water buffalo to the point that he could "paint" the entire hotel bar "red" with blood, which seems to allude to a scene in Kubrick's *The Shining*. Dinkins then laments that Hawaiians make him uneasy because

[444] Season 7 episode 14 "Person to Person" May 17, 2015.

[445] Season 6 episode 1 "The Doorway" April 7, 2013.

"they look just like the enemy (the Vietcong)."[446] Nine episodes later, Don smokes hashish for the first time at a party in the Hollywood Hills, which causes him to hallucinate and he nearly drowns in the swimming pool. While unconscious Don imagines seeing Dinkins, which seems to indicate that the newlywed Marine has died.[447] The previous season, Joan's husband, Greg Harris, also defends his decision to volunteer to go back to Vietnam by likening the Vietcong to the Japanese during World War II. "I'm glad the army makes you feel like a man," Joan seethes, "because I'm sick of trying to do it." Her ire underscores *Mad Men's* critique of the New Man as a glorified warrior supposedly protecting Americans' freedoms. "The army makes me feel like a good man," Greg says defensively. "You're not a good man," Joan says, "you never were, even before we were married and you know what I'm talking about (she references the time he raped her)." The fact that Greg is a rapist could also allude to the My Lai Massacre in 1968, or countless other atrocities to have happened during warfare throughout human history.[448]

The imagery in *Mad Men* of little boys dressed as soldiers and firing toy assault rifles ads greater depth to the fact that so many of the vets – Freddy Rumsen, Duck Phillips, Don Draper, and Roger Sterling in particular -- are depicted as seeming to suffer from arrested development. The notion that American men are

[446] Season 6 episode 1 "The Doorway" April 7, 2013.

[447] Season 6 episode 10 "A Tale of Two Cities" June 2, 2013.

[448] Season 5 episode 4 "Mystery Date" April 8, 2012. Greg rapes Joan season 2 episode 12 "The Mountain King" October 19, 2008.

little boys is a recurring theme throughout the series. In season two, for example, Betty says that she does not "need a book to tell" her "what little boys do," as she casts a long and somewhat accusatory gaze at Don as he lights a cigarette across the dining room table from her.[449] In season four, Joan tells some of the creatives in the office to "call the complaint line" in regards to a faulty vending machine and to "have an adult solve the problem."[450] In season five, Lane Pryce confides to Pete that "Roger Sterling is a child."[451] The sentiment is seconded by Megan's mother who says to Roger that "inside you is a little boy," as they flirt at the American Cancer Society Codfish Ball in season five.[452] The notion of Roger suffering from arrested development is later confirmed by his daughter, Margaret, as she scolds her father for taking her young son (who plays with toy guns) to see *The Planet of the Apes*, which gives the child nightmares.[453] Roger's mental health therapist confirms he suffers from arrested development in season six.[454]

Despite the obvious long-term physical, emotional, mental, and spiritual harm experienced by countless veterans during World War I, European fascists, prior to World War II, often championed military values such as courage, unquestioning obedience to

[449] Season 2 episode 2 "Flight 1" August 3, 2008.

[450] Season 4 episode 8 "The Summer Man" September 12, 2010.

[451] Season 4 episode 6 "Waldorf Stories" August 29, 2010.

[452] Season 5 episode 7 "At the Codfish Ball" April 29, 2012.

[453] Season 6 episode 9 "The Better Half" May 26, 2013.

[454] Season 6 episode 10 "A Tale of Two Cities" June 2, 2013.

authority, discipline, and physical strength – cultural traits likewise cherished in America's postwar military industrial complex. Movies, as alluded to by the real Don Draper in season two, perpetuated the notion that war was seductive and regenerative, especially World War II. The United States emerged from World War II as the premier imperial superpower, but the nation's newfound power is depicted in *Mad Men* as a kind of Faustian Bargain that has made the proverbial head that wears the crown especially heavy. "Three months after (Franklin) Roosevelt died," Mona Sterling's date to Margaret's wedding in season three says, "we bombed Hiroshima. That's how you get over these things," in reference to the national trauma suffered as a result of the assassination of John F. Kennedy.[455]

The notion of the genocidal violence associated with atomic weapons being a regenerative method of getting over trauma broached in the paragraph above smacks of Hitler's assertion that the Nazi's were "barbarians, and proud of it!"[456] The fuehrer and Benito Mussolini both ardently glorified violence as healthy and regenerative antidotes to effeminate decadence. Richard Slotkin, who studies nineteenth century American frontier violence and teaches English at Matthew Weiner's alma mater, Wesleyan, finds genocide and the notion that violence was regenerative to be as central an ethos to American history as it was to German history.[457]

[455] Season 3 episode 12 "The Grown Ups" November 1, 2009.

[456] John Weiss, *Ideology of Death Why the Holocaust Happened in Germany*, (Chicago, Ivan R. Dee, 1996) p. 111.

[457] See Richard Slotkin, *Regeneration Through Violence: The Mythology of the American Frontier, 1600 – 1860.* (Middletown, CT., Wesleyan University Press,

The notion of violence being restorative to a nation and a subsequent catalyst for turning boys into men also played a role in convincing young Italian, German, and American men to risk their lives for the nation.

The theme of death, destruction, and war being regenerative is further alluded to in season five as a Jaguar executive tells Lane Pryce that he was stationed in North Africa for three years, and they were the "best years" of his life and how he "associates to his youth." Lane explains that he was a supply assistant during the war. "Everybody did their part," the Jaguar executive fondly recalls, "that was Brittan at their best."[458] The theme of war being regenerative and as *the* quintessential institution that makes men of boys is explored more deeply in episode three when a somewhat peevish young copywriter laments that his father hopes he "gets drafted" (to fight in Vietnam), presumably to make a man of him.[459] In season seven, Glen Bishop's father is thrilled the younger flunked out of college because his draft status became 1-A. "You've obviously grown into a fine young man," patriotic Betty, who is obsessed and terrified by ageing, says as she encourages Glen to risk his life for the glory of the nation.[460] In season three, Bobby discovers his grandpa Gene's victory medal from France and a

1973.) Mad Men creator Mathew Weiner studied English at Wesleyan, where Slotkin is a professor.

[458] Season 5 episode 4 "Signal 30" April 15, 2012.

[459] Season 3 episode 6 "Guy Walks Into an Advertising Agency" September 20, 2009.

[460] Season 7 episode 10 "The Forecast" April 19, 2015.

Prussian helmet his grandfather kept as a spoil of war. Grandpa Gene places the helmet, which has a bullet hole and dry blood in it, on his grandson's head. Bobby then pretends to fire an imaginary rifle and kill people as he wears the helmet. Don demands his son take the helmet off because "there was a person in it." Gene snaps back, "an enemy!" as if to indicate that an enemy is not also a person. "War is bad," Bobby says. Gene, who thinks he shot a Prussian in the head, corrects his grandson by saying that "living off the land" and fighting next to one's "brothers" is sure to make a man of him.[461] Later in the episode, Bert Cooper says, "kill or be killed, eat or be eaten; That's how I was raised," to a shipping magnate war profiteer, thereby alluding to the Social Darwinist rationale central to European and American imperialism (and fascism) and the glorification of the New Man warrior that is such a central component to nationalistic militarism.[462]

This glorification of the New Man and fetish for youth fueled Nazi militarism in the decades before World War II, but it also, as depicted in *Mad Men*, was a central characteristic of postwar American popular culture, especially in westerns, war movies, politics, and the co-opting of tropes associated with the counterculture by corporate America, which *Mad Men* elaborates well. In season two, there is just one fleeting instance in which old age is depicted positively as it is connoted as synonymous with wisdom by Anna Draper when she gives Don a Tarot Card reading. For the most part, however, youth is fetishized concomitant to old age being denigrated by the characters on *Mad Men*. Early in season

[461] Season 3 episode 4 "The Arrangements" September 6, 2009.

[462] Ibid.

one, for example, Roger's daughter, Margaret, scoffs that her father's white hair makes him "look old."[463] In season five, Roger, on a head full of LSD, imagines himself having black hair.[464] In season two, Joy, Don's twenty-year-old paramour in Palm Springs, tells him that her father Willy (Phillip Brenninkmeyer), who has a German accent and whose hair is as white as Roger's, "doesn't want people to think he's old."[465] In season three, two Roman men flirt with Betty (who speaks Italian). When Don arrives at the table the Italians call him "old and ugly" in their native language.[466] In season two, Joan is made the butt of a joke when her real age (older than thirty) is exposed on the bulletin board of the secretarial break room.[467]

Nobody on the show seems more offended by old age than nationalistic Betty Draper. In season one, she expresses disgust at how old Joan Crawford looks in a movie she and Don had seen. The episode is set on Mother's Day. Betty seems consumed with ageing and is troubled by the recent death of her mother.[468] The following season, Betty senses that Don cheated on her with Bobbi Barrett. "How could you?" Betty asks, seemingly more mortified

---

[463] Season 1 episode 6 "Babylon" August 23, 2007.

[464] Season 5 episode 6 "Far Away Places" April 22, 2012.

[465] Season 2 episode 11 "The Jet Set" October 12, 2008.

[466] Season 3 episode 8 "Souvenir" October 4, 2009.

[467] Season 2 episode 7 "The Gold Violin" September 7, 2008.

[468] Season 1 episode 6 "Babylon" August 23, 2007.

than irate, "She's so old."[469] A season later, Betty frets that she needs to put her "face on," underscoring a prevalent theme throughout *Mad Men* that everyone – regardless of age, race, class, gender, et cetera -- wears masks and that identity is a character one, subconsciously or not, performs and all the world is a stage.[470]

Peggy, who for the most part is depicted as Betty's spiritual antithesis, is as petrified of ageing as her counterpart seems to be. In season four, for example, Peggy markets Ponds as a "ritual" that "allows you to look in the mirror for twenty minutes and feel good, not vain."[471] Two episodes earlier, Peggy struggles to figure out a stylish way of selling supposedly age-defying products. "Nothing makes an old lady look good," she frets to Freddy. Three seasons later, Peggy laments that she turned thirty and has become "one of those women lying about her age."[472] Freddy pitches Peggy an idea for an ad campaign in season four: "Use Ponds and you'll get married," he says, "or worse yet, don't use it and don't get married." Peggy seems offended and calls him "old fashioned."[473]

Peggy's assertion that Freddy is "old fashioned" alludes to Don's duplicitous New Man persona, in that his preferred drink is an Old Fashioned but, like Freddy and Peggy, shills "new and

[469] Season 2 episode 8 "A Night to Remember" September 14, 2008.

[470] Season 3 episode 5 "The Fog" September 13, 2009.

[471] Season 4 episode 4 "The Rejected" August 5, 2010.

[472] Season 7 episode 6 "The Strategy" May 18, 2014.

[473] Season 4 episode 2 "Christmas Comes But Once a Year" August 1, 2010.

improved" for a living. "My first job," Don regales Kodak executives in the season one finale, "I was in house at a fur company with this old pro copywriter, a Greek named Teddy, who told me the most important idea in advertising is 'new.'"[474] Two seasons later, Don tells a real estate developer bent on tearing down Penn Station in order to build Madison Square Garden, "I was in California. Everything is new. The people are full of hope. New York is a city in decay."[475] New and improved (progress) is, of course, the lifeblood of the planned obsolescence that fuels consumer capitalism.

Female youth in particular is depicted in *Mad Men* as cherished and fetishized in 1960s America. The most prominent men on the show all, in fact, enjoy affairs and/or marry much younger women, all of whom represent newness and progress. Betty is younger than Don. Megan is younger than Betty. Joy is even younger than Megan.[476] Duck is likewise much older than Peggy. Roger has an affair with a twenty-year-old twin named Mirabelle and later leaves his wife, Mona, who is of proximate age to him, for a secretary in her early twenties. Even the prim, proper, and English gentleman (so it seemed), Lane Pryce, indulges in an affair with a very young woman who works as a waitress at the Playboy Club.

[474] Season 1 episode 13 "The Wheel" October 18, 2007.

[475] Season 3 episode 2 "Love Among the Ruins" August 23, 2009.

[476] Season 2 episode 11 "The Jet Set" October 12, 2008.

"It doesn't matter how old I am," Jane says to Roger in bed early one morning, "our souls are the same age."[477] An episode later Roger indicates that Bert Cooper's sister, Alice (Mary Anne McGarry), a shareholder in the company, is attracted to Don, who is much younger than her. Alice later insinuates that Roger has married a child (Jane).[478] Her statement underscores a glaring and sexist double standard in which men seem to revel in dating younger women, concomitant to widespread revulsion to older women being attracted to younger men. In season six, Pete Campbell's mother marries Manolo (Andres Faucher), a closeted homosexual who is much younger than she is, who, allegedly, shoves her over the side of a cruise ship in the misguided belief that he will inherit her wealth.[479]

Mad Men also depicts the co-opting of the youthfully exuberant 1960s counterculture by corporate America. "I don't know whether we should be nostalgic or groovier," an executive from Avon frets to Peggy and Joan in season six, which underscores the central paradox of consumerism in which older consumers have more money to spend, but young people represent hipness and the future. *Mad Men* especially depicts the pandering of products to youth in season two; Martinson Coffee enlists Sterling & Cooper and the agency's young and hip creatives in the hopes of getting kids addicted to coffee and thus making them customers for life. A season later, Patio (Diet Pepsi) demands a

[477] Ibid.

[478] Season 2 episode 12 "The Mountain King" October 19, 2008.

[479] Season 6 episode 13 "In Care Of" June 23, 2013.

young model comparable to Anne Margaret for their ad campaign. Nine episodes later, Jane drunkenly laments that John Kennedy, who her husband, Roger (a devout Republican), did not support, was "so handsome," but will "never get to vote for him," underscoring the centrality of his tanned and youthful photogenic façade, which played much better on television than Nixon's sweaty upper lip, furrowed brow, and disheveled mien during their infamous debate in 1960. "The president is a product," Pete tells Harry, "don't forget that."[480] Even Heinz Baked Beans is depicted as being obsessed with youth. "Beans is the War, the Depression, Bomb shelters," a Heinz executive explains to the creatives at the agency, "we have to erase that. They (beans) have to be cool… They (kids) have the hot plate. They're sitting in. Maybe somebody with a picket sign saying, 'we want beans!'"[481] An episode later Don and his young wife, Megan, meet with the same Heinz executive at a Manhattan restaurant where he asks for the Rolling Stones to be in the commercial because his teenaged daughter is obsessed with the band.[482]

The border between the postwar American fetish for youth and pedophilia also blurs several times on *Mad Men*. In season one, for instance, Helen Bishop confronts Betty because she found a lock of her blond hair in Glen's room, and forbids contact between Betty and her son. The insinuation is that something sinister can be detected in Betty's seeming attraction to Glen, who has a crush on

[480] Season 1 episode 10 "Long Weekend" September 27, 2007.

[481] Season 5 episode 1 "A Little Kiss" March 25, 2012.

[482] Season 5 episode 3 "The Tea Leaves" April 1, 2012.

her.483 In season three, senile Gene Hofstadt gropes his daughter, Betty, who he seems to confuse for his dead wife. Moments later he thinks Betty is a small child and promises to take her for ice cream. The implication is that he may have sexually assaulted his daughter.484 The following season, Sally is found riding between the cars of a commuter train into Manhattan because she does not have enough money for the fare. "You're lucky I found her," Vivian Winters, the woman who finds Sally says to Don, "the types on those trains..."485 Childhood rape is alluded to later in season five, as Beth, Pete's reluctant mistress, says, "I've had men paying attention to me since before it was appropriate. They don't care what I say." She later explains that the view of earth taken from outer space published by *TIME* scares her because "it makes the world seem so unprotected."486 In season two, Carlton, Don's neighbor, confides to the Don (who was molested by a prostitute and beaten savagely by his stepmother as a child)487 that he is sexually attracted to his high school-aged babysitter. "I think Francine brings her in to torture me," Carlton confesses to Don; "There is a pie cooling on the window sill," he adds, "and I'm not even supposed to smell it?"488 In season three, Peggy notes how

---

483 Season 1 episode 11 "Indian Summer" October 4, 2007.

484 Season 2 episode 10 "The Inheritance" October 5, 2008."

485 Season 4 episode 9 "The Beautiful Girls" September 19, 2010.

486 Season 5 episode 8 "Lady Lazarus" May 6, 2012.

487 Season 6 episode 8 "The Crash" May 19, 2013.

488 Season 2 episode 2 "Flight 1" August 3, 2008.

odd it is that Ann Margaret is twenty-five years old in *Bye Bye Birdie* but acts fourteen years old, which seems to titillate men of all ages.[489] In season five, Don and Harry Crane go to a Rolling Stones concert in the hopes of obtaining the rights to one of the band's songs in order to make a commercial for Heinz Baked Beans. They meet two fourteen-year-old girls backstage. "Young girls are so much fun," Harry later says to Don, "they're all on drugs." Don, whose daughter, Sally, is only slightly younger than the girls backstage at the Stones concert, expresses his concern for kids enduring puberty in what seems to be an increasingly violent, militarized, sexualized and consumerist society.[490] Two episodes later Pete fantasizes about a recent high school graduate in his driver's education course.[491] An episode later Michael Ginsberg announces that "we (the agency) should sell adult bras to little girls." A bit later in the episode Megan's father says in a broken French accent to Don, "one day your little girl will spread her legs and fly away."[492]

The allusion to youth simultaneously fetishized and imperiled in postwar America's consumerist/militarist culture can often be detected in *Mad Men* and directed towards the youth of both genders. Early in season one, for instance, Rachel Menken seems frustrated as she asks Don, "why do I hire young girls?" To which he replies, "Because they cost next to nothing," underscoring

[489] Season 3 episode 2 "Love Among the Ruins" August 23, 2009.

[490] Season 5 episode 3 "The Tea Leaves" April 1, 2012.

[491] Season 5 episode 5 "Signal 30" April 15, 2012.

[492] Season 5 episode 7 "At the Codfish Ball" April 29, 2012.

how exploited young labor tends to be, especially in retail.[493] In season six, Dr. Rosen is upset that his son's Draft status is 1-A as a result of Mitchell sending his Draft card back in protest for what he perceives to be an unjust war. "Kids that are eighteen and nineteen, they have no sense of their own mortality," Rosen (a renowned cardiologist) confides. Don replies, "or anyone else's. That's what makes them good soldiers."[494] Don's line speaks volumes because it underscores the point that the creators of *Mad Men* seek to expose the fetish for the New Man and youth in general as ultimately being designed to convince young people of the "value" of both consuming products and risking their lives for the glory of the nation and, ultimately, to maintain the economic and political status quo. In fact, though the young are perhaps the most fetishized and commodified form depicted on *Mad Men*, especially by patriotic Betty, the young are also depicted as, perhaps, the most imperiled and scapegoated on the show.

Scapegoats are a central feature of any fascist enterprise. European fascists, in the decades prior to World War II, often blamed their nations' problems on Jews, Freemasons, Marxists, and immigrants. In Spain, much of the Falange's early violence was directed against students at the University of Madrid. In *Mad Men*, young liberals are predominately depicted by conservative neoliberals on the show as one of the greatest threats to America, thus foreshadowing the culture wars that defined American politics in the waning decades of the twentieth century and the early decades of the twenty-first century. In season six, for example, Ken

[493] Season 1 episode 3 "Marriage of Figaro" August 2, 2007.

[494] Season 6 episode 11 "Favors" June 9, 2013.

and Harry meet with Dow Chemical. They chat about Columbia students briefly occupying the lobby of Dow's New York City offices. "They acted like they were storming the Bastille," a Dow executive says, thereby insinuating that the student uprisings on Columbia University's campus, and in Prague, Paris, Mexico City, and dozens of other places throughout the world in 1968 were comparable the French Revolution.[495] In season six, in the wake of the "police riot" at the 1968 Democratic National Convention in Chicago, a Carnation Instant Breakfast executive in a meeting with Don and Pete held in Southern California fumes, "Last night was disgusting, seeing those long hairs shame this country."[496] Also in season six, anti-Semitic Jim Cutler feuds with Michal Ginsberg, a young artist; "I served in the Air Force, did you?"[497] Cutler, who dropped bombs on Dresden during World War II, rhetorically asks as a means of expressing that he has greater moral authority than young, naïve, and pacifist Ginsberg (who was born in a concentration camp). Close to the midway point of the final season of the show, Lou Avery, who is also a World War II vet, calls Stan Rizzo and Johnny Mathis (not the musician) "a bunch of flag burning snots" that have "got a thing to learn about patriotism and loyalty."[498] The massacre of student protestors at Kent State University (and, by implication, Jackson State University) in 1970 is likewise broached in season seven when Sally asks Glen Bishop,

[495] Season 6 episode 4 "To Have and Hold" April 21, 2013.

[496] Season 6 episode 10 "A Tale of Two Cities" June 2, 2013.

[497] Ibid.

[498] Season 7 episode 5 "The Runaways" May 11, 2014.

"What about Kent State? You were crying and going to join the movement." Glen rejoins her with, "What about a bunch of Negro kids dying while we stay at home and get stoned? It's immoral."[499]

In season three, Don picks up a hitchhiker on his way to Niagara Falls who explains that his Draft Status is 1-A and he is trying to get to Canada. "I have a target on my back," the young man says, "and for what?"[500] His statement underscores the terror experienced by tens of thousands of young American men who were drafted into the Armed Forces to fight an immoral war that American leaders knew could not be won. Three seasons later, Don mentions young people avoiding the Draft to a General Motors executive who sneers that, Draft dodging makes him "sick."[501] In season seven, an associate of Henry Francis denigrates the "wildness of the kids" as "a natural disaster." His wife adds, "I know all anyone wants to talk about is Vietnam, but things are falling apart here, too." Patriotic Betty wholeheartedly agrees and notes:

> "I don't know that they are unrelated; first the kids start protesting, next thing you know all authority is up for grabs. I mean, if they learned to support their country and sacrifice in hard times, we'd have the morale to win the war."[502]

---

[499] Season 7 episode 10 "The Forecast" April 19, 2015.

[500] Season 3 episode 7 "Seven Twenty Three" September 27, 2009.

[501] Season 6 episode 11 "Favors" June 9, 2013.

[502] Season 7 episode 5 "The Runaways" May 11, 2014.

Betty's blaming of the young for losing Vietnam underscores the scapegoating of young liberals and especially leftists by elder conservatives terrified of growing old. Her assertion also underscores the point that weapons manufacturers such as Dow, and politicians who waged the war, are not considered villains in contrast to the young men who refuse to risk their lives so that companies such as GM, Braniff, and North American Aviation can maximize shareholders' profits.

Mad Men does well illuminating how nationalism, military values associated with the New Man, and consumerism grew increasingly conflated in postwar American society due, in part, to the work of glib ad men, television, and movies that glorified war as regenerative to the nation as it made men of boys, if it did not kill them first. In both Europe, in the decades prior to World War II, and in postwar America mass-media makers often glorified concepts such as the New Man, which couched military values ultimately designed to manipulate young people into risking their lives to fight for the enrichment and aggrandizement of the nation's politicians, industries, executives, and corporate lobbyists. Youth was subsequently fetishized as a means of selling warfare as well as "new and improved" often "age defying" products. The young were, however, often subsequently denigrated as naïve idealists, if not also enemies of the state, when they had the audacity to resist being sent to war by their elders. And, though *Mad Men* does not seem to either overtly champion or chastise Marxist or neoliberal ideology, the show's stance on the perceived value of militarism and war, which has historically been incumbent on the willingness of young people to risk being slaughtered, seems far less ambivalent.

Chapter Six

"*Mad Men* and the American Empire"

An executive for London Fog in season three of *Mad Men* takes a meeting with Don Draper and Salvatore Romano at the raincoat maker's headquarters in Baltimore, Maryland. Even though London Fog proudly sold two thirds of all raincoats in the world the previous year, the executive fears that "everyone who needed a raincoat bought one already... A business needs to keep growing," he says, "that's capitalism."[503] That, according to Vladimir Lenin, is also imperialism.[504] Both the Italians and Nazis used hard power to expand the reach of their burgeoning empires during the 1930s. But both also, as did the American empire during the Cold War, skillfully used soft power in tandem with hard power to perpetuate the notion that imperialism was the Social Darwinist natural order of things.[505]

---

[503] Season 3 episode 1 "Out of Town" August 16, 2009.

[504] V.I. Lenin, *Imperialism, The Highest State of Capitalism*, 1917.

[505] See David Welch, *Nazi Propaganda: The Power and Limitations* (London, Croom Helm, 1983). See also Hans Speier, "Nazi Propaganda and its Decline," *Social Research*, Vol. 10, No. 3 (September, 1943), pp. 358-377; and Eugene J. D'souza, "Nazi Propaganda in India," *Social Scientist* Vol. 28, No. 5/6 (May - Jun., 2000), pp. 77-99. For a comparison between American imperialism and other empires throughout history see George Steinmetz, "Return to Empire: The New U.S. Imperialism in Comparative Historical Perspective," *Sociological Theory* Vol. 23, No. 4 (Dec., 2005), pp. 339-367; and also Joseph Lepgold and Timothy McKeown, "Is American Foreign Policy Exceptional? An Empirical Analysis," *Political Science Quarterly* Vol. 110, No. 3 (Autumn, 1995), pp. 369-384.

There are several allusions made to both hard and soft power imperialism in *Mad Men*. In season one, for example, Jim Hobart of McCann-Erickson promises Don Draper "the world" as he tries to woo the creative director from Sterling & Cooper to his agency, which has a transnational clientele and global presence.[506] There are, in fact, several globes in the set design of the show throughout seven seasons. There are, for example, globes in Don's, Roger Sterling's, and Peter Campbell's offices in the early seasons of the show. There is also a copper globe on the wall of Sterling & Cooper in season three.[507] Jim Cutler, the most obvious and unabashed fascist on the show, likewise has a globe on his desk in season seven.[508] The biggest globe, however, is a gold wall hanging in a conference room at McCann-Erickson's corporate headquarters in Manhattan, an agency with "international prestige" thanks to clients such as Coca-Cola – a multinational soft drink company symbolic of American soft power imperialism.[509]

There are also Roman victory arches adorning the walls of Lane Pryce's and Harry Crane's offices. In season seven, the wall of Ted Shaw's office is adorned with a work of art depicting a bird's eye view of numerous bridges leading to Manhattan, which seems to allude to the notion that "all bridges lead to Rome (the imperial metropole)." In the decades after World War II Manhattan replaced London and Paris, which had earlier replaced Rome and Istanbul,

[506] Season 1 episode 9 "Shoot" September 13, 2007.

[507] Season 3 episode 4 "The Arrangements" September 6, 2009.

[508] Season 7 episode 3 "Field Trip" April 27, 2014.

[509] Season 7 episode 9 "New Business" April 12, 2015.

as the center of the western imperial world. The globes, victory arches, and bridges leading to Manhattan seem to point viewers of *Mad Men* toward the fact that the show depicts the United States at the height of its imperial powers.

Soft power is an especially important part of *Mad Men's* depiction of the 1960s. There are, as the paragraph above indicates, a number of subliminal clues to imperialism woven into the show. In season one, for instance, the decorating scheme in Betty's beloved first floor bathroom seems a shrine to French aristocracy before the first revolution.[510] In season two, Betty and Don enjoy tall glasses of Tom Collins and listen to a Bing Crosby song, "Blue Room," that mentions *Robinson Crusoe*.[511] The story of *Robinson Crusoe* is an allegory of British Imperialism in the Pacific Ocean during the nineteenth century. In season three, Pete Campbell and Kenny Cosgrove are both made head of accounts by their new British overlords at Putnam, Powell & Lowe, which speaks to the ways in which the British deviously played Muslims and Hindus against each other in the interest of consolidating the Crown's power on the subcontinent in nineteenth-century India.[512] Episode four of season three foreshadows the July Fourth-weekend coup waged by Sterling & Cooper against Putnam, Powell and Lowe. The episode concludes with a rendition of George M. Cohan's "Over There," which hailed America's fighting men in World War I. The "Great War" was the point in American and world history

[510] Season 1 episode 3 "Marriage of Figaro" August 2, 2007.

[511] Season 2 episode 4 "Three Sundays" August 17, 2008.

[512] Season 3 episode 1 "Out of Town" August 16, 2009.

when the United States went from being a debtor to creditor nation and thus was established as a world power on par with England and France.[513] Peter Baehr indicates that the U.S. was a totalitarian state at the moment it became a truly global imperial force with the power to compete with and influence the old European empire's global reach and prestige.[514] In the second to last episode of the series, some drunken American Veterans of Foreign Wars, including Don, belt out "Over There," as if to remind viewers that the United States was the world hegemonic military, industrial, and economic power.[515] Another subliminal clue that *Mad Men* is a veiled critique of the soft power wielded by the American empire can be detected in season six as Peggy explains to Ted Shaw that margarine, which the agency is crafting an ad campaign for, nourished Napoleon III's imperial army as it plundered Europe in the nineteenth century. In the following scene Don's mistress (and neighbor) mentions her son participating in the 1968 general strike in which university students joined blue-collar workers in uprisings in France in protest of Charles De Gaulle's policies and regime.[516] Sherry Mangan and others consider De Gaulle, who

---

[513] Season 3 episode 4 "The Arrangements" September 6, 2009.

[514] For an interesting argument that the U.S. was a totalitarian state during World War I see: Peter Baehr's "Totalitarianism in America? Robert Nisbet on the 'Wilson War State' and Beyond," *The American Sociologist* Vol. 45, No. 1, A Conservative in Academe: Robert Nisbet and American Sociology (March 2014), pp. 84-102.

[515] Season 7 episode 13 "Person to Person" May 17, 2015.

[516] Season 6 episode 7 "Man With a Plan" May 12, 2013.

helped lure the United States into Indochina in the 1950s, to be both an imperialist and a fascist.[517]

Mad Men's depiction of Conrad Hilton, more than anyone in seven seasons of the series, characterizes postwar American soft power imperialism, and, arguably fascism. He wants Hilton Hotels all over the world, "like missions." He tells Don that he envisions Hiltons on "the moon." America is, he explains, wherever the empire looks. "It's my purpose in life to bring America to the world, whether they like it or not." He describes the American empire as a "force of good" because the U.S. has God, which is starkly contrasted to atheist communists. He also reminds Don about the Marshall Plan. "Everyone who saw our ways wanted to be us," he explains. "After all the things we threw at Khrushchev, you know what made him fall apart?" Hilton asks. "He couldn't get into Disneyland."[518] Don later gives a heartfelt presentation to the hotel baron with the tagline, "Hilton, It's The Same in Every Language." The hotelier is, however, deeply bemused and upset that the campaign failed to mention Hilton Hotels on the moon. "When I say I want the moon," Hilton fumes, "I expect the moon."[519] He ultimately decides not to do business with Don's agency. In season seven, the Burger Chef presentation is, not coincidentally, set the day after the Apollo 11 moon landing – the symbolic zenith of the American empire.[520] The final scene of *Mad*

[517] Sherry Mangan, "Two Democracies in Crisis: France: Is De Gaulle a Fascist?" *Commentary*, January 1, 1948.

[518] Season 7 Episode 1 "Time Zones" April 13, 2014.

[519] Season 3 episode 9 "Wee Small Hours" October 11, 2009.

[520] Season 7 episode 7 "Waterloo" May 25, 2014.

Men concludes with the utopian and iconic Coca-Cola commercial in which people all around the world drink Coke, hold hands, and sing, as if to indicate what would happen if and when the world learned to stop worrying, fussing, and fighting in order to consume advertised products in unison and perfect harmony.

Disney is in *Mad Men* depicted to be an even bigger indicator of American soft power and empire than is Coca-Cola and Hilton Hotels. There are, as Hilton's remark about Khrushchev alludes to, many winks to Disney in *Mad Men*. In season one, for example, Paul Kinsey calls Peggy "mouse ears."[521] In season three, Conrad Hilton shows Don an ad campaign the hotel baron had crafted which depicts a mouse similar to Mickey Mouse.[522] In season four, Don drunkenly calls a mouse in his office "Mickey."[523] Three episodes later Lane Pryce buys his son a stuffed Mickey Mouse doll.[524] One episode after that Sally promises that she will always "love Minnie Mouse."[525] In season five, Sally, in an episode titled "Tormorrowland," is seen wearing Mickey Mouse ears in the back of Don's Cadillac after their trip to Disneyland in California.[526] A season later, Don and Roger meet with Carnation Foods, which has

---

[521] Season 1 episode 6 "Babylon" August 23, 2007.

[522] Season 3 episode 6 "My Old Kentucky Home" August 30, 2009.

[523] Season 4 episode 7 "The Suitcase" September 5, 2010.

[524] Season 4 episode 10 "Hands and Knees" September 26, 2010.

[525] Season 3 episode 11 "The Gypsy and the Hobo" October 25, 2009.

[526] Season 5 episode 6 "Far Away Places" April 22, 2012.

a café on Main Street at Disneyland.527 In season seven, Don flirts with a widow (Neve Campbell) on a flight en route to New York from California in which she tells him that her recently deceased husband wanted his ashes scattered at Disneyland. Earlier in the episode the agency aches to land Burger Chef as a client, which, like Carnation, is entrée into Disneyland.528 It is important to note that Walt Disney, like Ronald Reagan, can be considered evidence of postwar American fascism, considering both men expressed no qualms about testifying before the House Un-American Activities Committee, which is evidence of Cold War American fascism, and which contributed to the blacklisting of dozens of artists in Hollywood who had committed no crimes.

Mad Men thus conflates Cold War America's war on communist ideology, and also the consumerism symbolized by Hilton, Disney, Coca-Cola, and the American advertising industry itself, to be evidence of both hard and soft power imperialism at the center of American society during the 1960s. This synergy between consumerism and militarism is a recurring theme throughout the series. The theme of couching militarism in consumer culture can, for example, be detected in a scene that seems inspired by Stanley Kubrick's Cold War classic *Dr. Strangelove or: How I Stopped Worrying and Learned to Love the Bomb* (1964); Pete takes a model he just met home for coitus. The girl turns on the television so her mother, hopefully, will not hear her and Pete as they get to know each other in a Biblical sense. A U2 spy plane appears on the television screen as a gruff and masculine voice compares

527 Season 6 episode 5 "The Flood" April 28, 2013.

528 Season 7 episode 1" Time Zones" April 13, 2014.

supersonic flying to touching "the face of God" just as Pete slides his hand up the woman's dress, which has a bow on it as if she were a present to be unwrapped.[529] In season five, an annoying insurance salesman who is riding on the commuter train with Pete, has little jets on his tie.[530] In season seven, Ted Shaw's desk is adorned with a model fighter jet.[531] In season four, Roger claims that a rival agency (Cutler, Gleason and Shaw) brought an actor dressed as a general to an award show in order to "impress" someone, underscoring the centrality of American militarism in postwar popular culture.[532] The episode "Tomorrowland" in season four of the series alludes to Don taking his kids to Disneyland. Bobby tells his father, as they are deciding what rides to enjoy at the theme park the next day, that he does not want to ride an elephant, he "wants to fly a jet," which elaborates how the utopian depiction of American popular culture at home and abroad, via entities such as Disney, is the other side of the coin in regard to the Sunbelt military industrial complex, which put California at the center of postwar American politics.[533] The tension between Shaw and Don in season four also seems to be a metaphor for the thawing of the Cold War in which the rival agents ultimately become business associates.

[529] Season 2 episode 6 "Maidenform" August 31, 2008.

[530] Season 5 episode 8 "Lady Lazarus" May 6, 2012.

[531] Season 7 episode 2 "A Day's Work" April 20, 2014.

[532] Season 4 episode 6 "Waldorf Stories" August 29, 2010.

[533] Season 4 episode 13 "Tomorrowland" October 17, 2010.

There are, as the numerous references to Disney allude to, symbolic messages embedded in the show that point towards imperialism. Early in season one, for example, Don visits Rachel Menken at her department store. She has a selection of dozens of cufflinks she could choose for him, but ultimately selects "medieval knights," which alludes to the Crusades.[534] Bert Cooper has Samurai armor as decoration in his office; Lane Pryce has Knights' armor in his office in season three. Both seem to conflate British and Japanese imperialism with postwar American imperialism.[535] In season six, an elderly Rough Rider, who can barely stand, is, along with Don and many other vets, cheered at a Memorial Day gathering at the country club.[536] The Rough Riders, which were led by unabashed imperialist Theodore Roosevelt, are, as is the Spanish-American War, symbolic of the United States' evolution from a continental to a global empire at the turn of the twentieth century. The Spanish-American War was sold to the American public in order for William Randolph Hearst and Joseph Pulitzer to sell papers, but most importantly to sell ads in the yellow press.

There are further allusions to imperialism in season six when Roger says, "we're conquistadors" to Don in the first-class cabin of a westbound flight from New York to California. "I'm Vasco de Gama," Roger adds, which provides a bit more meaning to the numerous globes in the show's set design.[537] In the third episode of

[534] Season 1 episode 3 "Marriage of Figaro" August 2, 2007.

[535] Season 3 episode 6 "Guy Walks Into an Advertising Agency" September 20, 2009.

[536] Season 2 episode 6 "Maidenform" August 31, 2008.

[537] Season 6 episode 10 "A Tale of Two Cities" June 2, 2013.

the following season, a statue of a conquistador and cannon adorns the desk in Harry Crane's office. There are also drawings of red-coated and blue-coated soldiers from the eighteenth century adorning his walls.[538] Close to the end of the series, Roger – quite out of the blue – shows Peggy a Free Mason totem and asks if she knows anything about the secretive organization, which harkens back to season two when Bert Cooper tells Don that "there are a few people who get to decide what happens in this world" and Don has become one of them.[539] The "few people" Cooper alludes to might be a metonym for the postwar world's premier superpower, which was an empire whose power derived largely from militarism and the seductive power of consumerism.

The United States emerged from World War II as the world's imperial powerbroker. "You're the dying empire! We're (America) the future."[540] Bert Peterson seethes while being fired from Putnam, Powell, and Lowe – a British advertising agency that acquired Sterling & Cooper in large part to acquire Don Draper's "unique American genius."[541] America's patriotic fervor was at a peak in the decades between World War II and the 1960s. That patriotism began to wane during America's war in Indochina, when the nation's imperialism began to increasingly betray the country's

---

[538] Season 7 episode 3 "Field Trip" April 27, 2014.

[539] Season 7 episode 12 "New Horizons" May 3, 2015. See also Season 2 episode 7: "The Gold Violin" September 7, 2008.

[540] Season 3 episode 1 "Out of Town" August 12, 2009.

[541] Season 3 episode 6 "Guy Walks Into an Advertising Agency" September 20, 2009.

fascist, particularly its racist, corporatist and technocratic tendencies.

Part of postwar America's pervasive patriotic fervor was sparked in part by the central role the United States played in aiding and abetting the Soviet Union's defeat of the Nazis during World War II. Also, many ethic Americans, most notably Irish and Italian-Catholics, were absorbed into the middle-class and, thus, American mainstream due to their close contact with Protestant Americans during World War II. Government programs such as the G.I. Bill further facilitated assimilation of white ethnics by making education and property-ownership (often in overwhelmingly white suburbs) more attainable than ever before.

America had been considered a great "melting pot" in the early decades of the twentieth century. But most ethic groups identified themselves more in terms of the lands their ancestors hailed from first, before, secondly, considering themselves Americans. Even southerners, many of whom still bitterly resented the federal government long after the end of the American Civil War, tended to first consider themselves as Georgians and Virginians, et cetera, well before identifying themselves as Americans, which was synonymous with being a Yankee. But by the Second Red Scare of the late 1940s and 1950s, the polity was more collectively conformist and nationalistic than it had been at any other point in the nation's history. This fervent brand of nationalism was a catalyst of postwar America's commercial empire.

Betty Draper's second husband, Henry Francis, who works first for New York Governor, Nelson Rockefeller, and then New

York City Mayor, John Lindsay, is a symbol of postwar American nationalism and Northern Republicans prior to Barry Goldwater's monumental impact on the reshaping of the American polity in 1964 and the decades thereafter. The American standard hanging from Henry's mansion flutters in the soft summer breeze as he and Betty watch her children giggle and twirl sparklers on the front lawn at dusk on July Fourth. "Model UN is a joke," Henry later says to Betty after Sally expresses interest in participating in that club at her school, which stokes his ire.[542] Though New York City was made home of the United Nations in the years after World War II, many conservatives in the American Sunbelt, Deep South, and the North saw the global organization as toothless and, therefore, as worthless, as the League of Nations was also widely perceived to be after World War I. Many conservatives also perceived the UN as an unnecessary impediment to American political and economic domination.

The creators of *Mad Men*, as Henry Francis and Conrad Hilton personify, seem to conscientiously point viewers to the sense of swelling nationalism bubbling to the surface of American society all through the Cold War. This fervent nationalism is most prominently depicted in *Mad Men* to be particularly championed by America's economic elites who benefited the most from drafting young men into the Armed Forces to fight on behalf of Bell Helicopters, Lockheed, Coca-Cola, etc. Cold War conformity, which was packaged and sold by advertisers and many Hollywood movies, also surely played a role in the ascendance of postwar America's newfound sense of nationalism, especially Westerns and

[542] Season 6 Episode 11 "Favors" June 9, 2013.

war movies that fondly remembered World War II. American Westerns in particular championed the ethos of American imperialism, which is part of the reason why Red Westerns, which offered consumers in Soviet Bloc countries an inversion of American Westerns, in which Indians were anti-colonial and communal-living good guys in contrast to capitalist/imperialist cowboys, became so popular behind the Iron Curtain during the Cold War.[543]

Mad Men thus provides a critique of the commoditization of patriotism in the postwar era. Cigarette baron Lee Garner, Sr. (John Cullum), for instance, in the very first episode of the series declares, "we're selling America."[544] Cigarettes are, it is important to note, also made synonymous with death, which seems to allude to poet Gil Scott-Heron's metaphor of the United States being equated to "free doom" rather than "freedom" in "Who Will Survive in America?" (1970). Later in season one, Don pitches Bethlehem Steel, which is used to make tanks and jets, as being emblematic of the American Dream -- "the acorn that grows."[545] In season six, Kenny Cosgrove and Harry Crane meet with Dow Chemical executives, including Ken's father-in-law, Ed Baxter (Ray Wise). Dow is enduring a lot of bad press as a result of, as Ken says, "dumping napalm on children." Ken and Harry propose an idea for a televised corporate image campaign intended to help restore the

[543] For more on Red Westerns see Gerd Gemünden, "Between Karl May and Karl Marx: The DEFA Indianerfilme (1965-1983)." *New German Critique*, No. 82, East German Film (Winter, 2001), pp. 25-38.

[544] Season 1 episode 1 "Smoke Gets in Your Eyes" July 19, 2007.

[545] Season 1 episode 4 "New Amsterdam" August 9, 2007.

corporation's public image. The proposed campaign is an hour-long special sponsored by Dow called *Broadway Joe on Broadway* that not only promises sexpot Joey Heatherton, but also John Wayne in a Shakespeare sketch, perhaps of *Julius Caesar*, one of the most infamous dictators in world history who is also symbolic of the corruption and decline of the Roman empire. "Is there anything that makes people smile more than Broadway and Football?" a booster in the service of Ken and Harry asks as he pitches the show to the keenly interested executives. "Yankee Doodle Dandy and the Notre Dame Fight Song playing at the same time," the booster regales." Ken adds the tagline, "Dow Chemical: Family Products for the American Family."[546]

In the premier episode of season four, Don sips beer and watches football alone, twice.[547] Though baseball has long been considered America's pastime, American football is considered America's game, especially since no other countries are too terribly serious about it. Part of the reason few other countries presumably invest much interest in American football is because it is so obviously a metaphor of American imperialism. The National Football League's logo, for example, is an American flag. College football in the twenty-first century has numerous bowl games sponsored by the military or weapons manufacturers. The Army-Navy game and pageant culminates each regular season of college football. American football, which was invented and popularized especially in the Ivy League and military academies as an anecdote to neurasthenia in the late-nineteenth century, as the United States

[546] Season 6 episode 4 "To Have and Hold" April 21, 2013.

[547] Season 4 episode 1 "Public Relations" July 25, 2010.

was rapidly growing into an urban-industrial continental empire, is based on taking and defending territory; The Cowboys and Redskins rivalry thus seems a metaphor of the ways in which American imperialism has been stealthily absorbed into American popular and consumer culture.

The notion that American patriotism, such as that commodified and marketed by the NFL and college football, is evidence of a hollow and vapid nationalistic marketing scheme that contributes to a beer-guzzling, gun-toting, and mostly impotent American polity that champions coaches as dictatorial figures and nonchalantly sanctions fascistic impulses (such as the Red Scares, the Vietnam War, and invective directed at athletes who kneel during the National Anthem to protest police brutality and inveterate racism in the American legal system) can especially be detected in season five of *Mad Men*. The show, for example, conflates American patriotism with consumerism when Megan takes Don to see a live performance of *America Hurrah*, what beatnik Roy Hazelitt would refer to as "conscious drama" in contrast to the consumer utopian "mediocrity of Broadway."[548] *America Hurrah* savagely critiques American consumer culture, including the nation's political system, both of which are sardonically conflated. "I like to have a can of beer in my hand when I watch the beer ads," the protagonist of the play says as Don shifts impatiently in his seat. "The ad was making me sick, so I used the remote control to change the channel, but each channel made me just as sick." At home after the play, Don defends his industry (and, by implication, soft power and the American

---

[548] Season 1 episode 6 "Babylon" August 23, 2007.

empire) by saying, "people buy things because it makes them feel better." Megan half-heartedly defends *America Hurrah* by qualifying that the play "wasn't as much a stand against advertising as much as the emptiness of consumerism."[549] The obvious question is: what's the difference? In *Mad Men* there seems to be no difference. Thus, the series uses *America Hurrah* as a means of critiquing the American empire, soft power, and fascism in the context of conspicuous consumerism and America's war in Indochina.

Even warfare, as *Mad Men* alludes to in season one, was packaged and sold to Americans as patriotism in the postwar period. Don Draper (the actual one played by Chris Gann) asks Dick Whitman (played by John Hamm) in an expository flashback set during the Korean War, "What misconception made you want to be here, a movie?"[550] The larger context of the hidden symbolism and subtext in *Mad Men* is the reality of the Cold War and Vietnam War, which seep into the series more and more each season. In season one, Sterling & Cooper are desperate for Richard Nixon as a client against John Kennedy in the 1960 general election. "He's a friend of United Fruit and Proctor and Gamble," Bert Cooper says as he fantasizes about the business that could be done with Richard Nixon doing the agency's bidding.[551] United Fruit was the largest landowner in Guatemala in the mid-1950s. Guatemalan President, Jacabo Arbenz, nationalized United Fruit's landholdings, which led

---

[549] Season 5 episode 10 "Christmas Waltz" May 20, 2012.

[550] Season 1 episode 12 "Nixon vs. Kennedy," October 11, 2007.

[551] Season1 episode 2 "Ladies Room" July 26, 2007.

to a CIA-backed coup that removed Arbenz from power. In short, United Fruit, like so many other corporations and their lobbyists and lawyers, was synonymous with American imperialism.

In season two, Pete Campbell reads a lengthy list of "rocket makers" attending the "Rocket Fair" in California. "Sounds like a great stock portfolio," Don says. Pete seems excited at the idea of making clients of weapons makers because one of those corporations "spends three times" on advertising "what Lucky Strike does." Lucky Strike was, in early seasons of the series, Sterling & Cooper's largest client and, essentially, kept the agency afloat. Pete further elaborates that the "congressmen control the purse strings." Don replies that the weapons manufacturers are all trying to "land on the moon, or blow up Moscow, whichever costs more." Don, thus, tasks Pete with selling politicians and aerospace industry executives on Sterling & Cooper's ability to help them engage in pork-barrel politics. "The congressman is the customer," Don says, "we can help bring these contracts home."[552] Pete and Don later go to the American Aviation and Rocket conference in California, the epicenter of America's postwar military industrial complex and home to Presidents Richard Nixon (1969 – 1974) and Ronald Reagan (1981 – 1989). Don attends a presentation in which an enthusiastic salesman hocks Multiple Independently-targetable Reentry Vehicles (MIRVs) and regales the audience by proudly explaining that the product promises "total annihilation."[553] An

[552] Season 2 episode 10 "The Inheritance" October 5, 2008.

[553] Season 2 episode 11 "The Jet Set" October 12, 2008. A MIRV is a ballistic missile payload containing several warheads, each capable of being aimed to hit one of a group of targets.

episode later, Pete extols the importance of advertising to the aerospace industry and American politics into his Dictaphone, as if the creators of *Mad Men* are keen to drive home the point that American soft power consumerism and militarism are two sides of the same coin.[554]

The blurred line between the Cold War/Vietnam War/advertising industry is made even fuzzier in season three when Sally, who struggles with her grandfather's recent death, throws a fit and is sent to watch television in order to "calm down." She turns on the TV to see Thích Quảng Đức's self-emollition in protest of the Diem family's corrupt and oppressive South Vietnamese puppet regime, which was backed by the U.S. state department.[555] Pete meets with North American Aviation three episodes later and convinces the corporation that they need to spend more on ads if they want to "get out of NASA and into the Pentagon." Pete later seems delighted that the corporation ordered several tons of tanks and helicopters bound for Vietnam.[556] In season four, a weapons manufacturer tells Pete he uses the euphemism, "guidance and control system" so he never has to say "bomb," which has the potential to be a public relations problem due to a growing anti-war movement. Don suggests the weapons manufacturer avoid the term "defense" altogether. An employee for North American Aviation likewise couches the destruction associated with "Minutemen Missiles" in the utopianism associated

---

[554] Season 2 episode 12 "The Mountain King" October 19, 2008.

[555] Season 3 episode 4 "The Arrangements" September 6, 2009.

[556] Season 3 episode 7 "Seven Twenty Three" September 27, 2009.

with "the moon."557 In season five, Don takes a meeting with Dow-Corning executives in the hope of winning the corporation's business. He regales them with anecdotes that champion napalm, which was, he notes, used in "flamethrowers against the Nazis" and "impact bombs against the Japanese. It was all over the place in Korea. Now it's in Vietnam. But the important thing is," Don adds, "when our boys are fighting and they need it -- when America needs it -- it works." Though the Dow executives seem somewhat impressed by Don's boldness and creativity, the more gregarious of them explains that the corporation is "happy" with their current advertising agency. "What is happiness?" Don prods. "It's a moment before we need more happiness. You don't want most of it, you want all of it. And I won't stop until you get it," which seems to be a euphemism for the nature of consumerism, capitalism and imperialism: more is never enough.558

The creators of *Mad Men*, as the paragraph above helps to illuminate, ostensibly depict ways in which the language of warfare was actively sanitized by advertising agents such as Don Draper as a means of selling it to the public and consequently making war a glorified, intractable, and seemingly natural part of American life in the half century-plus after World War II. The sanitization and glorification of war was concomitant to American imperialism being widely articulated by Hollywood movies and network news as undisputed champions of nebulously or never actually-defined high-minded concepts such as "freedom and liberty" – which was linguistically conflated in American mass media as consumerism

[557] Season 4 episode 10 "Hands and Knees" September 26, 2010.

[558] Season 5 episode 7 "At the Codfish Ball" April 29, 2012.

and imperialism – all, supposedly, heroically defended by America's warrior class.[559]

Though *Mad Men* depicts the United States at the zenith of the nation's imperial powers, the show originally aired as America was deeply mired in The War on Terror and War on Drugs, which had replaced the Cold War as the prime justification for exorbitant American military spending and a subsequent reigning in of domestic social programs and public services. Most of the show also premiered in the wake of the 2008 global economic collapse. Thus, it seems evident that *Mad Men* is as much about the United States in the twenty-first century, as the empire's political and economic power flagged, it is about the postwar era while the empire was at its peak. Roger Sterling, for instance, tells Betty and Don in season one that the Pacific was "all about gasoline, people forget that." In doing so, he underscores the continuity in the American military's dependence on nonrenewable and, often, foreign resources that power the empire's military supremacy since World War II.[560]

There are several other hints that *Mad Men* is as much about the rapid decline of the American empire as it is about the empire's crest. Anxiety, for example, regarding the precipitous decline of the American empire in the twenty-first century seems especially alluded to in season three of the show as Sally reads *The Decline and Fall of the Roman Empire* to her grandfather, who, like John Wayne,

[559] Richard Grenier, "Hollywood's Foreign Policy: Utopianism Tempered by Greed," *The National Interest* No. 24 (Summer 1991), pp. 67-77.

[560] Season 1 episode 7 "Red in the Face" August 30, 2007.

is a white, masculine, Protestant symbol of America's rugged past as fetishized in war movies, westerns, and American politics.[561] A season later, the agency's resident artist, Stan Rizzo, says to Peggy, "it's the last days of Rome," as it appears that the agency is collapsing.[562]

America's founding fathers conscientiously set out to define the United States as a shining city on a hill and, as the neoclassical architecture that defines Washington D.C. speaks to, style the new Republic as the Roman Empire's torchbearer in the New World. The tearing down of Penn Station, with its neoclassical design, in order to build the Madison Square Garden sports arena and concert hall in season three seems to be a tangible symbol of the beginning of empire's decline. As such, as much as *Mad Men* depicts America at the zenith of its imperial powers, the show, which aired between 2007 – 2015, is equally about the meltdown of capitalism as a result of the collapse of the dot.com bubble at the turn of the twenty-first century, followed shortly thereafter by the mortgage crisis of 2008, and the subsequent weakening of the American empire as a supposed moral, political and economic force in the world. *Mad Men*, the multi-Emmy and Golden Globe-award winning commercial juggernaut was made at an especially hostile and partisan time in American history, a moment arguably as tumultuous as the late-1960s. After September 11, 2001 the United States became mired in bloody and intractable conflicts in Afghanistan, Iraq and Syria, all unwinnable quagmires comparable to the American war in Indochina in the 1960s and 1970s, which

[561] Season 3 episode 3 "My Old Kentucky Home" August 30, 2009.

[562] Season 4 episode 11 "Chinese Wall" October 3, 2010.

plays such a central role in *Mad Men's* depiction of Cold War America. America's new twenty-first century quagmires ensured that the militarism, and, by implication, consumerism, that was thrust to the center of the American experience in the decades after World War II, would not abate anytime in the foreseeable future. Military spending, the funds of which were often loaned to the U.S. by China so that American politicians and economic powerbrokers could forestall the certain backlash associated with raising Americans' taxes, in fact, dwarfed Cold War expenditures during the time *Mad Men* was made and originally aired, which further underscored the American empire's dependence on other nations, thereby exposing the fact that the proverbial emperor had no clothes other than those loaned by the Communist Party of China.

Chapter Seven

"Death, Religion, Consumerism and Utopianism"

In season four, Peggy Olson goes to a party in downtown Manhattan with Joyce, who is a photo editor at *Time Life*; David Kellogg's experimental film, "Holy Eucharist," plays in the background. It artfully depicts missiles being readied for firing. Peggy meets a leftist journalist named Abe Drexler at the party. He later explains to her that "We have a religion in this country and it is business." Peggy tentatively defends her profession by saying, "I'm not a war criminal," in reaction to a story Abe later writes called, "Nuremberg on Madison Avenue," that conflates the Third Reich, the Jewish Holocaust, postwar America's consumerist/militarist society and the nation's war in Indochina. Peggy professes that she's "not a political person." Abe, however, attempts to educate her by saying, "you're a political person whether you think so or not."563 Abe, in short, indicates that commerce, religion, and politics are synonymous.

Lyman Tower Sargent's "Authority & Utopia: Utopianism in Political Thought;" Richard Grenier's "Hollywood's Foreign Policy: Utopianism Tempered by Greed;" and Paul A. Hummert's "Bernard Shaw's Marxist Utopias," all help to elaborate the centrality of utopianism to power and authority during the twentieth century.564 *Mad Men* also, as the paragraph above indicates, pays close attention to the relationship between political power and utopianism promised by religion, including consumerism.

The conflation of postwar American consumerism, religion, and politics is particularly personified in *Mad Men* by the shape-shifting Richard Nixon. In the first season of the show, the then-Vice President's business is up for grabs in the 1960 general election, which is widely considered the first TV campaign in American political history. Sterling & Cooper is desperate to get Nixon's business. For one, both Cooper and Sterling are devout Republicans and as neoliberal as Milton Friedman and Ayn Rand. Nixon, like Dwight Eisenhower, is also a staunch "anti-communist" and "not Catholic," which makes him seem to be a shoo-in for the Oval Office over Kennedy, who is Catholic. "Nixon is from

---

563 Season 4 episode 9 "The Beautiful Girls" September 19, 2010.

564 Lyman Tower Sargent, "Authority & Utopia: Utopianism in Political Thought," *Polity* Vol. 14, No. 4 (Summer, 1982), pp. 565-584. See also Richard Grenier, "Hollywood's Foreign Policy: Utopianism Tempered by Greed," *The National Interest* No. 24 (Summer 1991), pp. 67-77. And Paul A. Hummert, "Bernard Shaw's Marxist Utopias," *The Shaw Review* Vol. 2, No. 9, A Special Perspectives Number: The Later Plays – 1920-1950 (September, 1959), pp. 7-26.

nothing," Don declares as he packages Nixon into a commodity readymade for consumption by the American polity. Nixon is also, Don explains, "a self-made man, the Abe Lincoln of California, who was vice president of the United States six years after getting out of the Navy." Don, conversely, depicts John Kennedy's identity as an elitist trust-fund baby and "recent immigrant who bought his way into Harvard."[565] The show brings things full circle in season six, which is set in the incredibly tumultuous year of 1968, when a fear-mongering law-and-order Nixon commercial plays in the background while the Republican candidate in the 1968 general election cycle urges the silent majority to "vote like your life depended on it" in the interest of rolling back the tide of crime most commonly associated with the urban riots of the mid-1960s.[566]

Later in season six, Don slinks into a darkened bar. A "Nixon is the One" campaign poster adorns the wall. An Evangelist minister hones in on the seemingly lonesome ad-man as he bellies up to the bar as he drinks an Old Fashioned. "What if I told you Jesus can not only offer you eternal life," the itinerant preacher prods Don, "but freedom from pain in this life." Don snidely replies, "I'm doing just fine. Nixon is the president. Everything is back where Jesus wanted it." Don drunkenly goads the preacher and subsequently alludes to the rise of the Religious Right that became the most powerful voting bloc in American politics in the decades after 1968. Don rhetorically asks: Did "he (God) offer the same deal to (the recently shot Robert) Kennedy, Martin Luther King, and Vietnam, for Christ's sake?" Don further incites the

[565] Season 1 episode 10 "Long Weekend" September 27, 2007.

[566] Season 6 episode 12 "The Quality of Mercy" June 16, 2013.

preacher by adding, "Jesus had a bad year." The preacher callously informs Don that, "there's not one true believer on that list," thereby indicating that the murdered luminaries of American history deserved what they got and are surely in hell. The smug and arrogant insensitivity expressed by the Evangelist particularly stokes Don's wrath. "What the hell did you just say?" Don demands of the preacher just before he slips into a childhood memory in which a *Bible*-thumping Evangelist minister visits the brothel where young Dick Whitman resides and explains to the prostitutes in attendance that, "the only unpardonable sin is to believe that God cannot forgive you."[567]

Mad Men, as the paragraphs above indicate, does well to conflate politics and religion, but also to conflate the utopianism promised by religion and consumerism. "Who knows why people in history did good things?" hedonist Roger Sterling says in season five. Roger likewise conflates religion and advertising as similar brands of utopianism when he says, "For all we know, Jesus was trying to get the loaves and fishes account."[568] One distinct commonality between religion and consumerism is mass mobilization. One of the hallmarks of all fascist regimes is likewise mass mobilization. Fascists characteristically attempted to win popular support and consolidate power by mobilizing the masses in fervid meetings, parades, and other grand spectacles. Exploiting principles borrowed from traditional religious ritual and American advertising, which stressed the importance of appealing to the mob's emotions rather than to an individual's sense of reason and

[567] Season 6 episode 13 "In Care Of" June 23, 2013.

[568] Season 5 episode 7 "At The Codfish Ball," April 29, 2012.

rationality, fascists used mass mobilizations to create cultish patriotic fervor and to encourage fanatic enthusiasm for the espoused ideology being marketed to the masses in order to foster allegiance to the state and its leaders. Allegiance to the nation and its leaders (which were often conflated with divinity) promised followers utopia.

Mad Men is, above all, a series that depicts American mass mobilization to the postwar capitalist system, which was fueled most conspicuously by consumerism, which in many ways subsumed religion into the sphere of commoditization. In season one, for instance, shortly after being encouraged to exploit the notion that Americans have an inherent "death wish" that is, supposedly, as powerful as the urge to procreate, in the interest of selling cigarettes, Don explains to executives at Lucky Strike that he sells six identical products. Advertising is thus, he notes, based on one thing: selling happiness. Ads reassure consumers that "whatever you're doing is okay."[569] Don later explains to Rachel Menken that advertising agents invented romantic love to sell nylons. Later in the first season of the series the fetish for the utopianism associated with the Space Age is used to sell Gillette's Right Guard deodorant to men anxious about sweating too much. Don alludes to the fact that the search for new horizons, including the Moon, is fueled by anxiety associated with the specter of nuclear holocaust, whose associated ethos of "enjoy today because tomorrow is not guaranteed" dovetailed nicely with the interests of an economy fueled by conspicuous consumption of products.

[569] Season 1 episode 1 "Smoke Gets in Your Eyes," July 19, 2007.

The most common thread linking Judeo-Christianity, fascism, and postwar American consumerism is the specter of death, and congruent psychological need for utopianism, being central features of each. Thus, *Mad Men* rightly depicts consumerism and religion not in competition, but rather as fueling and reifying each other. The notion of utopia is therefore an especially fertile concept in *Mad Men's* depiction of 1960s America, especially in the realm of religion and consumerism. This chapter, as such, plumbs *Mad Men's* depiction of Christianity, consumerism as a quasi-religion, and the primal urge for utopianism that holistically conflate secularism and spirituality.

Mad Men casts an especially dark and dystopian shadow in its depiction of 1960s America. In season one, for example, an episode is titled "Babylon," which is a dystopia.[570] The following season, Betty Draper reads F. Scott Fitzgerald's *Babylon Revisited* (1931), which points viewers to the interplay between the dystopianism and utopianism that runs throughout the show.[571] In season six, the news of Martin Luther King, Jr's murder is announced during the Clio's Advertising Award Show, which seems to underscore the farce of consumer capitalism and advertising being anything remotely akin to utopian.[572]

The notion of postwar America being consumed with utopianism can be further detected in the season premiere of the final season of *Mad Men* as Don watches the television he recently

[570] Season 1 episode 6 "Babylon" August 23, 2007.

[571] Season 2 episode 4 "Three Sundays" August 17, 2008.

[572] Season 6 episode 5 "The Flood" April 28, 2013.

purchased for his wife's California home as the opening of Frank Capra's *Lost Horizon* (1937), a movie about a group of Westerners who crash land in a hidden Tibetan valley and discover paradise, crawls on his screen:

> "In these days of wars and rumors of wars - haven't you ever dreamed of a place where there was peace and security, where living was not a struggle but a lasting delight? Of course, you have. So has every man since time began. Always the same dream. Sometimes he calls it Utopia -- Sometimes the Fountain of Youth -- Sometimes merely 'that little chicken farm.'"[573]

The utopian chicken farm seems foreshadowed the prior season when Paul Kinsey tells Harry Crane that he dreams of having a little farm with his new love interest, Lakshmi. The overt and subliminal messages that allude to utopianism and dystopianism embedded in *Mad Men* points viewers to the fact that the creators of the show are especially conscious of the utopianism associated with Disneyland and sending men to the moon during the Cold War, both of which drew cultural force by the ever-present threat of nuclear holocaust. Matthew Weiner said as much to Michael Renov in *From Shtetl to Stardom*. "There was a constant discussion that the end of the world was imminent in some way or another and that we might lose," Weiner said. "It's how Ronald Reagan got to be the President."[574]

---

[573] Season 7 episode 1 "Time Zones" April 13, 2014.

[574] Steven J. Ross and Michael Renov, "An Outsider's View of Sixties America: Matthew Weiner Talks with Michael Renov about the Jews of *Mad Men*" in *From Shtetl to Stardom*, (West Lafayette, IN, Purdue University Press,

The specter of imminent death indeed casts a long, dark, and satirical shadow over *Mad Men* every bit as much as it does Stanley Kubrick's in *Dr. Strangelove or: How I Learned to Story Worrying and Love the Bomb* (1964). "We can all learn something from the funeral business," Jim Cutler tells Harry Crane in season seven, as the latter shows the former Jessica Mitford's *The American Way of Death* (1963), a groundbreaking exposé of the American funeral industry, which focused especially on the industry's exorbitant costs and the crass commercialization of death. Death, and often despair, indeed stalks the characters on the show. The series, in fact, is as much about the inherent existential crisis of life, which ultimately culminates in death, as the show is about advertising in 1960s America.

Cancer is especially depicted throughout the show from the first episode to last. Sterling & Cooper, for instance, is dependent on Lucky Strike Cigarettes for the agency's existence in early seasons, which is set in the midst of the surgeon general (federal government) beginning to regulate the tobacco industry. The wife of Dick Whitman's father dies of cancer; Burt's Peterson's wife dies of cancer; Dick Whitman's first wife, Anna, dies of cancer; Frank Gleason dies of cancer; the mother of Sally Draper's classmate, Carol (Juliette Angelo), dies of cancer; Rachel Menken dies of leukemia; and the series concludes with Betty Draper being diagnosed with stage-4 lung cancer and refusing treatment.

Fatalism and utopianism are, in short, both especially central themes in *Mad Men*. The greater the specter of death is, the more

2017), p. 166.

seductive utopianism is to congregant-consumers desperate to make sense of an increasingly violent, senseless, uncertain, and seemingly dystopian reality. Religion and consumerism, as depicted in *Mad Men*, thus seem to be intended as evidence that humans are desperate to find meaning in what seems to be an increasingly uncertain existence in which the specter of nuclear holocaust and cancer makes the notion of utopia, whether packaged as popsicles or Evangelical Christianity, seem more resonant in the decades after World War II than perhaps any other point in American history.

In *Mad Men* death is ultimately what makes the supposed certainty of utopianism – whether consumerist, fascist, or religious – so seductive to the advertisers and consumers depicted on the show. Late in season one, for instance, Roger suffers a heart attack and experiences an existential crisis. "Do you believe in a soul?" He worriedly prods Don. "I wish I was going somewhere" (when he dies).[575] The following season, Roger asks Don if he needs to remind him of the "finite nature of life."[576] Two episodes later, Roger laments that "it's your life, you don't know how long it's going to be but you know it's a bad ending."[577] The season after that, young Sally Draper says to her father, "I'm afraid what's going to happen when you turn off the light."[578] Sally's seemingly

[575] Season 1 episode 10 "Long Weekend" September 27, 2007.

[576] Season 2 episode 7 "The Gold Violin" September 7, 2008.

[577] Season 2 episode 9 "Six Month Leave" September 28, 2008.

[578] Season 3 episode 6 "Guy Walks Into an Advertising Agency" September 20, 2009.

childish fear of the dark actually speaks to a primal fear of the unknown signified by death. After Frank Gleason dies in season six, Peggy, who admits to liking her former boss at Cutler, Gleason and Shaw, does not seem sold on the notion that Frank is "in a better place" now that he is dead.[579] In season four, Don imagines seeing the ghost of Anna Draper (Melinda Page Hamilton) toting a Sampsonite suitcase as if she were set to take a vacation, perhaps to heaven. "She's in a better place," her niece, Stephanie, later says to Don as she breaks the news that her aunt had succumbed to bone cancer. "That's what they say," Don responds, as if doubtful of an afterlife.[580] Five episodes later, Sally tells Glen Bishop of a lucid dream she had in which she flew over London. "It smelled like I was going to heaven," she says, "except I don't believe in it." Glen seems somewhat puzzled as he asks, "Then what happens when you die?"[581] In the season two finale, which is set during the Cuban Missile Crisis, young Father John Gil tells Peggy that he believes God sent him to the parish in Brooklyn to save her soul "from hell." Peggy, however, expresses discomfort with Father Gil's unsolicited proselytizing and explains that she, to paraphrase, does not believe in a petty and vindictive God.[582]

Death and the aching for utopia, and the terror of dystopia, is an especially central feature of the season six premier of *Mad Men*. For example, Don's watch dies in the opening scene of the

[579] Season 6 episode 7 "Man With a Plan" May 12, 2013.

[580] Season 4 episode 7 "The Suitcase" September 5, 2010.

[581] Season 4 episode 12 "Blowing Smoke" October 10, 2010.

[582] Season 2 episode 13 "Meditations in Crisis" October 26, 2008.

episode. Roger's mother also dies later in the episode, which triggers in him an emotional breakdown. Roger also references a door as a metaphor for life and death. But in reality, he says to Don, "it's just a straight line to you know where (death)." Later in the episode Don drunkenly demands to know what Jonesy (Ray Abruzzo), the doorman at the luxury midtown-Manhattan high-rise where he and Megan live, saw while suffering cardiac arrest. Jonsey reluctantly concedes that he did not see anything divine. Still later in the episode, Bob Grange, an executive at The Hawaiian Royal Palm, visits Manhattan to discuss the progress of the advertising campaign Don's agency has been enlisted to craft. Don pitches the campaign with the tagline, "Hawaii, The Jumping Off Point;" a storyboard depicts a businessman's black wingtips, crumpled blue suit, and discarded fedora atop the sandy white beach as lonesome footsteps lead into the blue abyss of the Pacific Ocean. The client is, however, distressed because he feels as though the campaign is "a little morbid." Don seems defensive as he says, "Heaven is a little morbid," because one "has to die" to get to heaven (the utopia). Don later, after the largely unsuccessful meeting, asks resident artist Stan Rizzo, "does that (the storyboard) make you think of suicide?" Stan replies, "Of course it does, that's what is so great about it." Roger then says to Don, "We sold death for twenty-five years with Lucky Strike. You know how? We ignored it." Close to the conclusion of the episode, Dr. Rosen, a world-class cardiologist who has life and death in his hands nearly every day, is called away from Megan's New Year's Eve gathering in order to rush to the hospital for an emergency surgery. "The whole life and death thing," Rosen admits to Don, who seems increasingly obsessed with the concept, "it doesn't bother me… Guys like us," Rosen elaborates, "that's why we get paid. You get paid to think about things people don't want to think about. I get paid not to. People will do anything to alleviate their anxiety." As Rosen leaves on his cross-country skis into a driving snowstorm en route to the hospital, Don immediately takes the elevator to Rosen's apartment and makes love to the cardiologist's wife, Sylvia. A crucifix hangs on the wall over the bed.[583]

Mad Men, in short, depicts utopia and dystopia to be different sides of the same coin. In season one, for instance, Rachel Menken informs Don that "Israel is more of an idea" than an actual place. "The Greeks," she elaborates, "have two meanings of utopia – 'the good place' and also 'the place that can't be.'[584] In the season one finale Don presents an ad campaign for a slide projector to Kodak executives. He defines utopia as "pain from an old wound more powerful than memory alone. This machine (the Kodak wheel)," he adds, "is a time machine. It takes us to a place we long to go again… a place where we are loved."[585]

In season five, both LSD and love are depicted as utopian. Roger Sterling and his wife, Jane, for example, attend a dinner party with urbane and sophisticated intellectuals that seem to be plucked from the pages of Tom Wolfe's *Radical Chic and Mau-Mauing the Flak Catchers* (1970). The cadre assembled at the soiree discuss high-minded concepts such as truth, goodness, love, and the *Tibetan Book of the Dead: A Guide for Dying* (1949). Jane's psychiatrist, who is in attendance at the soiree, explains that "it is a

[583] Season 6 episode 1 "The Doorway" April 7, 2013.

[584] Season 1 episode 6 "Babylon" August 23, 2007.

[585] Season 1 episode 13 "Wheel" October 18, 2007.

myth that tracing logic all the way down to the truth is a cure for neurosis or anything else." Jane affably asks, "is there a cure for neurosis?" A party attendee, who later crawls on the floor declaring, "I don't want to die," smiles warmly as she says, "Love works." Roger later hallucinates seeing Don at the gathering; Don assures Roger that, "Everything is okay. You are okay... Now go to your wife. She wants to be alone in the truth with you."[586]

The utopian assurance that no matter what one is doing "it is okay" is a recurring theme throughout the show. In season one, for example, Don explains to Lucky Strike Cigarette executives that all "advertising is based on one thing: happiness. And you know what happiness is?" he asks. "Happiness is the smell of a new car; it's freedom from fear; it's a billboard at the side of the road that screams with reassurance that whatever you're doing, it's okay... You are okay."[587] In the season one finale Betty cries and tells Glen Bishop how sad she is and urges him to assure her that things will be okay. But he seems terribly doubtful.[588] A season later, Freddy Rumsen, who has been forced out of Sterling & Cooper due to alcoholism, assures Don that "everything is going to be okay."[589] The following season, Don assures Betty at Margaret's wedding, which is set during John Kennedy's funeral, that "everything is going to be fine." She pessimistically responds, "how do you know that?" as if Don is simply telling another of many lies or selling her

[586] Season 5 episode 6 "Far Away Places" April 22, 2012.

[587] Season 1 episode 1 "Smoke Gets In Your Eyes" July 19, 2007.

[588] Season 1 episode 13 "The Wheel" October 18, 2007.

[589] Season 2 episode 9 "Six Month Leave" September 28, 2008.

a product. In season four, Megan promises Sally, who is suffering an existential crisis caused by the onset of puberty, that everything is "going to be alright." Sally, who begins to understand the inherent suffering associated with mortality after her grandfather's death in season three, echoes her mother's pessimism when she says quite matter-of-factly, "no, it's not." In the same episode, Roger assures Joan that "it" will be okay. "People love to say that," she responds, as if to disagree.[590] Two episodes later Megan assures Don that he will "get through" his own existential crisis and that everything is going "to be okay." Echoing his daughter from two episodes prior, Don says, "You don't know that."[591] In season five, Betty has a cancer scare; while waiting to get the results of her test back from a world renowned oncologist, she urges Don to assuage her fears by saying "that thing you always say." He then assures her, "Everything's going to be okay."[592] Late in the final season of *Mad Men* Roger assures Don that he is "okay" at McCann-Erickson not long before his friend heads west.[593] In the series finale of the show the theme of "you are okay" resurfaces one last time as Don tells Stephanie to put the past behind her and move forward. He promises her that "it'll get easier" the further away she runs from the problem (not having custody of her infant son). "I don't think you're right about that," Stephanie says shortly before abandoning

[590] Season 4 episode 9 "The Beautiful Girls" September 19, 2010.

[591] Season 4 episode 11 "Chinese Wall" October 3, 2010.

[592] Season 5 episode 3 "The Tea Leaves" April 1, 2012.

[593] Season 7 episode 11 "Time & Life" April 26, 2015. The mythic American west has long been associated with utopianism and new beginnings. It is also a common theme in *Mad Men*.

Don at a New Age retreat on the coast of California.[594] The irony is that Don is constantly running from one problem to another, yet never really getting to a higher spiritual plane.

The utopianism associated with traditional western religion, particularly Judaism and Christianity, is also centrally featured on *Mad Men*. Eastern religion and New Ageism, as the paragraph above speaks to, also grows somewhat central to the series in later episodes. Despite the affluence commonly associated with postwar American society, *Mad Men* depicts Americans as especially angst ridden in part due to the specter of total annihilation and mutually assured destruction that were at the forefront of Americans' collective consciousness during the Cold War. Ancient religions coupled with the modern pleasures promised by consumerism were increasingly conflated as the breakdown of the traditional family grew more profoundly common in the American experience in the decades after World War II. Both religion and consumerism were, as *Mad Men* helps to illuminate, utopian and ultimately designed in part to capitalize on people's desperation to cope with the reality that life is, above all, a process of dying. But utopianism, whether packaged as fascism, consumerism, or eastern and/or western religion, is viewed in *Mad Men* with great skepticism and, ultimately, depicted as inseparable from business.

Christianity is especially central to *Mad Men's* depiction of 1960s American society. No one man personifies Evangelicalism and big business in *Mad Men* more than Conrad Hilton. In season three, Hilton unexpectedly drops by Don's midtown Manhattan office early one morning. "You need a *Bible* and pictures of your

[594] Season 7 episode 7 "Person to Person" May 15, 2015.

family," Hilton grills the polite but unreceptive ad man.[595] Don seems to particularly view Christianity with skepticism, if not disdain. Early in season four, for example, he visits Anna Draper and her niece, Stephanie, in California. Stephanie laments that her roommate at the University of California at Berkeley woke her one morning to creepily ask, "Have you heard the good news?" Anna laughs as she says, "There are worse (roommates)." Don matter-of-factly replies, "No there aren't."[596] A few episodes later Don's geriatric secretary, Mrs. Blankenship, references born again Christian discourse when she refers to her recent eye surgery, "I was blind," she quips. "Now I see."[597] The following season Pete Campbell develops a crush on a recent high school graduate in his driver's education course. He had previously told her about a botanical garden his patrician family had a hand in building several years earlier. He later reminds her that she promised to save a Sunday to visit the gardens with him. "What about Church?" she says, while gently trying to reject him. "God's all over the Gardens," he replies.[598] In season three, Sally asks her mother, "Why don't we go to church? Carla's family goes every Sunday." Betty explains, "We don't need to go every week," indicating that she is perhaps freer from sin than her maid's family.[599] Betty's hardly-concealed defensiveness and guilty conscience points to the

[595] Season 3 episode 10 "The Color Blue" October 18, 2009.

[596] Season 4 episode 3 "The Good News" August 8, 2010.

[597] Season 4 episode 8 "The Summer Man" September 12, 2010.

[598] Season 5 episode 4 "Signal 30" April 8, 2012.

[599] Season 3 episode 10 "The Color Blue" October 18, 2009.

fact that white Protestant Americans regularly attended church far less in the decades after World War II than at any point in the country's history. Religion, as Pete and Betty's comments likewise allude to, was largely subsumed by and/or conflated with consumerism in the postwar period. Church thus became less and less of a cultural institution central to Americans' daily lives throughout the 1960s, especially compared to the cultural force of network television. Church, in short, ceased to have the aura of utopian sanctuary from the outside world that it had for so many in previous generations due, in part, to the fact that it was increasingly subsumed by consumerism. The diminished cultural importance of organized religion in the decades following World War II is often, rightly or not, associated with the perceived breakdown of the traditional family.

Mad Men depicts myriad broken families, including the Drapers, Sterlings, Phillips, the Bishops and several others. The breakdown of traditional religious values, including the nuclear family, is a common theme meticulously explored in *Mad Men*. In season six, for instance, Don wakes suddenly in a dark and seedy Manhattan drunk tank, where he was evidently taken after assaulting the preacher who declared that Martin Luther King, Jr. was a faux Christian. "You should be in Rikers (Island) for punching a minister," a surly bailiff grills Don. Moments later in the same episode, Betty Draper expresses deep and profound regret that her daughter, Sally, is increasingly acting out because she is the product of "a broken home."[600]

[600] Season 6 episode 13 "In Care Of" June 23, 2013.

Mad Men hints at advertisers playing a central role in the breakdown of the traditional family. In season two, for instance, Belle Jolie rejects Harry's idea of advertising the cosmetics company during a controversial episode of *The Defenders* that depicts a young girl contemplating abortion. "Belle Jolie is a family company," Elliot Lawrence, a Belle Jolie executive who is also a closeted homosexual, says, "this is not wholesome."[601] In season four, bathing suit company Jantzen resists making their bikini smaller because they are a "family company."[602] In season seven, Peggy – who, in season two, gave her child up for adoption in order to pursue her career – notes the fact that the concept of family has been forever altered as a result of consumerism as she explains her Burger Chef idea to Pete and Don as they share a "family meal" at the fast food restaurant.[603]

At the start of season six, Don reads *The Inferno* on a Hawaiian beach, which was given to him by Sylvia, a married and devout Catholic he has an affair with. The notion of devout women being sexually promiscuous is referenced again two episodes later when Dawn says to Shirley that it is impossible to standout (in Church in order to attract a man) in that group of harlots." Later in the episode, Don urges Sylvia, his neighbor, to remove the crucifix around her neck before they have sex. "I pray for you to find peace," she says just before he slides the crucifix behind her neck

---

[601] Season 2 episode 2 "Flight 1" August 3, 2008.

[602] Season 4 episode 1 "Out of Town" August 16, 2008.

[603] Season 7 episode 6 "The Strategy" May 18, 2014.

and kisses her.[604] Promiscuous women and philandering men are, however, depicted in *Mad Men* as both symptom and disease of the breakdown of the traditional Judeo-Christian family, in which the man was the primary breadwinner and well-to-do white women largely stayed home. In season seven, Peggy is filled with angst about selling Burger Chef an ad campaign that celebrates the nuclear family. "Does this family even exist anymore? Are there really people who eat dinner together and smile instead of watching TV?" she asks.[605] Peggy scoffs at the idea of Burger Chef executives being seduced by ads that seem to champion the nuclear family as the cornerstone of postwar American life. Three episodes later she laments having to pitch the traditional Judeo-Christian family in order to sell hamburgers a day after "man touches the face of God" (the Apollo 11 moon landing). Her presentation particularly speaks to the increased anxiety associated with the perceived breakdown of traditional religion and "family values" in modern American society as a result of consumerism, which helped fuel the resurgent political conservatism of Evangelical Christians in the 1970s and 1980s. "Vietnam on in the background, the TV wins every night," Peggy says as she regales Burger Chef executives with her sales pitch. "We can have the connection we are craving for… There may be chaos at home, but there is Burger Chef for dinner."[606]

[604] Season 6 episode 4 "To Have and Hold" April 21, 2013.

[605] Season 7 episode 6 "The Strategy" May 18, 2014.

[606] Season 7 episode 7 "Waterloo" May 25, 2014.

The perceived anxiety associated with the breakdown of traditional religion and family values is further expressed five episodes later when Don goes to Wisconsin in the hope of finding his most recent lover, Diana Baur (Elizabeth Reaser), who has disappeared. "I lost my daughter to God and my wife to the devil," Diana's ex-husband, Cliff (Mackenzie Astin), concedes to Don. "You can't save her," Cliff adds, "only Jesus can. He can help you too."[607] Don, however, as alluded to in season one when Bert Cooper urges him to read Ayn Rand's libertarian classic, *Atlas Shrugged*, seems to believe only in business.[608]

But religion and business, particularly consumerism, are often conflated in *Mad Men*, which exacerbates Don's enduring existential crisis. In season one, for instance, beatnik Roy Hazelitt impugns Don, "You hucksters (ad men) created religion and mass consumption."[609] Though it is a bit of a stretch to say ad men created religion, they surely helped conflate it with big business in the decades after World War II. Part of the reason for Billy Graham's incredible commercial success during the Cold War was the showman's skillful use of mass media to market himself and his message at a moment in human history when mutually assured nuclear destruction made the notion of religious redemption and revivalism especially resonant to millions of terrified Americans clamoring to make sense of what seemed to be an increasingly

[607] Season 7 episode 12 "Lost Horizons" May 3, 2015.

[608] Season 1 episode 13 "The Wheel" October 18, 2007.

[609] Season 1 episode 6 "Babylon" August 23, 2007.

mechanistic and dystopian reality hurling humanity towards oblivion.

Mad Men, in short, makes it seem as though the advertising industry is complicit in the sadistic specter of Cold War nuclear holocaust. Mrs. Blankenship, Don's elderly secretary says to Peggy "this (the advertising industry) is the business of sadists and masochists," not long before dying at her desk. Just after the sixteenth minute in the same episode, Sally sits in the lobby of the midtown Manhattan high-rise where her father's agency is located; outside the window is "666" emblazoned in big bold black print just above Abe Drexler's head. The point that the "666" is directly over Abe's head seems particularly significant because he has just dropped off an article he wrote entitled "Nuremberg on Madison Avenue" to his new love interest, Peggy. The title of the story is an obvious allusion to the Jewish Holocaust. The "666" high above Madison Avenue, however, also seems to subliminally indicate that the American advertising industry represents the same banality of evil associated with the Nazis. [610] Two seasons later, Sally reads *Rosemary's Baby* (1967), a book made into a movie by child rapist Roman Polanski, whose pregnant wife, Sharon Tate, was murdered in 1969 by the Manson Family.[611] Consumerism, as the subliminal "666" outside the window of the agency alludes, did not replace but rather repackaged, Judeo-Christian notions of good and evil, and utopia and dystopia, and is, ultimately, evidence of the

[610] Season 4 episode 9 "The Beautiful Girls" September 19, 2010.

[611] Season 6 episode 8 "The Crash" May 19, 2013.

continuity that actually collapses the distinction between ancient and modern in the realm of consumerism.

Old time Christianity, like Judaism, is also often depicted as commoditized in *Mad Men*. In season one, for instance, Don grows especially impatient with a reluctant client. "You're a nonbeliever," Don impatiently fumes. "Why should we waste time on Kabuki? You've tried your plan; you're number four. I'm not here to tell you about Jesus. You already know about Jesus. He either lives in your heart or he doesn't." Later in the episode, Don has a childhood flashback set during the Great Depression in which he recalls his father telling a transient hobo, "We're not Christians here anymore." The episode concludes with the folk gospel hymn, "(Gimme That) Old Time Religion."[612] The lyrics are as follows:

"It was good for the Hebrew children
It's good enough for me
It was good for dad and mother
And it's good enough for me.
It will do when I am dying'
Gimme that old time religion
It's good enough for me"[613]

The Jim Reeves song is a prime example of one of the myriad ways in which

---

[612] Season 1 episode 8 "The Hobo Code" September 6, 2007.

[613] J Baird and Jim Reeves, "(Gimme That) Old Time Religion," (Nashville, TN, Warner/Chappell Music, Inc).

communication technology (such as the gramophone, radio, television, et cetera) helped to transform religion into a commodity.[614]

Episode four of season two opens with Peggy, who is hungover, and her family attending mass at The Church of the Holy Innocents. The priest rails against "indulging in pleasures of the flesh...The rational soul," he says, "is supported by the cross of Christ." Peggy soon excuses herself from mass and happens upon Father John Gil, who is close to her age, in the narthex. Father Gil informs Peggy that he is in need of her marketing acumen in order to attract young congregants to Youth Group functions, which gives viewers a sense of the increased syncretism of religion and consumerism (and ancient/modern) in the postwar period.

The exchange between Peggy and Father Gil also alludes to the Second Vatican Council, informally known as Vatican II, which lasted from 1962 to 1965. Vatican II addressed strained relations between the Catholic Church and the modern world. The Church had often aided and abetted fascist regimes, including Germany and Italy, in the years before and during World War II. The Church's long held claim to moral authority was thus terribly diminished in the wake of the war. In the postwar period the Church's popularity, institutional importance, and power went into swift and steep recess all around the world. In other words, the Church had a branding problem that the clergy was desperate to address. Peggy, who represents mass marketers, ultimately helps Father Gil, who represents the Church, a great deal by writing his Palm Sunday Sermon, which was very well received. "I felt like I

---

[614] See Alex Hall, "'A Way of Revealing:' Technology and Utopianism in Contemporary Culture," *The Journal of Technology Studies* Vol. 35, No. 1 (Fall 2009), pp. 58-66.

was the only one you were talking to," Peggy's mother, Katherine (Myra Turley), says to Father Gil after the sermon. The notion of an ad making the consumer feel as though it is directed solely at that particular consumer is earlier defined by Peggy as the basis of a great ad. Peggy's mom, in other words, is unwittingly drawing the connection that religion is consumerism and vice versa;[615] both shill utopianism.

Later in season two, the conflation of religion and consumerism continues as Peggy and Salvatore are tasked with marketing popsicles while Don is on the lam in California in the wake of the dissolution of his marriage to Betty. "You break the popsicle in two, like Jesus at the last supper," Salvatore says. Peggy adds that, "The ritual… it's like communion… The Catholic Church sure knows how to sell things." *Mad Men* here clearly depicts ancient religion and modern consumerism not in competition, but rather feeding and reifying the other.[616] The theme is further elaborated in the finale of season two when Father Gil preaches a message of taking control of one's own soul to the congregants at The Church of Holy Innocents; "We are all sinners," Father Gil's voice fills the nave, "every one of us. The one thing that unites all, according to Christians, is that all are sinners," much like all are consumers.[617]

In season three, consumerism and Christianity, continue to be conflated, though more subliminally. Henry Francis, for

[615] Season 2 episode 4 "Three Sundays" August 17, 2008.

[616] Season 2 episode 12 "The Mountain King" October 19, 2008.

[617] Season 2 episode 13 "Meditations in Crisis" October 26, 2008.

instance, is called away to do business on behalf Nelson Rockefeller, who is in the midst of a primary election campaign against Barry Goldwater and George Romney. "His master's voice," Henry says to Betty, thereby alluding to the classic 1930s RCA Radio commercial in which a curious dog listens intently to a gramophone. Henry, in short, artfully explains to his wife that Rockefeller is his master and that the underling is at his beck and call, which merges politics and consumerism with religion. Smitty Smith likewise conveys the same message the previous season when he says, "His master's voice" to Don.[618] Two episodes after Henry alludes to the RCA ad, Conrad Hilton lectures Don about the importance of regularly talking to God. "Do you ever pray on things?" Hilton asks Don. "God speaks and we act on it," Hilton adds. Don, like Henry and Smitty, alludes to the RCA commercial when he snidely quips, "So you're just like a dog?"[619]

Consumerism is, in *Mad Men*, often tangled up in religion much like ancient and modern are often conflated in the form of nostalgia and vintage. In season five, for instance, Don brainstorms ideas to market Snoball Ice Cream by imagining the devil boasting, "it's sinfully delicious."[620] In the first season of the Emmy Award winning series Salvatore Romano likewise pitches Don an idea for selling Israeli tourism as "glamorous" by having Moses part the Red Sea to reveal a utopian four-star resort.[621] In the season three

[618] Season 2 episode 1 "For Those Who Think Young" July 27, 2008.

[619] Season 3 episode 9 "Wee Small Hours" October 11, 2009.

[620] Season 5 episode 9 "Dark Shadows" May 13, 2012.

[621] Season 1 episode 6 "Babylon" August 23, 2007.

finale, Bobby and Sally Draper intently watch a Christmas program on television, which further underscores the conflation of Christianity and consumerism in postwar American society.[622] As Vatican II and the commercialization of formerly Pagan-turned-Christian holidays such as Easter and Christmas help to illuminate, traditional religion was profoundly subsumed by modernist consumerism in the decades after World War II. The point is further underscored in season one when the Israeli Tourist Board enlists Don to produce an ad campaign because he was the man responsible for seducing countless Christians/consumers to Rio de Janeiro, Brazil, by associating the Christ the Redeemer Statue with the city and nation.[623]

But Eastern as well as Western religion are both ultimately treated by the creators of *Mad Men* with minimally concealed skepticism and contempt. Paul Kinsey, for example, returns to the show late in season five after a long hiatus. During his absence, he has become a member of the Hare Krishnas sect of Hinduism, which, by the late-1960s, had a massive following throughout the world, including the United States and England (as evidence by the organization's influence on The Beatles). Krishna is, however, treated with the same veiled condescension that Western religions tend to be depicted in *Mad Men*. "I don't understand why I have to live that way (in austerity) to love God," Kinsey confides to Harry Crane. Kinsey experiences an existential crisis rooted in not "feeling Krishna's love," but desperately wanting to continue his sexual relationship and what he believes to be a budding partnership with

[622] Season 3 episode 13 "Shut the Door. Have a Seat" November 8, 2009.

[623] Season 1 episode 9 "Shoot" September 13, 2007.

Lakshmi, the young woman who seduced him into the organization. Kinsey explains to Harry that he only joined the movement after "degrading" himself terribly. "Nobody likes me," he admits, "but Lakshmi." Lakshmi later assails Harry for wanting to make Kinsey "into a gross materialist when he's living in the spiritual world." The notion that the Krishnas are, like the Evangelist Christian minister Don punches in the face in season six, ultimately selling fearful consumers facing the specter of mortality nothing but hollow utopian fantasies, is expressed when Lakshmi informs Harry that Kinsey "is our best closer," she says. "He really can close."[624]

The dystopian and fatalist notion that life is a process of dying is fertile field for utopianism, whether masked as Eastern or Western religion, or as conspicuous consumption and conformity. The most distinct commonality between Marxism, fascism, religion, and consumerism is that all shill the notion of utopianism to people forced to confront the dystopian reality of travail leading to certain death. As *Mad Men* makes plain, politics, religion, and business cannot be pried apart. And rather than being in competition as secular modern consumerism versus ancient traditional religion, *Mad Men* artfully depicts a fusion of the ancient and modern in the increased conflation of politics, religion and consumerism in postwar American society, all of which are informed by the dystopian fear and reality of inevitable death.

Chapter Eight

---

[624] Season 5 episode 10 "Christmas Waltz" May 20, 2012.

"*Mad Men*, the Culture Industry, and the Vanishing Border Between High and Low Art"

High art, which is sometimes contrasted with low art, appeals predominately to experts such as art critics, art historians, scholars and curators, rather than to the often pejoratively referred to "masses." Low art, in contrast to high art, includes pop music, blockbuster movies, and advertisements, all of which are often deemed to lack texture, subtlety, sophistication, and nuance in contrast to high art. So, what does one make of *Mad Men*, a television show made for the masses? Is it high or low art? Can television, which is a medium made primarily to sell ad space, ideology, and products, even be high art?

Stephen Bayley of the *Telegraph* describes *Mad Men* as not just superb television, but art.[625] Mary McNamara of *The Los Angeles Times* hails *Mad Men* for "bringing high art to the masses."[626] In several scenes of *Mad Men*, framed advertisements adorn the walls of offices next to abstract expressionist paintings, the juxtaposition of which seems to illuminate that the creators of the series are conscious of the complex challenges of attempting to make high art in a low art medium, to ultimately sell products and the very idea of consumerism itself. Although *Mad Men*, at times, reeks of a melodrama, together with the fact that it is a commercial juggernaut that hocks myriad consumer goods (such as Lucky Strike Cigarettes, Heineken Beer, General Motors, Buick, Jaguar,

[625] Stephen Bayley, "Mad Men was more than just superb TV - it was art," (*The Telegraph*, May 17, 2015.

[626] Mary McNamara, "'*Mad Men's*' true legacy: Bringing high art to the TV masses," (May 9, 2014).

Ortho Pharmaceuticals, Dow Chemical, Topaz, Ponds, Avon, Nabisco, Life Cereal, and dozens of others) the show is also cloaked in the trappings of high art, such as allegory, symbolism, subliminal messages, and is often beautifully shot and edited.

In other ways *Mad Men* evinces the characteristic of high art; it even has a number of references to high art, such as Mark Rothko's abstract expressionist paintings and Frank O'Hara's poetry, and myriad other references that might otherwise go unnoticed by the so called "masses." In season two, for instance, a drunken Freddy Rumsen plays a Mozart tune with the zipper of his pants, which seems to be the show's creators' tongue-in-cheek way of expressing – much like the abstract expressionism next to framed print ads on the walls of offices -- a consciousness of *Mad Men* blurring the line between high and low art, concomitant to blurring the line between art and commoditized product.

The show's use of doors as metaphor for the beginning and end of life, and as a metonym of the existential crisis of life being a process of dying, is evidence that the show does indeed have moments of being genuinely high art, even though it is ultimately made for the masses. In season six and seven doors grow increasingly important to conveying meaning in terms of new horizons and closed chapters (including music by the band The Doors), all used as literary devices. The numerous dance numbers on the show, such as Pete and Trudy Campbell's rendition of the Charleston, followed by Roger Sterling's performance of "My Old Kentucky Home,"[627] and Joan Harris's accordion solo in season

---

[627] Season 3 episode 3 "My Old Kentucky Home" August 30, 2009.

three;[628] Megan Draper's *Zou Bisou Bisou* performance in season five;[629] Ken Cosgrove's tap dance numbers,[630] and Roger's juggling act in season six;[631] Megan's dance number with a hipster at her party;[632] and Don and Peggy's slow dance to Frank Sinatra's "My Way" in season seven;[633] followed an episode later by Bert Cooper's "The Best Things in Life Are Free" song and dance number,[634] all of which are wedged into the storyline of the show without pushing the plot forward, particularly seem to speak to the fact that the creators of *Mad Men* have fun with the idea of being high art in a low art medium. The show's numerous references to Broadway performances, reference to *America Hurrah*, and especially the unidentified drag queen in the Mache cake who receives raucous applause from drunken American Veterans of Foreign Wars late in season seven all likewise point to the creators of *Mad Men* making satire, and, arguably, high art.[635]

As much as the creators of *Mad Men* toy with whether the show is or is not high or low art, or simply a sophisticated commercial, the show actually criticizes the advertising industry it

[628] Ibid.

[629] Season 5 episode 1 "A Little Kiss" March 25, 2012.

[630] Season 6 episode 8 "The Crash" May 19, 2013.

[631] Season 6 episode 10 "Favors" June 9, 2013.

[632] Season 7 episode 5 "The Runaways" May 11, 2014.

[633] Season 7 episode 6 "The Strategy" May 18, 2014.

[634] Season 7 episode 7 "Waterloo" May 25, 2014.

[635] Season 7 episode 14 "Person to Person" May 17, 2015.

simultaneously romanticizes. Anna Draper's niece, Stephanie, for instance – who majors in political science at the University of California at Berkeley during the free speech movement -- tells Don that advertising is "pollution." Don explains to her that her generation is the driving force in advertising, as if she is as culpable in the "pollution" as ad men are.[636] Perhaps one of the greatest subliminal messages that speaks to the point that the creators of *Mad Men* quite self-consciously poke fun at the notion of the series being high art trapped in a medium made for the all-consuming masses can be detected ever so subtly in the season four premier as Joey Baird and Peggy Olson seductively say "John" and "Marsha" to each other on a few occasions in husky and melodramatic tones, as if the pair share a private joke.[637] "John" and "Marsha," however, speaks to the incredible research and hidden meaning embedded in *Mad Men*. In 1951, comedian Stan Freberg recorded an album titled *John and Marsha* that, in part, parodied the soap operatic language stylistically employed by Peggy and Joey early in season four. Freberg later became an ad man himself, working on Madison Avenue in the 1960s. The references to *John and Marsha* thus speak to the point that *Mad Men* is a critique of melodrama at the same time it is a melodrama, as well as a commercial as it critiques the commercialization of art.

The creators of *Mad Men* can be compared to Andy Warhol and Banksy in the sense that their product makes light of its own commoditization and consumer spectacle. The point seems underscored further close to the end of the series as Peggy informs

[636] Season 4 episode 3 "The Good News" August 8, 2010.

[637] Season 4 episode 1 "Public Relations" July 25, 2010.

Don that she dreams of "creating something with lasting value." Don scoffs, "You think you're going to do that in advertising?"[638] Peggy's line and Don's retort seem to speak to the show's creators' quandary in creating high art for the television masses and ultimately selling advertising space (commercials) on *AMC*. The Coca-Cola commercial Don imagines at the very end of the series seems to be Matthew Weiner and the other creators' acknowledgment that *Mad Men* was as much a name brand and elaborate commercial as it was art.[639]

In season four, for instance, Sally Draper mentions the Land 'O Lakes Indian holding a box of herself holding a box of herself.[640] Also in season four Peggy's friend, Joyce, introduces her to artist David Kellogg at a party in downtown Manhattan. Peggy suggests that Kellogg might, perhaps, be interested in doing some work for the ad agency where she makes a living. "Art and advertising?" Kellogg smugly asks, "Why would anyone do that after Warhol?"[641] Sally's mentioning of the Land 'O Lakes box and Kellogg's snide comment help to demonstrate that the makers of *Mad Men* are clearly self-referential towards the duality embedded in *Mad Men* as a result of trying to be high art for the consuming masses. The same can be said of the show's numerous references to soap operas, such as *Peyton Place* and *Dark Shadows*, both of which were popular during the 1960s, as well as the fact that Don's wife,

[638] Season 7 episode 10 "The Forecast" April 19, 2015.

[639] Season 7 episode 14 "Person to Person" May 17, 2015.

[640] Season 4 episode 12 "Blowing Smoke" October 10, 2010.

[641] Season 4 episode 4 "The Rejected" August 15, 2010.

Megan, who seems offended by the commercialization or art, is a soap star in season six.

The constraints of making art for a television audience, and the process of advertising are poignantly alluded to in season two when Harry Crane tries to convince Belle Jolie to buy ad space during an episode of *The Defenders,* which broaches the controversial subject of abortion. Belle Jolie is impressed with the boldness of Harry's idea to buy ad space during the airing of the show. But Belle Jolie, in a scene reminiscent of Admiral Television refusing to be an "integrated company" in season three, balks at the idea of buying cheaper ad space during the controversial show because it is a "family company" and abortion is "not wholesome."[642] The Belle Jolie abortion controversy speaks to the constraints of corporate hierarchy, family values discourse, et cetera, that dictates the boundaries of what can and cannot be traversed on television. In other words, television might be considered an art form, yet it is ultimately designed to sell products. Television was not designed to propagate revolutionary art that might lead to the eventual toppling of the economic and political system it perpetuates.

The duality and tension between individual liberty promised by consumerism and Cold War conformity in postwar American society is particularly elaborated by the specter of the Vietnam War in season six of the series. Don, his young wife Megan, and the producers on her soap opera, for instance, dine at an upscale Manhattan restaurant where they discuss the *Smothers Brothers* controversy, which ensued after the comedians' public

[642] Season 2 episode 3 "The Benefactor" August 10, 2008.

criticism of the Vietnam War. "I think the sponsors are for the war," the producer (Ted McGinley) of Megan's soap opera says. "They don't want any dissent… This is censorship." Don defends the sponsors by explaining, "When you buy an ad you are hoping the consumer is in a good mood when they hear your message. If you agree on a wholesome variety show and all of a sudden it is a satire (like *Mad Men*), the most threatening humor there is, you're worried about people hating what you're selling."[643] Don's line illuminates how consumer culture affects politics and vice versa. The exchange is also a reminder that free speech of artists is often conscribed and marginalized by the culture in which the artist exists without the artist even being aware of it. The lines above regarding censorship of artists such as the creators of *Mad Men*, who were actually discouraged from using the word abortion by *AMC* executives fearful of alienating conservative consumers, speaks to the limitations placed on artists who make commercial products, such as television programs, for the masses.[644] No matter how sophisticated or brilliant, high art for the masses is inevitably captive to the condition it diagnoses. In other words, all art is captive to the form, which is captive to consumer capitalism.

The blurred line between art and consumer spectacle, as well as between commercial and show (work of art), is especially alluded to late in the final season of the show when Pima Ryan (Mimi Rogers), an acclaimed photographer hired to shoot an ad for the agency, says to Stan Rizzo, "All art is selling something." Stan

[643] Season 6 episode 4 "To Have and Hold" April 21, 2013.

[644] James Poniewozik, "Making History: A Q & A with *Mad Men's* Matthew Weiner." *TIME*, March 27, 2014.

matter-of-factly replies, "No... we're actually selling something; today it's vermouth."[645] This seems to be the creators of *Mad Men* telling their audience that 'we are artists but also pitchmen.' *Mad Men* is also self-referential in the sense that the creators of the show highlight being bound by the constraints of the art form (primetime television) as they point consumers to the ways in which marketers seek to exploit their fears, hopes, dreams and anxieties. The fact that the show somewhat demystifies the process of exploiting consumers is what makes the show a groundbreaking work of art, even in light of the franchise's shameless hocking of consumer products, such as the *Mad Men* clothing line at Banana Republic.

But *Mad Men* also alludes to the exploitative nature of consumerism, especially ads that promise social mobility for consumers. "It's a great sin to take advantage of people's hopes," Marie says to Megan in response to her daughter being sent a letter suggesting she purchase sessions of advanced acting classes in order to land an agent and gain entry into the industry. Megan had thought she had found an agent and congruent promise of social mobility, but instead was sold a bill of goods.[646] *Mad Men*, in short, on numerous occasions pulls the proverbial curtain back on the culture industry, which exploits consumers by shilling empty promises of happiness, hope, freedom, and mobility, regardless of the actual product being marketed.

The duality between high and low art in *Mad Men* thus mirrors postwar America's duality between liberty and

[645] Season 7 episode 9 "New Business" April 12, 2015.

[646] Season 5 episode 13 "The Phantom" June 10, 2012.

authoritarianism. The creators of *Mad Men* seem conscious of this fact with their uses of abstract expressionism and allusions to the New York School, both of which determinedly sought to be revolutionary. The art, especially the abstract expressionism on the interior walls at the ad agency, speaks to the theme of individual liberty versus fascism that is a prominently portrayed throughout *Mad Men*. This duality can particularly be discerned in season two when Paul Kinsey describes the Mark Rothko painting hanging in Bert Cooper's office as "abstract expressionism," to which Harry Crane replies, "what the hell does that mean?"[647] Viewers of *Mad Men* with a background in art history may have been particularly fascinated by the abundance of abstract expressionist paintings on the walls at the advertising agencies and in many homes depicted on the show. The backdrop of most of Don and Peggy's presentations to clients, for example, is usually an abstract expressionist painting. Conversely, however, art in the homes of conservatives such as the Dykman and Francis families and in high-end restaurants, tends to be patrician portraits or impressionistic landscapes. At the wake of David Montgomery in season four, and at the funeral held for Roger Sterling's mother in season six, two separate transcendentalist paintings depicting a lonesome tempest tossed wooden ship helps to illuminate that the works of art displayed in the background are not merely props, decoration, or simply meant to set an atmosphere;[648] the art is actually meant to deep convey meaning.

[647] Season 2 episode 7 "The Gold Violin" September 7, 2007.

[648] Season 6 episode 1 "The Doorway" April 7, 2013.

The value (or lack thereof) of art is also often alluded to in *Mad Men*. In season three, for example, as Sterling, Cooper, Draper, and Pryce wage a July Fourth-weekend coup against Putnam, Powell, and Lowe (the British firm that recently acquired it), a presumably pricey abstract expressionist painting is left behind on the floor of Don's office, which might be a jab at the value (or lack thereof) of modern art.[649] In the season five premier, Roger gives Harry more than $1,000 (which is pocket change for Sterling) to trade offices with Pete, an account man who often hosts clients. "Here," Roger says to Harry as he hands his surly underling the wad of cash, "you can buy a pretty picture to look at."[650] A painting of a Roman victory arch and a statue of a conquistador adorn Harry's office in subsequent episodes. In season two, Don compares the crass comedian Jimmy Barrett, whom he hates, to an artist in the employ of the Medici Family during the Italian Renaissance. Later in the season, Jane Siegal, Salvatore Romano, and Kenny Cosgrove sneak into Cooper's office to look at his newly purchased Rothko painting. "I'm an artist," Salvatore says as he struggles to make sense of the masterpiece, "it must have meaning." Ken (who moonlights as a short story writer) adds, "I don't think it is supposed to be explained. I think you're supposed to feel something… It's like looking into something very deep. You could fall in."[651] The very next scene after Jane, Sal, and Kenny discuss the Rothko painting in Cooper's office, the transition shot leading into the next scene scales the side of a high-rise building

[649] Season 3 episode 13 "Shut the Door. Have a Seat" November 8, 2009.

[650] Season 5 episode 1 "A Little Kiss" March 25, 2012.

[651] Season 2 episode 7 "The Gold Violin" September 7, 2008.

leading up to a partly cloudy sky. The sleek and shiny geometric squares of the building take up half the screen and the natural sky the other. The shot is abstract expressionist.[652] Two seasons later, Freddy Rumsen says, "I feel like I'm getting sucked into this thing," as he gazes at the black and white polka dot piece adorning a wall in Roger's office.[653] A season later, Michael Ginsberg says to Roger, "I like the connect the dots," in reference to the piece in his boss' office, "what does it end up being?" Roger replies, "Actually, it's reminiscent of certain experiences with some people."[654]

Mad Men has been revered for the show's painstaking attention to detail, including ice cubes hand-cut to smaller 1960s dimensions; nicotine stains painted on the fingers of actors; furniture, clothing, kitchenware, and whiskey tumblers that are all genuine vintage items, not replicas; even real fruit, when used, was selected to match the size of produce from the bygone era that predates genetic modification.[655] It seems evident, then, that abstract expressionist paintings in Mad Men are by no means mere decoration. The paintings are, in fact, meant to convey deep meaning. This point is particularly illuminated by Bert Cooper explaining to Lane Pryce that the Japanese painting in his office depicting an octopus giving oral sex to an enraptured young woman reminds the elder of the advertising industry. "We were

[652] Ibid.

[653] Season 4 episode 2 "Christmas Comes But Once a Year" August 1, 2010.

[654] Season 5 episode 9 "Dark Shadows" May 13, 2012.

[655] Yi-Ping Ong, "Smoke Gets in Your Eyes: *Mad Men* and Moral Ambiguity," *Philosophy And New American TV Series,* Vol. 127, No. 5, (December 2012), pp. 1013-1039, p. 1017.

just talking about you," Cooper says to Don as he enters the office just a moment after he explains the meaning of the work of art to Lane.[656] Cooper's cryptic statement might inspire viewers to wonder: is Don the octopus, the girl being devoured by it, or both? Either way, the instance is evidence of the show being high art.

The plethora of abstract expressionism and references to the New York School throughout *Mad Men* provide viewers with a sense of the aesthetics that inspired the creators of the show. The New York School, which includes Frank O'Hara and Mark Rothko, both of whose works are prominently featured on *Mad Men*, were heavily influenced by several European artists, such as Willem de Kooning, who fled fascism in Europe for New York City in the years preceding World War II. The New York School was an informal group of poets, painters, dancers, and musicians active in the 1950s and 1960s, particularly in New York City. The artists often drew inspiration from surrealism and the contemporary avant-garde art movements, in particular action painting, abstract expressionism, jazz, improvisational theater and experimental music – all of which the Nazis would have considered decadent and depraved. German Fascists, which Jim Cutler seems to be a metonym for, praised the *Volk* and pandered to populist anti-intellectualism. Nazi art criticism, for example, perpetuated the populist view that the common man was the best judge of art and that art that did not appeal to the masses was overly intellectual, decadent, and thus, morally bankrupt.

One of the things that connected the disparate artists, intellectuals, and genres into a collective whole known as The New

[656] Season 3 episode 1 "Out of Town" August 16, 2009.

York School was that the participants conscientiously set out to make the kind of democratic art that fascists would have likely denigrated as offensive to the masses. The New York School was, in part, as Jed Perl notes in *New Art City* (2005), a response to fascism and often sought to take art back to its prehistoric origins when it was a spiritual experience more so than a product fetishized by art collectors and investors, which is alluded to in the show.657 In season one, for instance, Harry references the redoubtable and visceral splendor of the cave paintings and the handprints in Lascaux, France.658 In season four, Don is coerced by his former mistress, Midge, who is a heroin junkie, into buying "#4," an abstract expressionist piece she painted. It is described as what she sees when she "closes her eyes." Later, Don, who is enduring a grueling existential crisis as his business seems to be falling apart due to Lucky Strike Cigarettes abandoning the agency, fully absorbs himself in Midge's painting as he sits alone in his darkened lower Manhattan apartment. The sensual experience he has with "#4" ultimately inspires him to pen his controversial, "Why I'm Quitting Tobacco" open letter published in *The New York Times*, which shapes the rest of his life on the series.659

Many artists and intellectuals of the Beat Generation, including Allan Ginsberg and Jack Kerouac were, according to Perl, greatly influenced by the energy, spirit, and revolutionary potential

---

657 Jed Perl, *New Art City: Manhattan at Mid-Century*. (New York: Knopf, 2005) p. 402. See also, Jane de Hart Mathews, "Art and Politics in Cold War America," *The American Historical Review* Vol. 81, No. 4 (Oct., 1976), pp. 762-787.

658 Season 1 episode 13 "The Wheel" October 18, 2007.

659 Season 4 episode 12 "Blowing Smoke" October 10, 2010.

of the New York School. The influence of both the New York School and Beat Generation is thus also evident in *Mad Men*. Don, the creative, albeit deeply flawed genius, at times seems to be both an authoritarian man and yet a beatnik, which might be a metaphor for the duality and tension between liberty and fascism that helped to shape the postwar American experience. Late in the final season of the series, Don heads west in search of true freedom. "You like to play the stranger," the ghost of Bert Cooper says to Don. Don replies, "Remember *On The Road* (by Jack Kerouac)? I'm riding the rails." Cooper replies by quoting Kerouac, "Whither goest America in thy shiny car in the night."[660] Cooper's cryptic line underscores the point that Don is a metaphor of modern consumerist America. It is also another example of the show being high art trapped in a medium made for the masses.

As much as Don is a metaphor for postwar America's duality between individual liberty and corporatist conformity, no one character in seven seasons of *Mad Men* personifies the influence of the Beat Generation more so than Michael Ginsberg, who -- it seems -- is meant to personify Allen Ginsberg's poem, *Howl* (1955), particularly the line:

> "I saw the best minds of my generation destroyed by madness... who were burned alive in their innocent flannel suits on Madison Avenue amid blasts of leaden verse & the tanked-up clatter of the iron regiments of fashion & the nitroglycerine shrieks of the fairies of advertising & the

[660] Season 7 episode 12 "New Horizons" May 3, 2015.

mustard gas of sinister intelligent editors, or were run down by the drunken taxicabs of Absolute Reality."[661]

Like *Howl, Mad Men* also, often, critiques industrialization, urbanization, and postwar American capitalism as a tyrannical and dystopian Moloch. The Moloch described in *Howl* and alluded to in *Mad Men* via Michael Ginsberg's character, which is in perpetual conflict with the technocratic capitalist modernity that devours the young as they "break their backs" lifting Moloch (which is a metaphor for postwar American capitalism and militarism and evidence of the nation's collective madness) to "the sky." Late in season one, Pete Campbell seems to unwittingly evoke the Moloch in *Howl* to the agency's creative director when he laments that, "there isn't a man in this room that isn't holding Don Draper on their shoulders so he can reach partner."[662] Again, Don represents the duplicity in American society between the conformist authoritarianism represented by consumerism and quest for liberty represented by the Beat Generation.

But there is no such duplicity between freedom and fascism in Michael Ginsberg, who represents both madness and morality. In his initial job interview, Ginsberg openly admits to that the line in his resume that indicates he is related to Allen Ginsberg, who worked on Madison Avenue during the 1950s, is a lie. And, though Peggy seems afraid that Michael Ginsberg might be a madman, his portfolio of ads is very good. Plus, Roger, despite Peggy's reservations, insists that she hire him because "Mohawk (Airlines)

---

[661] Allen Ginsberg, *Howl and Other Poems*. (New York, City Lights Books, 1956).

[662] Season 1 episode 11 "Indian Summer" October 4, 2007.

insists" and that all the agencies have a Jewish employee now, which he equates with "modern." Thus, Ginsberg personifies the mania of modernity depicted in *Howl*, including modern art's visceral rejection of amoral groupthink conformity.[663]

"One could argue," M. Keith Booker and Bob Batchelor write in *Mad Men: A Cultural History* (2016), "that Ginsberg's mental illness is a sign of the general sickness of modern society."[664] To be sure. Ginsberg actually alludes to this point himself in season six when he says, "I believe I'm the only person in the *Time-Life* Building who's not out of his mind.[665] Ginsberg's mania particularly personifies the line *in Howl*, "Moloch whose mind is pure machinery! Moloch whose blood is running money!"[666] The interplay between Ginsberg's hysteria towards technology and capitalists' obsession with maximizing profits by any means necessary is embodied by both the IBM360 supercomputer that Jim Cutler and Harry Crane acquire for the agency, and Ginsberg's visceral, manic, and violent reaction to the soulless machine. Cutler, who in season seven boasts to Harry, "we can all learn something about the funeral business," as he holds Jessica Mitford's *The American Way of Death* (1963) aloft,[667]

---

[663] Season 5 episode 3 "The Tea Leaves" April 1, 2012.

[664] M. Keith Booker and Bob Batchelor, *Mad Men: A Cultural History*. (Lanham, Md. Rowman & Littlefield, 2016). pg 113.

[665] Season 6 episode 8 "The Crash" May 19, 2013.

[666] Allen Ginsberg, *Howl and Other Poems*. (New York, City Lights Books, 1956).

[667] Season 7 episode 3 "Field Trip" April 27, 2014.

particularly personifies technocratic fascism, in contrast to Ginsberg -- the creative genius whose talent and energy is gradually marginalized and silenced, as is his aura; the concept of which is described, perhaps most famously, by Walter Benjamin in his seminal critique of modernism in *The Work of Art in the Age of Mechanical Reproduction* (1936).[668]

"You're for the war!" Ginsberg assails Cutler shortly after the Peace Plank at the 1968 Democratic National Convention is rejected. "There's two hundred body bags every week. Figure out how to get into that business yet?" The ever-glib Cutler, who firebombed Dresden (which was completely destroyed close to the end of World War II, though it had a dearth of strategically valuable targets), shows no emotion as he coolly, almost robotically, replies, "I refuse to take an interest in events in which I have no participation or stake." Ginsberg screams, "You're disgusting, you know that! This whole thing works because people like you look the other way… Be friendly and charming after you've stuck your fascist boot on my neck… You're a fascist because you love business and hate everything else -- freedom, blacks, Jews." Cutler's facial expression never changes as he says, "I hate hypocrites, like hippies who cash checks from Dow Chemical and General Motors." Ginsberg responds with, "you rooting for the Soviets in Prague too, you Nazi? You're a truncheon!"[669]

---

[668] Benjamin's concept of loss of aura in reproduced art also seems alluded to in season 3 episode 4 "The Arrangements" September 6, 2009. "It's not Anne Margaret," Roger explains to Harry why the Patio "Bye Bye Birdie" commercial does not work. It is a replica sans Anne Margaret and thus lacks authenticity and aura. The camera holds on the replica of a painting hanging on the wall as Roger leaves the conference room.

[669] Season 6 episode 10 "A Tale of Two Cities" June 2, 2013.

Cutler later demands to his business partner, Ted Shaw, that Ginsberg be fired for gross insubordination. Shaw, however, protects Ginsberg because "he's lightning in a bottle" and the most creative artist at the agency – even more creative than Don. Later in the episode it seems evident that Cutler's line to Ginsberg about being a "hypocrite who cashes checks from Dow and GM" pushes the fragile creative genius one step closer to the gaping chasm of madness. "I'm part of the problem," Ginsberg regretfully admits close to the end of the episode and quotes Robert Openheimer, the mastermind behind the atomic bomb, who famously quoted *The Vedas* after the Trinity detonation by saying, "'Now I am death, destroyer of worlds.'"[670] Ginsberg's nervous breakdown in season seven is likewise foreshadowed in season five when he quotes *Ozymandias*, a poem by Percey Bysshe Shelley, to Peggy and Stan Rizzo after a successful presentation to clients. "'Look on My Works, Ye Mighty, and Despair!'" Ginsberg says. Stan condescendingly scoffs, "You should read the rest of that poem, you boob."[671] The lines Stan refers to are:

Nothing beside remains.
Round the decay
Of that colossal Wreck,
boundless and bare
The lone and level sands stretch far away."[672]

[670] Season 6 episode 10 "A Tale of Two Cities" June 2, 2013.

[671] Season 5 episode 9 "Dark Shadows" May 13, 2012.

[672] Percey Bysshe Shelley, *Ozymandias,* January 11, 1818, *The Examiner.*

The creators of *Mad Men*, including Weiner, who studied poetry at Wesleyan before studying film and television production at the University of Southern California, later reveal Cutler to be anti-Semitic when he indicates to his shape-shifting and ambitious underling, Bob Benson, that he cannot detect a difference between Ginsberg (a Jew) and Manischewitz executives (also Jewish) and refuses to take a meeting with any of them, which seems to particularly expose Cutler as a fascist comparable to the Nazis depicted in Hannah Arendt's *Eichmann in Jerusalem* (1963).[673]

The supercomputer and Cutler both represent the soulless lack of sentimentality associated with corporatist fascism. The IBM360, Cutler, and Lloyd Hawley (Robert Baker) all also represent the increasingly mechanized and dehumanized society represented in *Howl*. "I know what this company should look like," Cutler, who especially aches to invest more money in computers and less in creative personalities after his conflict with Ginsberg, says, "media buys with pinpoint accuracy… It's the agency of the future."[674] A season earlier, Kenny explains that Chevy is using a computer to make the "perfect car."[675] The following season, the viewer learns that Koss Headphones is interested in doing business with Gray, a rival agency, because of their new computer. "This computer situation is an arms race," Cutler says to the agency's partners. "There's no point in winning if people don't know about it," which seems to allude to the doomsday device in Stanley Kubrick's Cold War classic, *Dr. Strangelove or: How I learned to Stop Worrying and*

[673] Season 6 episode 10 "A Tale of Two Cities" June 2, 2013.

[674] Season 7 episode 7 "Waterloo" May 25, 2014.

[675] Season 6 episode 6 "For Immediate Release" May 5, 2013.

Love The Bomb (1964).676 In season five, Kenny Cosgrove writes a science fiction story about a rogue robot who unfastens a bolt on a bridge that connects planets, which seems to allude to the HAL9000 computer in Kubrick's *Space Odyssey 2001* (1968), which seems to be the inspiration of the Agency's new super computer in season seven.677 "This agency has entered the future," Cutler says as he fawns over the newly acquired machine. The agency's creatives – especially Ginsberg -- are, however, far less enthusiastic because they are literally forced out of their creative lounge in order to make room for the massive supercomputer, concomitant to being metaphorically pushed out of the industry altogether. "They are trying to erase us," Ginsberg frets, which seems to allude to Hitler's Final Solution of the Jews (the Holocaust).

The creeping fascism of soulless technology that ultimately leads to the "hydrogen bomb" in Ginsberg's head "exploding" and his complete nervous breakdown in season seven is quite the pervasive theme on *Mad Men*.678 And, though the most obvious allusion to Ludditism can be detected in Ginsberg's visceral reaction to the IBM360, the fear of technology is actually a recurring theme throughout the series. One of the most ominous allusions to Ludditism can be found in season one when Freddy mentions the execution of Ethel Rosenberg (a Jewish-American mother) in the electric chair, followed by Pete asking when they are going to start running electricity through the chairs of the secretaries taking part

---

676 Season 7 episode 3 "Field Trip" April 27, 2014.

677 Season 5 episode 10 "Christmas Waltz" May 20, 2012.

678 Season 7 episode 5 "The Runaways" May 11, 2014.

in the Belle Jolie lipstick panel.679 The concealed theme of Ludditism can, likewise, be detected as early as season one when Peggy describes the "Relaxicizer" (a vibrator marketed as an exercise contraption) as providing "the pleasure of a man without the man." Freddy nervously quips, "You mean we've been replaced?"680 The Xerox machine that takes up so much space in the premier episode of season two foreshadows the IBM360 supercomputer that contributes to Ginsberg's loss of sanity in the final season of the show. Likewise, the presence of many soda machines throughout the series speaks to the anxiety associated with the obsolescence of laborers as a result of technological advancements, most notably the wholesale replacement of soda jerks and mom-and-pop Main Street pharmacies in the decades following World War II. The theme of machines replacing human workers can also be detected late in season four when it appears that all the predominately African-American sandwich and coffee salespeople that frequented the office in early seasons of the show have been replaced by a mostly defective snack machine, which foreshadows the agency's supercomputer that gradually marginalizes and silences the creatives (such as Ginsberg and Don).681

There are also a number of concealed references to Ludditism in terms of the specter of cars and planes crashing. In season two, for example, Pete Campbell's father dies in a plane crash. Don later tells Peggy, who has never flown, a story about the

[679] Season 1 episode 6 "Babylon" August 23, 2007.

[680] Season 1 episode 11 "Indian Summer" October 4, 2007.

[681] Season 4 episode 8 "The Summer Man" September 12, 2010.

time he and many other soldiers were shipped to Korea. He reminisces about some terrified "rube" hollering, "man ain't supposed to fly."[682] On wo separate occasions in later episodes of the series the viewer is exposed to the specter of Ted Shaw's plane crashing.[683] In season three, Peggy goes on a date with a young man who explains that he decided to pursue being an engineer instead of being a lawyer because, "if the world is going to be run by machines, it's smarter to be an engineer than a lawyer." Peggy jokes that, "you could be a robot."[684] In season four, the science of consumer evaluation, with its "precision of a surgeon's scalpel" (which is a humorous jab aimed at Greg Harris who earlier in the series botches a surgery), is introduced via two freelance psychologists hired to maximize the agency's ability to predict consumer behavior and "better serve clients' needs."[685]

Three seasons later, the psychologists are replaced by the much more cost effective and precisely designed IBM360 computer. "These machines can be a metaphor for whatever is on people's minds," an engineer named Lloyd says to Don, who seems only slightly less uneasy by the computer's presence than Ginsberg is. "They" (computers), Lloyd explains, represent a "cosmic disturbance because they can contain infinite amounts of information. That's threatening, because human existence is finite.

[682] Season 5 episode 4 "Mystery Date" April 8, 2012.

[683] In episode 6 season 6 "Man With a Plan" May 12, 2013. it appears that Ted Shaw's plane might crash. In episode 7 season 7 "Waterloo" May 25, 2014, Ted cuts the engine of his plane in midair as Sunkist executives panic and plead for their lives.

[684] Season 3 episode 7 "Seven Twenty Three" September 27, 2009.

[685] Season 4 episode 2 "Christmas Comes But Once a Year" August 1, 2010.

But isn't it godlike that we've mastered the infinite?"[686] Later in the episode, Don, who is very drunk, says to Lloyd (who represents soulless technocracy), "You go by many names. I know who you are. You don't need an (ad) campaign. You have the greatest campaign since the dawn of time," which seems to allude to the Moloch in Allen Ginsberg's *Howl* and the fascism alluded to in Frank Capra's *Meet John Doe* (1941).

The jarring mechanistic sound of construction that invades the office as the computer is being installed, together with the incessant tapping of Selectric typewriters, phones ringing, and the muddled hum of employees chatting, gradually grates on Ginsberg's nerves. But the HAL9000-like hum of the monolith IBM360 ultimately causes the delicate creative genius to shatter. "The machine came for us one by one," Ginsberg says to Peggy as he wanders aimlessly out of what was formerly the creative lounge towards the abyss of insanity. "That machine," he pleads with Peggy later in the episode, "makes men do unnatural things, like be a homo." The creators of *Mad Men* thus depict Ginsberg's manic reaction to the IBM360 as evidence of his repressed homosexuality. In season six, Stan Rizzo, Johnny Mathis, and a few of the other "fellas" at the office are highly entertained as Julia, Megan's short-skirted friend crawls seductively across the conference table pretending to be a jaguar. Ginsberg (a virgin), however, is completely disinterested in the seductive spectacle.[687] A season later, Ginsberg lets slip to Peggy that he is sexually attracted to

---

[686] Season 7 episode 4 "The Monolith" May 4, 2014.

[687] Season 6 episode 10 "A Tale of Two Cities" June 2, 2013.

Stan, which he believes is a result of the computer's perverse "waves" of energy.[688]

Ginsberg, who was born in a Nazi concentration camp and claims to be a Martian, represents the danger of the self-hatred associated with homophobia and repressed homosexuality fostered during the conformist decades after World War II.[689] He is ultimately driven completely mad at the prospect of the computer turning him into a homosexual. "The waves of data were filling me up," he pleads with Peggy. "I had to find a release. I removed the pressure, now it flows through me without any trouble at all," he says as he gives her a box with his nipple ("the valve") inside, which seems to allude to Vincent Van Gogh giving a prostitute his ear as a present during his own nervous breakdown. "Get out while you can!" Ginsberg screams as he is being rolled out of the agency on a gurney.[690] Ginsberg, the personification of "lightning in a bottle,'" likewise represents the madness of the greatest minds of the Beat Generation destroyed in part as a result of the increasingly mechanized, militarist, conformist, and consumerist Cold War American society described in Allen Ginsberg's *Howl*.

The influence of the New York School and the Beat Generation, both of which are most often associated with high art, is in *Mad Men* personified most by Michael Ginsberg, particularly his breakdown under the weight of the homophobic and technocratic tendencies deeply imbued in American society during

---

[688] Season 7 episode 5 "The Runaways" May 11, 2014.

[689] Season 5 episode 6 "Far Away Places" April 22, 2012.

[690] Season 7 episode 5 "The Runaways" May 11, 2014.

the Cold War. But the influence of the Beat Generation is, likewise, satirically alluded to in season one as Don's mistress, Midge, and a few of her beatnik buddies cajole Don into going to the Gaslight Café in the Village to listen to poetry and music. A busty redheaded woman wearing a wool sweater seductively recites a poem to the audience in which she declares:

> "I dreamed of making love to Fidel Castro on a king-size bed at the Waldorf Astoria Hotel. 'Viva la Revolution,' he roared as he vanquished my dress. Outside the window Nikita Khrushchev watched while plucking a chicken."

A man and women in the crowd at the Gaslight yell, "take your shirt off!" The poet gladly complies. Don snidely replies, "too much art for me."[691]

"People buy things to realize their aspirations," Cooper says to Harry in season two. "It's the foundation of our business. But between you, me, and the lamppost that thing (the Rothko painting) should double by next Christmas."[692] Cooper, who does not seem to value art as anything more than an investment, later sits in front of a Jackson Pollock painting (also a great investment) in his apartment as he watches the Apollo 11 moon landing moments before his death.[693] Both the Rothko and Pollock owned by Cooper seem to speak to the increased commodification and co-opting of high art as consumer goods in the postwar period. The

[691] Season 1 episode 6 "Babylon" August 23, 2007.

[692] Season 2 episode 7 "The Gold Violin" September 7, 2008.

[693] Season 2 episode 5 "The New Girl" August 24, 2008 and Season 7 episode 7 "Waterloo" May 25, 2014.

duplicity inherent in *Mad Men's* self-reflective anti-ideological stance is further underscored by the irony of the poet taking her shirt off to please her audience and by Cooper valuing his Rothko painting as little more than a healthy investment that will soon make him slightly richer.

This duplicity is particularly evident in *Mad Men*, which is high art made to sell advertising space to multinational corporations who aim to sell products and ideology to the masses. Don, who seems fascist at times and like a beatnik at others, particularly exhibits the blurring of the line between high and low art and between the commercial and the actual television show, which is ultimately a vehicle to sell ads and products. Don, for instance, is interviewed about his award-winning ad for Glocoat in the season four premiere. "I wanted it (the ad) to be indistinguishable from the movies," he says, which alludes to the numerous products stealth marketed in *Mad Men*, most notably Lucky Strike Cigarettes and Coca-Cola.[694] In season one, Joan paraphrases Marshal McLuhan when she tells Peggy, "the medium is the message."[695] The camera holds steady as Joan sashays away in a scarlet a-line that hugs tight to her bodacious curves. Joan's evoking of McLuhan's notion that the form of a medium (such as television, which is designed to sell products) embeds itself in any message (ideology) it would transmit or convey, creating a symbiotic relationship by which the medium influences how the message is perceived, seems to be the creators of *Mad Men* expressing their quandary at creating high art for a low art medium

[694] Season 4 episode 1 "Public Relations" July 25, 2010.

[695] Season 1 episode 6 "Babylon" August 23, 2007.

and the masses. Don's award winning Glocoat commercial was, for example, not just selling floor shine, it was selling the fetish for American westerns, which is a metaphor for imperialism and capitalism. In other words, regardless of the product or ideology seemingly promulgated over the airwaves, consumption is always the message. Even the Red Westerns that were so popular behind the Iron Curtain during the Cold War (which espoused communist ideology by making communal-living Native Americans the good guys and the cowboys the bad capitalists) the practice of going to the movies, drinking Pepsi, and eating popcorn crafted consumers of communists, which – like The Beatles and Levi's blue jeans – ultimately contributed to the collapse of the Soviet Union and communist ideology around the globe in the waning decades of the twentieth century.

The creators of *Mad Men* seem to revel in the duplicity, as evidenced by the prevalence of stealth marketing of products throughout the series. One of the most glaring examples of stealth marketing of Coca-Cola in *Mad Men* can be found at the very beginning of episode nine in season four when the sound of a man and woman (Don and Dr. Miller) mid-coitus can be heard in the next room as the camera holds steady on a sleek Coke bottle atop an otherwise barren coffee table, as if to make a joke in reference to the adage, "sex sells."[696] In the second to last episode of the series, Don is cajoled into fixing a vintage vending machine at the motel where he is stranded while his Cadillac is being fixed. The machine reads, "Have a Coke" on the side in bright red and white cursive letters. There are also numerous instances of vintage Coke bottles

---

[696] Season 4 episode 9 "The Beautiful Girls" September 19, 2010.

and cans on conference room tables and coffee tables throughout the series, underscoring that *Mad Men* is as much a commercial for myriad stealth-marketed products as it is a critique of the specter of fascism ensconced in postwar American consumer culture. Late in season one, for instance, Peggy goes on a date with a truck driver who says, "Advertising doesn't work on me. It's just a lot of screaming at you from the walls and TV." Peggy replies, "If advertising is good, people never think it works."[697]

It is therefore a bit of a paradox that the creators of *Mad Men* seem fully conscious of the fact that they were crafting both art and commercial at once. The show, of course, concludes with Don meditating at a New Age retreat on the coast of Northern California and envisioning the classic and iconic, "I'd Like to Teach the World to Sing" Coca-Cola television spot. In season seven, Megan has a copy of *Playboy* in her living room in California.[698] It is certainly a great ad for *Playboy*, which was surely as glad to cash in on *Mad Men's* popularity as *Mad Men* was to cash in on *Playboy's* popularity and cultural relevance. It is also, however, a bit Orwellian that the show seems to critique the objectification of women and implied and overt masculine violence directed towards females concomitant to being a commercial for *Playboy*, which amassed a fortune for chauvinist Hugh Hefner, who actually undermined the primary goals of second-wave feminism by both objectifying women as sexual objects while conflating the movement, which was about economic and political equality for all, with the sexual revolution. In other words, *Mad Men* is cloaked in symbols of social

[697] Season 1 episode 11 "Indian Summer" October 4, 2007.

[698] Season 7 episode 1 "Time Zones" April 13, 2014.

revolution as it perpetuates the economic and political status quo. It is interesting that in the second half of the final season of *Mad Men*, which is set in 1970, Ted Shaw and Roger Sterling have shaggier hair, Fu Manchu moustaches, and wear looser fitting suits. The advertising agents – like the creators of *Mad Men* – have, in short, appropriated symbols of counterculture to put in service of mainstream consumerism and militarism, which, as the show rightly alludes to, is inherently conformist and conservative.

Mad Men is, in short, both high art that critiques consumer capitalism and exposes its fascist features while at the same time, it perpetuates the conformity and power structure it critiques, which makes it, by definition, post-modern. *Mad Men* is indeed art, but also, like a Che Guevara t-shirt or the Red Westerns that were wildly popular in Cold War eastern bloc countries, the show ultimately perpetuates consumerism at the same time it critiques the exploitative nature of capitalism. The fact that Megan can be seen in season six wearing a t-shirt with the five-pointed red star synonymous with Marxist movements seems to underscore the point that symbols of revolution as well as religion have been subsumed into consumer culture as a means of perpetuating the global economic and political status quo.[699]

Fascists, in the decades prior to World War II, like advertisers in postwar America, marketed the notion that they alone represented "new," "revolutionary," and "progressive" ideals that appealed not just to the young, but to older literary

---

[699] Season six episode 10 "A Tale of Two Cities" June 2, 2013.

modernists such as Ezra Pound and T.S. Eliot.[700] "'This is the way the world ends,'" Paul Kinsey quotes Eliot in season three, "not with a bang, with a whimper."[701] In season two, Kinsey, who seems to personify the duplicity between revolution and Cold War conformity, plans to flake out on his girlfriend, an African-American woman who is going on a Freedom Ride to Mississippi in order to register voters, so that he can instead go to the "Rocket Fair" in California with Pete Campbell. Kinsey is thus portrayed as a self-absorbed pseudo-liberal masquerading as an enlightened social activist, but is really just a sleazy and self-absorbed libertarian ad man. Later in the episode, Kinsey pretends to his girlfriend that he has decided to go to Mississippi after all because he is genuinely invested in civil rights for African Americans. But in reality, Kinsey lost his seat on the plane because his superior at the agency, creative director Don, decides to go on the trip, after all. Kinsey's duplicity seems a metaphor for the creators of *Mad Men*, who ultimately make what might appear to be a revolutionary critique of consumer capitalism as being evidence of postwar American fascism at the same time they perpetuate the authoritarian conformity embedded in the consumerism they simultaneously critique.

Mad Men, in short, is both subject and object, high and low art, commercial and work of art, whore and john, liberal and conservative, revolutionary and fascist. Though *Mad Men* clearly

---

[700] Weiner mentions being enthralled with Eliot's *The Waste Land*. *See* Steven J. Ross and Michael Renov, "An Outsider's View of Sixties America: Matthew Weiner Talks with Michael Renov about the Jews of *Mad Men*" in *From Shtetl to Stardom*, (West Lafayette, IN, Purdue University Press, 2017), p. 165.

[701] Season 3 episode 3 "My Old Kentucky Home" August 30, 2009.

has characteristics of high art, the show ultimately perpetuates the star culture that reifies society into social hierarchies in which celebrities, such as Jon Hamm, January Jones, and Matthew Weiner are American aristocracy in the realm of popular consumer culture. The inherent star culture entrenched in consumer culture led Frankfurt School critical theorists such as Theodor Adorno and Max Horkheimer to assail popular culture as inherently fascistic.[702] According to Adorno and Horkheimer, the culture industry is a main phenomenon of late capitalism, one which encompasses all products and forms of light entertainment – from Hollywood films, television shows, such as *Mad Men*, to elevator music. Adorno specifically notes that the term "culture industry," which is often synonymous with "low art," was chosen over "mass culture" in order to make sure that it was not misunderstood as something which spontaneously flowered from the masses, but was a creature of advertisers, such as Don Draper, and television producers such as Matthew Weiner.

Products of the culture economy sometimes take the appearance of artwork but are in fact dependent on industry and economy, meaning they are subject to the interests of money and power. All products of the culture industry, including high art, are ultimately, whether the artist is conscious of it or not, designed for profit. According to Adorno and Horkheimer, this means that every work of art is turned into a consumer product and is shaped by the logic of capitalist rationality. Thus, art is thus no longer autonomous, but is, rather, a commodified product of the economic relations of production, which is what Benjamin argues in *The Work*

---

[702] Don is also somewhat oddly akin to the scholars in the Frankfurt School, especially Adorno, in the sense that he is suspicious of all ideology and orthodoxy.

of Art in the Age of Mechanical Reproduction. The main argument of "Culture Industry: Enlightenment as Mass Deception" is that the commodification of culture is the commodification of human conciseness. Adorno and Horkheimer therefore agree that the culture industry eradicates individual critical thinking, which serves to preserve the reigning order. The culture industry offers easy entertainment, which distracts the masses from their own exploitation. Adorno and Horkheimer argue that the culture industry had, by 1960, subsumed the very notion of reality as the prism through which people experience life, thereby completely shaping and conditioning their experience of life without most being conscious of it, which is a theme explored in HBO's dystopian *West World*. The concept of the culture industry also serves to keep workers busy, as expressed by Adorno and Horkheimer's assertion that amusement had become an *extension* of labor under late capitalism.[703] Popular culture, as such, appears to offer a utopian refuge and distraction for labor, but in truth traps the worker into a reality shaped by desire for products and consumerism itself. In other words, rather than being liberatory, the culture industry is the very device that prevents workers from gaining true economic, political, and social equality. The only true freedom the culture industry offers, Adorno and Horkheimer asserted, was a freedom from critical thinking. The final argument posed by Adorno and Horkheimer was that people under capitalism suffered the same fate of art under the culture industry as they did under fascist regimes. To wit, the inability to think

---

[703] See Max Horkheimer and Theodor W. Adorno, *Dialectic of Enlightenment, Philosophical Fragments.* (Frankfurt, S. Fishcher Verlag, 1987), especially "The Culture Industry: Enlightenment as Mass Deception, pp. 137 – 136.

critically as a result of conformity to consumerism, thereby turning people into passive and subordinated subjects, unable to fully take critical responsibility for their own actions, which is crucial for a functioning democracy. And so, although the creators of *Mad Men* help to expose the specter of fascism deeply embedded in postwar American society, particularly consumerism and militarism, they simultaneously break their backs lifting the Moloch of the culture industry closer to the sky.

Epilogue

Whether he realized it or not, William Faulkner's point in *Requiem for a Nun* (1951) "that the past is never dead; it is not even past" essentially offers the argument: history is prologue.[704] But critic Mark Greif erroneously remarked of *Mad Men* that the show was an exercise in "now we know better."[705] Weiner, however, told Michael Renov that "the exact opposite" was what he "was trying to do."[706] Weiner believed *Mad Men* to be an exercise in historical continuity.

Mad Men, in other words, is as much about the specter of American fascism in the Digital Age as it is about the specter of fascism in the Cold War/Space Age/Vietnam Era in American

---

[704] William Faulkner, *Requiem For a Nun*, (New York, Random House, 1951).

[705] Mark Greif, "You'll Love the Way it Makes You Feel," (*London Review of Books*, October 23, 2008.

[706] Steven J. Ross and Michael Renov, "An Outsider's View of Sixties America: Matthew Weiner Talks with Michael Renov about the Jews of *Mad Men*" in *From Shtetl to Stardom*, (West Lafayette, IN, Purdue University Press, 2017), p. 160.

history. Weiner admitted as much in a 2014 interview with *TIME* in which he mentioned John Kenneth Galbraith's *The Affluent Society* (1958), Rachel Carson's *Silent Spring* (1962), and Ralph Nader's *Unsafe at Any Speed* (1965) as a means of underscoring the point that the United States had yet to adequately address many of the most pressing issues central to American society in the 1960s:

> "We are screwing up the environment. We are the richest country in the world and we have poverty in it. And corporations do not care about you; you are not part of the bottom line… That's like part of our personality – that if we don't watch out, businesspeople will have us all working twelve hours a day in a room with no windows."

He elaborated that he sensed Americans in the post-bailout twenty-first century had grown "exhausted and terrified" as a result of the economic calamity of the early twenty-first century and that they had "very low self-esteem." He also detected a "national anxiety" about the nation's "place in the world."[707] *Mad Men*, Weiner added, was, in part, a reaction to the collapse of the cratering of the global economy in the early twenty-first century, which was triggered by the dot.com boom/bust at the turn of the century, and which was soon followed by the mortgage crisis of 2008. Combined, they proved to be a global economic crisis in scope and scale the nation had not witnessed since the Great Depression of the 1930s (Don Draper's childhood).

And, much like the Great Depression, the economic collapse

---

[707] James Poniewozik, "Making History: A Q & A with *Mad Men's* Matthew Weiner." *TIME*, March 27, 2014.

early in the twenty-first century fostered the rise of fascist demagogues across the globe who mass mobilized voters by stoking fear in the hearts and minds of folks aching for scapegoats and who were desperate for simple solutions and answers that might solve the very complex problems in their lives,[708] which prompted scholars such as Roger Eatwell to caution, "Beware of men — and women — wearing smart Italian suits who promote free-market capitalism and lower taxes. The color is now gray, the material is cut to fit the times, but the aim is still power... fascism is on the move once more, even if its most sophisticated forms have learned to dress to suit the times."[709] Historian Richard Wolin likewise describes these movements as "designer fascism," which seems to allude to both the nattily dressed ad men depicted in *Mad Men* and also the sharply dressed executives and politicians with whom corporations (advertisers) and voters (advertised to) buy into.[710]

As Siegfried Kracauer argues in *From Caligari to Hitler: A Psychological History of the German Film* (1947), Weimer German cinema foreshadowed the rise of Adolf Hitler and the Nazis, so too the creators of *Mad Men's* depiction of the American Sixties seem to have foreshadowed the stylish rise of neo-fascism in the early twenty-first century. Neo-fascism is, however, a bit of a misnomer because as both *Mad Men* and this study elaborate, fascism has long been deeply rooted in American society and in the nation's

---

[708] See Peter Baker, "Rise of Donald Trump Tracks Growing Debate Over Global Fascism," *The New York Times,* May 28, 2016.

[709] Roger Eatwell, *Fascism: A History*, (New York, Penguin Press, 1996).

[710] Richard Wolin, *The Seduction of Unreason: The Intellectual Romance With Fascism From Nietzsche to Postmodernism,* (Princeton NJ; Princeton University Press, 2004), p. 256.

collective identity. As such, when the drinking, sex, melodrama, stealth marketing, and sleek mid-century design of *Mad Men* is stripped away, the show poignantly unveils Cold War America, and, by implication, twenty-first century America, as having the same deep strains of the banality of evil associated with Nazi consumer culture and militarism also deeply embedded in American consumer culture, military industrial complex, political system, and collective identity.

www.ingramcontent.com/pod-product-compliance
Lightning Source LLC
Chambersburg PA
CBHW080333170426
43194CB00014B/2545